ROMANIA

Hippocrene Companion Guide to
ROMANIA

Lydle Brinkle

HIPPOCRENE BOOKS
New York

ACKNOWLEDGMENTS

The author wishes to acknowledge the following individuals and organizations for their contributions:

—The Carpati-Bucureşti National Tourist Office in Bucharest
—The Romanian Tourist Information Office in New York
—The Hotel Bucureşti in Bucharest.
—Editura Ştinnţifica şi Enciclopedică (Bucharest) for its map of Romania
—Margie Hudak, Carolyn Brinkle, and Joann Carlson, who typed the major portions of the manuscript
—Mike McCormick of the Canadian Embassy in Bucharest
—Liz Doyle of Sunny Land Tours, New Jersey
—The Faculty Research Committee of Gannon University, Erie, Pennsylvania
—Dr. Tom Ostrowski, Dean of Humanities, and Dr. Thomas Szendrey, Professor of History, Gannon University
—Simone Brinkle of Nashville, Tennessee
—George Blagowidow, president of Hippocrene Books, New York

Second Printing

Copyright ©1992 Lydle Brinkle

All rights reserved.

For information address:
Hippocrene Books, Inc.
171 Madison Ave.
New York, NY 10016

ISBN 0-87052-634-0

Printed in the United States.

To
Carolyn, Dale, Bryan, and Craig

Contents

Administrative Map of Romania	x
Map of Historic Romania	xi

CHAPTER 1. *Introduction to Romania* — 1
Geographical Setting — 2
People — 10
Brief History — 11
Folklore, Folk Art, Ethnography — 19

CHAPTER 2. *Bucharest* — 25

CHAPTER 3. *Wallachia and Dobruja: Major Cities and Historic Sites* — 41
Constanţa — 41
Brăila — 47
Ploieşti — 49
Craiova — 52
Buzău — 58
Piteşti — 59
Drobeta-Turnu Severin — 60
Tîrgoviste — 61
Slatina — 63
Rîmnicu Vîlcea — 63
Histria — 64

CHAPTER 4. *Transylvania: Major Cities and Historic Sites* ... 65
Braşov ... 65
Timişoara ... 69
Cluj-Napoca ... 75
Oradea ... 79
Arad ... 82
Sibiu ... 87
Tîrgu Mureş ... 91
Baia Mare ... 92
Satu Mare ... 93
Resiţa ... 94
Alba Iulia ... 94
Mediaş ... 101
Deva ... 101
Sighişoara ... 108
Sfîntu Gheorghe ... 109
Sarmizegethusa (Dacian) ... 109
Sarmizegethusa (Roman) ... 110
Micia (Ruins) ... 111

CHAPTER 5. *Moldavia: Major Cities and Historic Sites* ... 113
Iaşi ... 113
Galaţi ... 120
Bacău ... 122
Botosani ... 123
Suceava ... 124
Gheorghe Gheorghiu-Dej ... 130

CHAPTER 6. *Monasteries of Bukovina* ... 133

CHAPTER 7. *Danube River and Delta* ... 143

CHAPTER 8. *Health Resorts, Spas, Treatments* ... 161

CHAPTER 9. *Practical Information*   193
Visa Regulations   193
Customs   194
Currency Regulations   194
Tourist Seasons   195
Food and Drink   195
Show Times   195
Credit Cards, Shopping   195
Electricity   196
Photography   196
Admissions Fees   196
Shops, Salons, Business Hours   196
Entertainment   196
Independent Travel   197
Entry Points and Means of Travel   197
Sightseeing and Tours, Rental Cars   198
Gas, Speed Limits   199
Useful Addresses   200
Useful Words and Vocabulary   202
Mileage Chart   204
European Distances, Temperature Tables   204
Train Schedule   204
Romanian Menu Terms   205

Index   207

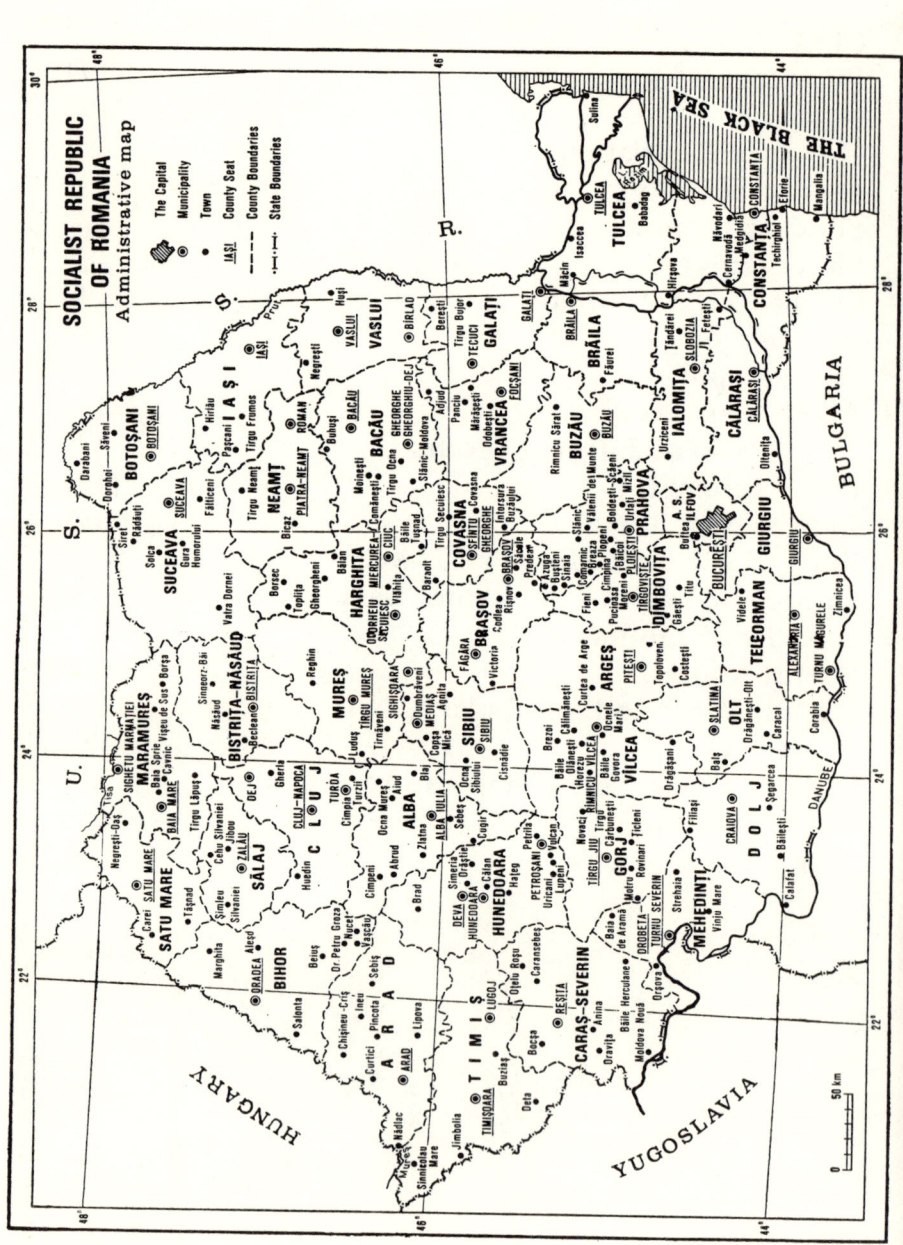

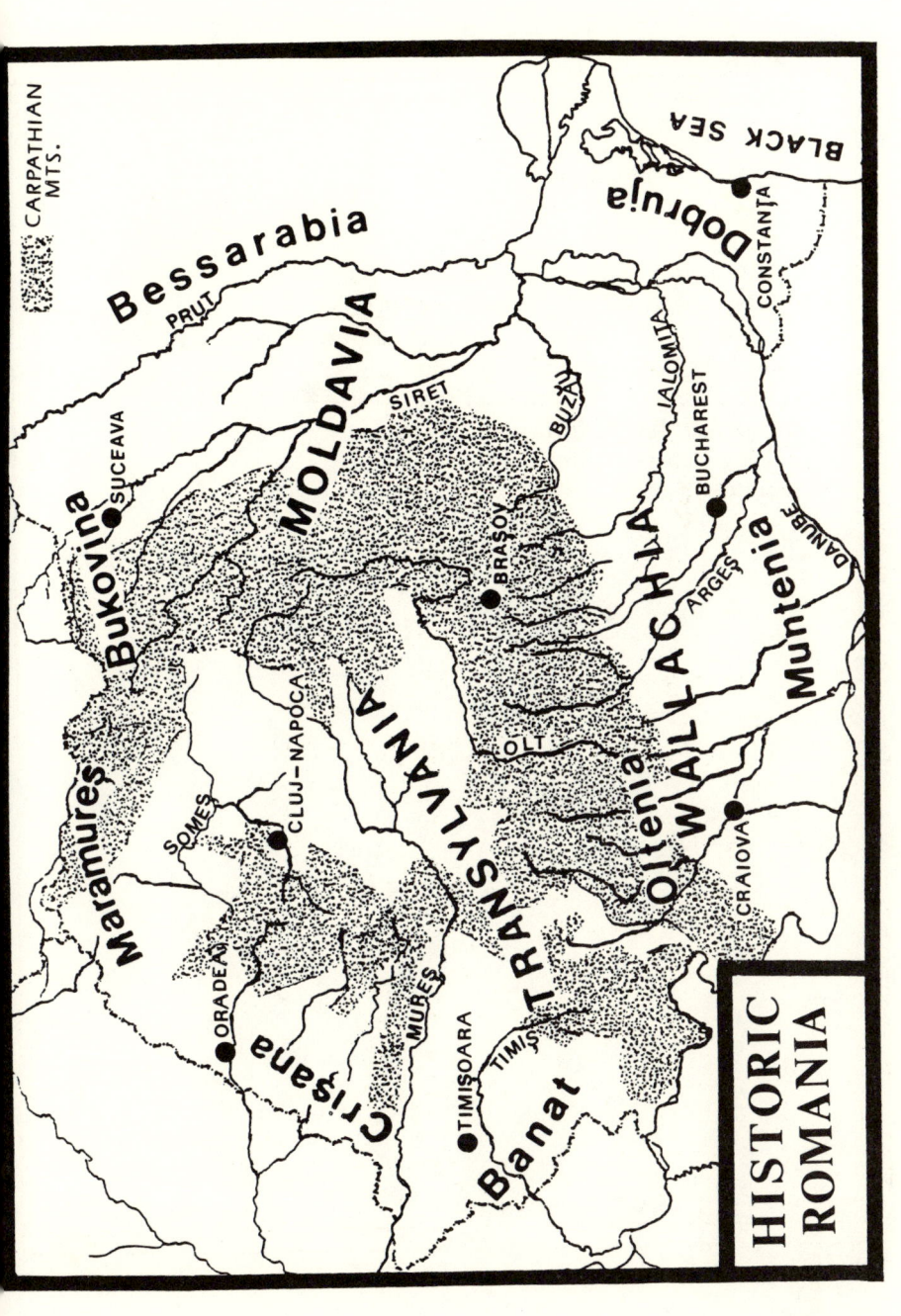

Look upon those high and verdant hills,
On those broad glades, covered with flowers,
Look at those Romanian shepherds, strangers to the world,
Beside their flocks guarded by their dogs,
Leading a gentle life in mysterious nature,
With horn in hand, flute at their lips,
Heavenly clearness, as within a spring,
Mirrors itself calm in their spirits.

—Grigore Alexandrescu (1812–85)

CHAPTER 1

Introduction to Romania

You will find Romania a country where Old World romance is still alive in a thousand quaint villages, in the Latin sophistication of Bucharest, in the valleys of the legendary Carpathians, and in the unspoiled natural beauty of the Danube delta. If you want to trace the relics of Romania's past you will cherish the precious treasures of art and architecture from the Roman, Byzantine, and Brancovan periods highlighted by the famous painted churches of Moldavia, the imposing feudal castles of Transylvania, and the unique native dwellings that abound in all of Romania's provinces. Romanian folk art, crafts, and native costumes have a special character reflecting the creativeness of the people.

Romania is a country of pleasant surprises, traditional hospitality, and friendly people. It is a vast museum of a thousand-year history. Every corner of the country reflects an image of its heritage and historical evolution. Many tour operators include Romania in their itineraries at prices that are reasonable and affordable.

Travel in Romania is possible without speaking Romanian. Local offices of the Romanian National Tourist Office employ staff well trained in speaking English, French, German, and a variety of other languages. Hotels customarily have trained personnel speaking these widely used languages as well. Airline offices, museums, train stations, telephone exchanges, embassies, colleges and universities, and other widely used public facilities and institutions are normally places where multilingual persons can be found. Informative literature in English and other languages is also freely available to tourists.

Geographical Setting

Romania covers an area of 91,725 square miles, is almost as large as the state of Oregon, and is twice the size of Pennsylvania. It has 1,609 miles of frontiers. It borders on Hungary and Yugoslavia in the west, on Bulgaria in the south, and on the Soviet Union in the east and north. Romania lies in the north of the Balkan Peninsula and in the southeastern part of central Europe. Latitudinally, it lies between 43 degrees and 37 minutes north, and its longitude stretches between 20 degrees and 15 minutes and 29 degrees and 41 minutes east. Its distance from the Atlantic Ocean is approximately 1,550 miles, and the Mediterranean Sea is about 559 miles away.

Topographically, Romania resembles a huge amphitheater. The lofty peaks of the Carpathian Mountains rise to more than 8,240 feet, surrounding the Transylvanian plateau, which averages 2,640 feet above sea level. The southern foothills of the Carpathians slope gently toward the fertile plains, the country's granary. The plains stretch toward the Black Sea, the Danube River, and the Mureș, Prut, and Olt rivers. Romania's Black Sea coast stretches for 152 sandy miles. The highest summits of the country are Moldoveanu (8,392 feet), Negolu (8,365 feet), Paringu Mare (8,309 feet), and Omul (8,273 feet). The Carpathians make up about 31 percent of Romania's territory; hills and tablelands comprise about 36 percent; and the plains cover approximately 33 percent of the country's surface. In the northeast the Moldavian tableland averages 1,312 to 1,969 feet in elevation, while in southeastern Romania the Dobruja Tableland is of approximately the same elevation. About 41 percent of Romania's area is classified as arable;

forests cover roughly 27 percent of the country; grazing and pastureland account for 19 percent of its surface; orchards and grapes grow on 3 percent of the land; and lakes and waterways cover another 3 percent of the country's area.

Romania's geographical position—approximately equidistant between the North Pole and the Equator—as well as its temperate continental climate, account for the abundance of its vegetation species. These are distributed across the country accordingly: approximately 31 percent are found in the mountains; 36 percent grow in the hills and plateaus; and 33 percent of the species thrive in the plains.

The former bottom of a Mesozoic sea (245–65 million years ago), the territory of today's Romania contains large fossil deposits and ancient mountain ranges on the one hand and some of the youngest land in Europe, still being formed, on the other hand. The Carpathians, which form the predominant relief features of the country, are of Tertiary origin (largely uplifted 50–65 million years ago) and belong to the Alpine mountain system.

The Romanian Carpathians cover an area of about 27,027 square miles and stretch in a semicircle for 621 miles through the country. They are young mountains which were folded during the Alpine orogeny and are low to medium in altitude compared to the Alps and Pyrenees. Numerous flatlands and deep valleys are common in the Carpathians and are an asset to transportation. The Transylvanian basin, which is surrounded by mountains, has more than thirty highways and rail lines connecting it with areas outside the Carpathians.

The Carpathians in Romania may be subdivided into three large ranges: the Eastern, Southern, and Western Carpathians. These divisions are based on their morphology, altitude, and relationship to the Transylvanian basin. Many of the ridges in the Carpathians have been dissected, eroded, and leveled into raised platforms exceeding 3,200 feet in elevation, with some over 6,500 feet high. These platforms provide suitable conditions for sheep raising, which is common in the Carpathians.

The Eastern Carpathians

This range extends from the northern boundary of Romania along the Soviet-Hungarian border southward to the Prahova valley. It consists of three parallel zones which are geologically distinct from one another. From east to west these are: (1) a zone of sandstone ridges, (2) the central zone of crystalline and limestone formations, and (3) a zone of volcanic material. Past glaciation had little impact on the Eastern Carpathians, whose peaks generally range between 5,000 to 7,000 feet in elevation. In general, however, the peaks of the Carpathians display much rounding due to the effects of weathering. The Eastern Carpathians extend southward as far as the Prahova Valley. The Bicaz gorges, along the Bicaz River in the northern part of the Eastern Carpathians, are among the most impressive and frequently visited mountain passes in Romania. The gorges are flanked by high limestone walls hundreds of feet high, and stretch for approximately five miles through the mountains. There are many fossil limestone formations in the gorges. The Eastern Carpathians also contain the "Ceahlău conglomerates," hard rocks over which flows the impressive Duruitoarea waterfall.

The highest peak in the Eastern Carpathians is Pietrosu, which is 7,565 feet high and is located in the central zone of the mountains. The volcanic zone in the west is comprised of a chain of extinct cones and craters. Local massifs in this chain include the Birgau, Călimani, Gurghiu, Gutii, Harghita, Oaş, and Tibleş. Depressions are common in the western zone and include those of Braşov (the largest in the Carpathians), Ciuc, Maramureş, and Giurgeu. This zone is the principal forested area in Romania, containing large stands of fir and spruce trees.

The Southern Carpathians

This mountainous zone, commonly called the Transylvanian Alps, stretches from the Prahova valley on the east to the Timiş-Cerna and Bistra valleys toward the west where they form a tectonic corridor. Glacial activity was common in the Southern Carpathians in past times, carving many cirques into the sides of the mountains, particularly in the Retezat and Făgăraş ranges. These two ranges and those of the Bucegi and Paring are the four main ranges of the Southern Carpathians. Crystalline schists, limestone formations, and volcanic rocks are common in the area. The many glacial features present in the Southern Carpathians have prompted their comparison to the Swiss Alps, leading many scientists and writers to call them the Transylvanian Alps. Their ranges are wooded, and the highest mountain in Romania, Moldoveanu in the Făgăraş range, reaches 8,392 feet.

The Bucegi Mountains in the Southern Carpathians are a traditional trekking area for Romanians, who begin their treks in the Sinaia health and winter sports resort. The three nature reserves in the area (about 17,500 acres) are located on the eastern and western slopes of the Bucegi. They contain numerous rare plants, karst formations, and gorges, as well as the Bucegi plateau with its well-known and mysterious formations of eroded rock: the "Old Woman" and the "Sphinx." The Sphinx formation is a close resemblance to the one in Egypt.

The Retezat Mountains, situated in the western part of the Southern Carpathians, are the most imposing rocky range in the Carpathians. The first national park in Romania was established here in 1935, comprising about 33,750 acres. It is a unique place due to its more than 100 permanent or temporary glacial lakes, and it also shelters over 300 flora species.

Mount Domogled, also in the Southern Carpathians, stands by the 1,000 year-old Băile Herculane spa. It is a nature reserve founded in 1932 and consists of 150,000 acres. Its specimens include rare forest species, cave butterflies and other fauna, the horned adder, and the tortoise.

Podul Uriașilor (the Giants' Bridge) is a natural monument found in the western part of the Southern Carpathians. At present it is a bridge used for traffic, formed after a cave fell in. There are temporary lakes, karst formations, and lilac forests in the area.

Peștera Muierilor (Women's Cave) is found on the northern slope of the Căpăținii Mountains in the Southern Carpathians. In this cave, traces of human habitation go back to the Paleolithic period. Fossil remains of cave bears have been found. The cave has electrical lighting. The Topolnita Cave was formed in the Mehedinti Mountains in the western part of the Southern Carpathians by four rivers disappearing under the ground. It contains terraced galleries, halls, wells, pits, lakes, and cave fauna.

In the Retezat Massif in the Southern Carpathians is the Retezat National Park, an area of over 50,000 acres. There are access roads for cars via Riu de Mori, Gura Apei, the Berhina meadow, and the Nucsorului valley. The park was founded in 1935 to honor the scientists Emil Racovita (1868–1945) and Alexander Borza (1887–1970). The area chosen for the park was due to the unspoiled natural beauty of the area and its varied relief with its rich fauna and flora, rivers, and lakes. The Retezat Massif dominates the Mureș valley with more than 20 peaks that surpass 7,500 feet in elevation and approximately 40 others that reach 6,500 feet in height. The entire area is structured into two ranges running in a northeast-southwest direction. There are 82 lakes in the massif, almost all of them of glacial origin, the largest of which is Bucura Lake lying at 6,696 feet in elevation and covering an area of 25 acres. The remains of 18 moraines created by Quaternary glaciers are found inside the park. Some of the park's principal sights are the large Gemenele and Birles hollows, Bilea waterfall, the Gemenele and Taul Negru lakes, Riul Mare valley, Buta and Retezat peaks, and its abundant vegetation and fauna. The park protects the existent flora and is a shelter for wild animals and migratory birds. The park has been included in catalogs on world parks and recognized in other international literature. More than 1,200 species of plants are found in Retezat National Park. A floral treasure of the park is the *Hieracium,* with more than 30 species growing in the area. Juniper trees are common above 5,900 feet in elevation, as are the beautiful "zimbru" plants *(Pinus cembra).* Interesting and abundant fauna in the park include bear, chamois, deer, wild boar, lynx, wild cat, eagles, and ravens. Continuous scientific research is performed at a laboratory in the park.

The chamois (mountain goat) is common in the Southern Carpathians. It is a ruminating wild animal whose hair changes from brown to black according to the season. It has two white stripes on the front side of the head and short horns curved at the top. The chamois is encountered in the Caucasus, Pyrenees, the Appenines, the Carpathians, and some other areas. *R.R. carpatica,* the Romanian breed of chamois, is the most vigorous and remarkable for its size and weight. Protected in the mountain massifs of Romania, their number has increased there.

The Western Carpathians

These mountains comprise the western end of the Carpathian arc and are located between the Danube River on the south and the Someş valley in the north. They are the lowest in elevation of the three zones of the Carpathians. Their average elevation is about 2,132 feet, while the highest is 6,063 feet in Curcubata Mare. The largest caves in Romania are found in the Western Carpathians. These include Cetatile Ponorului, Meziad, Scari şoara, Vintului, and Virtop. The Western Carpathians are themost fragmented of the three zones of the Carpathians, and their landscape is comprised of volcanic, sedimentary, and crystalline formations. The branches of the Western Carpathians include the

Banat, Poiana-Ruscă, and the Apuseni mountains (the northern branch). The Apuseni range consists of many basalt rocks on which many high columns and vertical pillars have formed. In the Apuseni are several beautiful gorges carved into the varied landscape. Hollows, underground glaciers, over twenty waterfalls and vertical springs *(izbucuri)*, botanical and dendrological reserves, and fossil remains add to the attractions of these mountains.

The Scarişoara Glacier, located near the village of Gîrda de Sus in Alba County in the Bihor Mountains, is a nature reserve set amidst picturesque scenery. Located at an altitude of 3,609 feet above the left slope of the Gîrda Saca valley, it is the largest ice cavern in Romania. Its entrance has vertical walls approximately 164 feet high. The cornices are covered with vegetation made up of flowering plants and moss. In the summertime, the lower section of the vertical opening is filled with cold air, while the upper part has a temperature resembling the surface climate. This phenomenon creates a vertical zonation of plants at different levels, and it is possible to follow the various periods of blooming. The block of ice is located on the bottom of the vertical entrance. It is 59 to 66 feet thick, separating the cavern into several halls, with the Great Hall having a circular shape that is 154 feet in diameter and 62 feet high. Several abysses run out of the ice floor and along the lateral walls. The southern abyss descends on a 35 degree slope, 180 feet long, into an enormous vaulted hall sustained by a group of ice columns known as stalagmites which were studied by the Romanian scientist Emil Racovita (1868–1947), the founder of Speology. By way of a threshold of blocks, one reaches the hall adorned by limestone structures, stalactites, stalagmites, and columns. The walls of the cavern look like a waterfall frozen into ice folds. A guide provides visitors with carbide lamps.

The Transylvanian Tableland

This large geographical area is cut into by the Mureş River valley and consists of dome-shaped structures that range between 1,312 and 1,969 feet in elevation. South of the Mureş lies the Tirnave tableland with an undulating relief that reaches over 1,900 feet high. North of the Mureş valley is the Transylvanian plain, which is less rugged than the Tirnave tableland, with elevations around 1,600 feet.

Until 1918, Transylvania was part of Hungary, and the Hungarians referred to it as "the land beyond the forest." The name Transylvania is somewhat unclear in terms of its geographical boundaries. One definition has it as meaning the area surrounded by the three zones of the Carpathian Mountains. This area would include the cities of Bistrița, Cluj, Sibiu, Alba Iulia, and Sighișoara, in other words that area in the north-central part of Romania. However, the name has also been applied at times to include the Banat area bordering on Yugoslavia in the southwest, the Crisana area bordering on Hungary in the west, and the Maramureș area bordering on Hungary and the Soviet Union in the northwest of Romania. Transylvania has vast forests and fertile soil and is amply endowed with mineral deposits such as iron ore, coal, gold, mercury, salt, and gas deposits.

The Getae or the Dacian tribes lived in the lands of Transylvania as early as the Iron Age. They fought with the Greeks, Persians, Romans, and barbarian tribes. An independent Dacian state formed in the 1st century B.C. lasted until A.D. 106 when it fell to the Romans under the Emperor Trajan. Wave after wave of invaders followed the Romans until finally, when the Turks defeated the Hungarians in 1526, Transylvania became semi-independent under the rule of Magyar princes. In the 16th century, Transylvania supported Michael the Brave (ruler of Wallachia) in defeating the Turks, and in 1600 joined Wallachia and Moldavia in a union of the Romanian lands.

The Subcarpathian Hills

This is an area of gentle relief consisting of low rolling hills (1,640 to 3,280 feet in elevation) lying east and south of the main Carpathian highlands. The Subcarpathians are folded and have a similar geologic origin as the Carpathians. They reach their highest altitude in Dealu Chicera (3,369 feet). The Subcarpathians contain many depressions, the largest of which is Tara Vrancei. The hills contain important mineral deposits including oil, salt, and lignite (brown coal). They are also the main fruit-growing area and the principal center of vineyards in Romania.

The Moldavian Tableland

Located in the eastern part of Romania between the Subcarpathians and the River Prut along the Soviet border, this is an area of eroded hills. In the northwest is the Suceava tableland, whose altitude varies between 984 and 1,640 feet high. The southern part of Moldavia is the Bîrlad tableland, which is 984 to 1,312 feet in elevation. In the central northwest area is the Jijia plain, with an altitude of 656 feet. Moldavia's favorable climate makes it an important grain-producing area. Sugar beets are also widely grown, and in the Suceava tableland potatoes are an important crop. Moldavian soils consist of both alluviums and chernozems in which wheat and maize grow abundantly.

The Dobruja Tableland

This tableland is an ancient Hercynian area of relief eroded into a low undulating and flat area with an elevation ranging between 656 and 984 feet high, with the exception of the Macin Mountains in the north which rise to 1,532 feet in altitude. Geologically speaking, these are the oldest mountains in Romania. Dobruja lies in the southeast part of Romania between the Danube River and the Black Sea coast. Dobruja has a dry climate and irrigation is widely used for farming. Sheep raising and the growing of grains are important activities on this tableland.

The Danube Delta

This triangle-shaped area is located in the southeastern part of Romania, bordering the Black Sea. The triangle is formed by the three main branches of the Danube—Chilia, Sulina and Sfîntu Gheorghe—by which the river flows into the sea. Permanent and temporary nature reserves in the delta cover over 100,000 acres where one can encounter pelicans, floating islands and salt-water vegetation, sandbanks, tropical forests, ducks, and geese. The delta was formed out of a sea gulf filled with mud and sediments by the waters of the Danube, a process still going on today. The area is a multitude of relief form: old mountains, seacoast, ridges, sand dunes, marshes, lakes, and canals. About 80 percent of the delta is covered with water. The most important delta settlements are Tulcea and Sulina. Villages of fishermen abound in the area. See the chapter on the Danube delta for more information about this area.

The Romanian Plain (Wallachia)

The Romanian plain is divided by the Olt River, which lies about 114 miles west of Bucharest. The Olt runs basically north-south and has its origin in the Eastern Carpathians near the headwaters of the Mureş. It is a tributary of the Danube. West of the Olt the Oltenian plain is a series of terraces reaching up to 984 feet in elevation. East of the Olt is the Baragan plain, a flat region which is the granary of Romania. The Oltenian area was largely forested in the past, but in the last two centuries much of its forests were cut. The Baragan area had fewer forests, and most of these have disappeared. Many dams have been built on the Romanian plain and the waters behind them have been widely used for irrigation, particularly in the south along the Danube River. Parts of the Romanian plain have been drained for agriculture. The soils of the plain are thick and consist largely of alluvial material.

Also known as Wallachia, a name derived from the Vlachs, as the people were called who lived here at the beginning of the 10th century, the plain is about 30,000 square miles in area, or roughly one-third of Romania's territory. Wallachia stretches from the Carpathians on the west to the Danube on the south and southeast and to the Siret River on the northeast. After 1310, Wallachia was a collection of feudal states which united with Moldavia in 1859 to form the Romanian union.

The Western Plain

This plain is largely a low-lying and smooth-surfaced area lying in the western part of Romania bordering on Yugoslavia and Hungary. Many rivers drain its surface. Its areas of lower elevations include the Timiş plain, Someş plain, and the Crisuri plain. The higher portions of the Western plain include the Arad plain, Carei plain, and the Gataia plain. After the Romanian plain, it is the second most important agricultural area of Romania. Major cities on this plain include Arad and Timişoara.

People

The population of Romania is over 23 million people, with females making up a slightly larger percentage of the population than males (50.7 percent to 49.3 percent respectively). The average life expectancy is about 70 years. About 56 percent of the population live in towns and cities. Women make up 40 percent of the labor force. The Romanian government lists the percentages of the country's nationalities accordingly: 89.1 percent Romanian nationals; 7.7 percent Magyar; 1.5 percent German; 0.2 percent Ukrainian; 0.2 percent Serbian and Croatian.

By faith or belief, 85 percent of the people worship as Romanian Orthodox. There are 40,000 Moslems in the country and about 30,000 Jews (half of whom live in Bucharest). Roman Catholics number 1,200,000, and Protestants 600,000 (most belonging to the Reformed [Calvinist] Church).

Over 56 percent of Romania's people live in the lowland areas of the country. There are 11 cities with more than 200,000 population. In 1990 the population will be near the 23.5 million mark. There are more than 13,100 villages in the country. The Romanian language is derived from the Latin and uses the Roman alphabet, as does English.

Romanian girls are noted for their beauty, charm, and friendliness. Their lovely dark eyes and hair can be traced back to the ancient Romans. Romanians are proud of their Roman descent. Many Romanian girls are as graceful and voluptuous as the statues of Roman goddesses.

Brief History

It is impossible to describe the history of a nation such as Romania in a few pages; and since this book is written with the tourist in mind rather than the scholar, an attempt is made to present a brief, but succinct, acquaintance with this country and its past events. More details about its history are provided in the chapters which follow.

Prehistory

Archeological finds and excavations reveal that Romania has been inhabited continually since the Paleolithic or Old Stone Age. This was the epoch of carved stone implements. The first Paleolithic discoveries in Romania were made in northern Moldavia during the 19th century. More recently, about 1,000 flint implements were discovered in the area between the Argeş and Olt rivers (i.e., to the west and northwest of Bucharest in the Subcarpathians). Their dating suggests a time before 600,000 B.C.

The oldest work of art discovered in Romania was found in 1978 on the ceiling of a cave in northwest Transylvania near Cuciulat village in Sălaj County. On the cave ceiling is a painting which appears to be an outline of a horse. The painting is 9.6 inches long and 4.9 inches tall. A second and larger figure on the ceiling resembles that of a feline or bear. The paintings are dated prior to 10,000 B.C. Some artifacts of a subsequent period have been found in the Iron Gates area of the Danube River.

Evidence of a Neolithic (New Stone Age) culture in Romania is the painted pottery of Cucuteni dated back to the 4th–3rd millennia B.C. There is evidence of a burnt clay art in all the Romanian territory since the Neolithic period.

In the third millennium B.C., Indo-European migration altered the ethnic composition of the peoples of the Carpathian and Danubian areas of the country. From the Bronze Age onward, historians speak of a Thracian population (2nd millennium B.C.) on Romanian territory.

The Geto-Dacians

The Dacians (or Getae), who lived in the Carpathian-Danubian area during the Iron Age in the first half of the 1st millennium B.C., became ethnically distinct from the Thracian tribes and founded a civilization of their own. In spite of some influence by the Greeks, they never came to accept the Greek tongue. The Greeks established colonies on the shore of the Black Sea—Histria, Tomi (now Constanța) and Callatis (now Mangalia)—during the 7th–6th centuries B.C. In 514 B.C. the Dacians strongly resisted a Persian army of King Darius I. In the 3rd century B.C., Geto-Dacian tribes on the Wallachian plain withstood attack by King Lysimachus of Thrace under their leader, Dromichaetes.

Burebista (70–44 B.C.), a strong Dacian ruler, extended his control over the Greek Black Sea cities and as far north as Bohemia. Another Dacian ruler, Decebalus (A.D. 87–106) brought the Dacian state to the pinnacle of its centralization and independence. He was finally slain after two campaigns (A.D. 101–2 and 105–6) against the Roman legions of the Emperor Trajan. Dacia then became a Roman province, and the Romans brought in colonists to settle it. These colonists covered roughly the present area of Romania, but Romanization was most complete in the areas of western Wallachia, Transylvania, and the Banat. The Romans had earlier occupied Dobrudja, where the great poet Ovid was banished.

Roman Dacia

Dacia remained Roman from A.D. 106 to 271, and the Latin tongue replaced the old Thraco-Illyrian, although some of its common words remained in usage. Gradually the Daco-Roman population was assimilated and became Romanized. The Romans built roads, bridges, fortifications, and other works in Dacia. The ruins or remains of many of these can still be seen. These were left behind as the frontiers of the empire came under attack by successive waves of barbarian invaders. These invasions would last a thousand years. Decius temporarily halted the Goths at Nicopolis on the Danube, and in 251 perished at Abritum in another battle with the Goths. Claudius defeated the Goths in Serbia in 268. Aurelian beat back the Alemanni but decided Rome could not hold Dacia and ordered it evacuated in 271, yielding the land north of the Danube to the barbarian hordes. Nearly all the invaders that swarmed into southern Europe until the 10th century marched into Romanian lands.

From the Romans to the Principalities

After the 4th century, waves of migratory peoples passed over the Wallachian and Moldavian plains. The Goths stayed long on Romanian soil, but there is little or no trace of their having been there. Their language had no effect on that spoken by the Latinized populace. Later, a Mongolian race, the Huns, occupied the area between the Danube and Tisza rivers from 375-453. On the heels of the Huns came a Gothic stock people, the Gepidae (453-566), who allied themselves with the eastern Roman Empire headquartered at Constantinople. They were followed by a relative of the Huns, the Avars (566-799), who came in just ahead of the Slavs. The Slavs had been infiltrating the area for some time, and now they came in great numbers. Settling on the plains of Romania with the Romanized people, they later moved to the Carpathian highlands, settling in its valleys. Many of the place names in Romania are of Slavic origin. In time the Slavs became assimilated with the Romanians. The Bulgars, a people related to the Huns, swept in during 679, adopted the Slavic language, and became assimilated with the Slavs. One of the Bulgar leaders, Boris I, was baptized in 865 in the Orthodox Church. Legend says his Christian motives occurred after a Byzantine painted a gruesome picture of hell on his palace wall. The Daco-Roman population had already accepted Christianity in the 2nd and 3rd centuries. In 840 and 890 the Hunnish Magyars occupied the Danubian plains but eventually gave them up and settled in what is now Hungary and Yugoslavia. The Transylvanian province of Romania was ruled by Hungary from the 11th century until 1918. Of the hordes of migratory people, the Magyars planted the last permanent settlements on European soil. The Pechenegs succeeded the Magyars on the plains of Romania and then disappeared, probably in wars with their neighbors and Byzantium. In 1050 there came the Cumans, a Finno-Ugric tribe, who also eventually settled in Hungary. In 1241 the last of the conquering hordes, the Mongolian Tatars, seized the coastal areas of Romania. At the beginning of modern times, the Ottoman Turks extended their empire into Romania in the 1300s.

The Rise of the Principalities

The first mention of the Romanians in the lands that eventually became their kingdom appear in documents dated in the 1160s. According to a Byzantine chronicler, a large force of Wallachs (or ancient Italian colonists) assisted the Byzantine army in a campaign against the Hungarians. Later a strong Bulgaro-Romanian kingdom was defeated by Hungary in 1230, and Wallachia continued as a fief of the Hungarians. From 1290 to 1308 Prince Basarb established a principality over Wallachia that was semi-independent of Hungary. Subsequently, in the middle of the 1300s another prince, Bogdan, created the principality of Moldavia. The beginnings of the national consciousness of the Romanians blossomed in the formation of these two principalities. Meanwhile, Transylvania under Hungarian rule enjoyed a high level of autonomy until 1526; and Dobruja, another feudal state, gained independence in the early 14th century and would later unite with Wallachia.

At the end of the 14th century the Turks stood on the shores of the Danube, and there now came to the forefront several Romanian leaders who became prominent in their struggles with the Ottoman Empire. The first of these was Mircea the Old of Wallachia (1386–1418). He annexed Dobruja and won a victory over the Turks in 1394 but later accepted Turkish suzerainty. Other Wallachian princes, Dan II (1420–31) and Vlad the Impaler (1456–62, 1476), continued the struggle. Vlad had some success fighting the Turks, but in 1462 they marched into Wallachia. Meanwhile, Alexander the Good of Moldavia (1401–31) helped to stabilize his principality. Another remarkable Moldavian ruler was Stephen the Great (1457–1504). He defeated the Hungarians, Turks, and

Poles while building nearly fifty monasteries and churches. He had a strong influence on Moldavian art and architecture and ruled part of Transylvania.

In the 16th century, Michael the Brave (1593–1601) ascended to the throne of Wallachia and proceeded to unite his principality with those of Moldavia and Transylvania to cast out the Turks. He won several famous battles against larger Turkish forces, an accomplishment that would not be repeated until the War of Independence in the 19th century. Michael was assassinated in 1601, and the alliance he forged fell apart. The Turks reasserted their control over the principalities and between 1716 and 1821 and sent their own officials to govern the principalities. These officials were largely Greeks who bribed Turkish officers for their positions. This period in Romanian history is known as the Phanariote Period, named after the Phanar quarter of Constantinople from where the Greeks came. The principalities had to pay tribute, but Wallachia and later Moldavia were allowed to have their own law codes. Greek became the language of the government and the cultural tongue.

During the 1700s, Russia and Austria also vied with each other for chunks of Romanian territory. Russia briefly occupied Moldavia, and then Austria took the area of Bukovina and its religious center of Suceava. Russia then seized the district of Bessarabia. In 1821 a popular uprising occurred when Tudor Vladimirescu, a Wallachian captain, seized Bucharest in an attempt to expel the Greeks and improve the lot of the peasants. The Greeks captured and executed him, but he inflamed the passions of Romanian independence and became a martyr for its cause. In 1848 a new uprising occurred, but the Turks and Russians quelled it. In Transylvania, fighting continued into 1849 with Austrian, Hungarian, and Russian forces involved. There the fighting evolved around racial lines, with the Saxons and Romanians pitted against the Magyars. Transylvania remained under Hungarian control until 1918.

Union of the Principalities and National Independence

The 1848 revolution rekindled the spirit of national unity on the part of the three principalities. Further, the Romanians knew from past experience that they could not rely upon any of their neighbors for assistance. Following Russia's defeat in the Crimean War (1854–56), the Congress of Paris in 1856 announced a joint protectorate of Wallachia and Moldavia by Great Britain, France, Russia, Austria, Prussia, Turkey, and Piedmont, with Turkey continuing its suzerainty over the Romanians. In 1857 the assemblies of Wallachia and Moldavia voted to create a union of the two principalities. They followed this action by electing Prince Alexandru Iaon Cuza to rule the union in 1859. In 1862 the state of Romania was officially proclaimed. A number of reforms were carried out after the 1859 union, including educational and land reform and the secularization of the property of the monasteries. In 1866 Cuza resigned, and the joint protectorate meeting in Paris proposed that Charles of Hohenzollern-Sigmaringen be confirmed as ruler of the union by a plebiscite in Romania. After confirmation he went to Romania, called a constitutional convention which ratified the constitution he submitted, and then visited the sultan of Turkey, who graciously received him. Charles took the title of Prince Carol I and had a long and contented reign. He married a Prussian princess (Elizabeth of Wied) who became better known as Carmen Sylva. In 1877 Charles took personal command of a Russian and Romanian force (at the request of the tsar) and defeated a huge Turkish force at the battle of Plevna. At the Congress of Berlin in 1878, Romania was forced to cede Bessarabia to Russia, but it was rewarded with the area of Dobruja along the Black Sea. It had been 460 years since Mircea the Old had annexed it. In 1881 Prince Charles was proclaimed King Carol and donned a crown made of steel from a cannon he captured at Plevna from the Turks.

Romania remained neutral during the first Balkan War (1912–13), although one plan called for it to offer Bulgaria part of its army to help take Adrianople from the Turks. In the second Balkan War (June–July 1913), Romania joined Greece, Serbia, and Turkey against Bulgaria. The Romanian army entered Bulgaria which, after the short-lived war, ceded southern Dobruja to the Romanians. King Carol I died in 1914, and Romania's new ruler became Ferdinand I (1914–27). Queen Marie was his admired wife.

The First World War and its close set the stage for the creation of Romanian national state unity. During the first two years of the war, Romania remained neutral. There was much pro-German sympathy, but Romania's distrust of the Germans in addition to its dislike of Turkey, Hungary, and Bulgaria decided it in favor of joining the Allies in August 1916. The Romanians, ill-prepared, marched into Transylvania; but German forces under Von Machensen defeated them, then pushed through the passes in the Carpathians down on the Wallachian plain. Meanwhile, German, Turkish, and Bulgarian forces pushed into Dobruja. Bucharest was captured in December, but Romanian forces continued to hold out in Moldavia. The Romanians won a victory at Marasesti in 1917, but this was in vain as they were forced to sign the Treaty of Bucharest in May 1918 and leave the war. Romania reentered the war prior to the armistice in 1918 and Allied victory. Romanian forces returned to Transylvania, occupied it, and then drove into Hungary in 1919 after Communist and Socialist forces there gained control under Bela Kun, who launched an attack across the Tiza River against the Romanians. The Romanians captured Budapest and occupied it for several months. The Romanian union was accomplished on December 1, 1918, when the national assembly met at Alba Iulia and Transylvania cast its lot with Romania. Bessarabia and Bukovina had earlier declared their union with Romania, and by the Treaty of Trianon in 1920 a portion of Banat Province was given to Romania.

From National Unity to the Present

In the interwar period the land reform act of 1921 and the new constitution of 1923 were among the major events in the country. The Romanian Communist Party was organized in 1921 but outlawed in 1924. Romania, Yugoslavia, and Czechoslovakia founded the Little Entente (1920–21); and in 1934 Romania joined with Yugoslavia, Greece, and Turkey in the Balkan Entente. The depression of 1929–33 caused social unrest and instability within the country and paved the way for the return of Carol, King Ferdinand's son who was in exile with Magda Lupescu, his mistress. He ascended the throne as Carol II and brought Lupescu to Bucharest. A Fascist movement was founded in 1927 by Codreanu, who later renamed his followers the Iron Guard. The Iron Guard grew in strength during the 1930s, and King Carol had thousands of them imprisoned and Codreanu shot. In 1938, King Carol II abolished the constitution and proclaimed a royal dictatorship. Romania declared its neutrality after Hitler invaded Poland in 1939. With the fall of France, Romania lost its close ally, and King Carol turned to Germany as its protector. It also lost Bessarabia and northern Bukovina in June 1940 when these areas were demanded from it by the Soviet Union, and Hitler advised Romania to relinquish them. Next, Romania lost southern

Dobrudja to Bulgaria and, finally, had to cede the northern part of Transylvania to Hungary in August 1940 by terms of the Vienna Award. King Carol II abdicated and Michael became king, although largely as a figurehead, since General Ion Antonescu directed the course of the country over the next several years. Antonescu allied Romania with Hitler in the Tripartite Pact and on June 22, 1941, marched thirty Romanian divisions into Bessarabia and Bukovina as German forces were invading Soviet territory. Romanian forces continued on into the Soviet Union, where their losses were heavy at the siege of Odessa. They fought bravely alongside the Germans, but by March 1944 the Russians were back in Bukovina and by that summer had moved into northern Moldavia. Romania then made contact with the Allies to arrange an armistice, and King Michael had Antonescu arrested and ordered the cessation of fighting. On August 26 Romania declared war on Germany, and the Russians took Bucharest without opposition on August 31. Bessarabia and northern Bukovina were lost to the Soviet Union, but Romania had Transylvania returned to it.

The Communists gradually increased their ranks in the government with the backing of Soviet pressure and by 1947 had effectively taken control of it and the country. King Michael abdicated, the monarchy was abolished, and Romania was declared a People's Republic. A Communist government headed by Petru Groza took power.

Soviet-style nationalization and collectivization followed the Communist takeover. Industrial enterprises, mines, banks, and transport facilities came under a planned economy. In 1951, five-year plans were introduced to develop industry and agriculture. Gheorghiu-Dej became one of the main leaders of the Romanian Communist Party and president of the Council of Ministers. After Stalin died in 1953, Gheorghiu-Dej attempted to improve relations with the West, China, and other countries. Romania followed a policy of independence in its foreign relations, one which did not always meet with the approval of the Soviet Union. In 1965 Nicolae Ceauşescu became Romania's leader when Gheorghiu-Dej died. He continued the policy of Romanian independence and challenged the Soviet right to unilaterally dictate to its partners in the Warsaw Pact, especially its military policy and actions. Born in 1918, Ceauşescu was re-elected head of state in 1985. He strongly resisted the reform movement sweeping Eastern Europe in the 1980s, and was deposed from power and executed in December 1989.

Folklore, Folk Art, Ethnography

Romania is a land of contrasts and paradoxes and a vast museum of ancient heritage. Here the Old World is still alive in thousands of quaint villages. Its treasures of art and architecture include Roman, Byzantine, and Brancovan styles. The famous painted churches of Moldavia are astonishing treasures of art. Romanian folk art, crafts, and native costumes have their own special character. And, of course, there is the legendary Carpathian Mountains with their imposing feudal castles.

Count Dracula

Who has not heard of Transylvania and the legend of Count Dracula! The legend of the count is associated with the ancient province of Transylvania, whose mysterious-looking old castles are perched on hillsides with slopes covered by shadowy forests. Add the sound of a few wolves, a moonlit night, and the wind whistling through the trees, and it's enough to cause goosebumps on the skin. Come to Romania and discover for yourself whether the story of Dracula is fact or fiction.

Most people who have heard of the story of Count Dracula know the version of it as told by Bram Stoker in his novel *Dracula* or the Hollywood version made by film makers. Yet every legend seems to have in fact some historical basis, as does that of Count Dracula (actually Vlad Dracula). Further, Vlad Dracula was a prince and not a count. Castle Dracula, or at least the one adopted by tourists, lies sixty-seven miles northwest of Bucharest in the zone of the Carpathians known as the Transylvanian Alps. Castle Bran is a medieval fortification which hugs the top of a peak on a mountain road that winds down into the area of Transylvania. The castle, located near the city of Braşov, was built in 1377 in a Gothic type of architecture. A museum displaying medieval art is located in the castle. Around the castle are located a number of villages and several tourist huts; paradoxically, it lies amidst a small health resort. The victims of Vlad Dracula would hardly consider it that. Nevertheless, the medieval weapons and decorations inside the castle are sufficient to conjure up in the mind lurid images from a bygone era. The real Vlad Dracula or Vlad

Țepeș (the Impaler) was a Wallachian prince whose reign was relatively short. He swore an oath to the Hungarian king in 1456 as Prince Vlad IV. His mind was abnormal, and he apparently was a psychopath. His tortured and depraved mind delighted in killing, maiming, and all sorts of bloodthirsty acts. The age, sex, or race of his victims mattered little to him. According to a Greek historian, a Romanian taken prisoner by the Turks refused to divulge any information about Vlad Țepeș because he feared death less than he feared the wrath of his prince. The Turkish sultan marveled that any man could inspire such fear into the minds of others and remarked that such a man would make a great leader. Mohammed the Conquerer felt that Vlad posed a threat to his conquering southeast Europe and decided to capture him. He sent two of his followers to arrange a trap and seize Vlad. Vlad discovered their secret and had them impaled. Vlad's sinister and diseased mind gave orders to his followers to cover the Turkish pasha in a ceremonial robe and impale him with a longer stake than the other victims, to honor his title and position. Whem Mohammed entered Wallachia in pursuit of Vlad, he found an entire valley covered with bodies impaled by his adversary, including that of the pasha. The sultan was so distraught that he cried at the scene of the vicious slaughter. Vlad fled to Hungary, was imprisoned there, and reportedly turned to Catholicism during his twelve years as a prisoner. In 1476 the Hungarians returned his title and throne to him as ruler of Wallachia. He died in the same year.

Vlad Dracula was born in the medieval town of Sighișoara, in Transylvania. The ancient house in which he was born is occupied by a restaurant displaying the emblem of a dragon, symbol of a royal order united to fight the Turks. In Romanian folklore the dragon symbolizes the devil, who is called *dracul*. Accordingly, the Romanians called him Vlad Dracula ("son of the devil") or Vlad Țepeș (Vlad the Impaler). The legend of Vlad says that while passing through the town of Brașov, near Bran Castle, he sought to raise money from local merchants to finance an army against the Turks. The merchants refused his request, and later he stopped at Bran Castle where he captured a large number of them and had them impaled nearby. Another time he is said to have had the turbans of a group of emissaries sent to him by the sultan nailed to their heads when they did not remove them in his presence. In his famous novel, Bram Stoker cast Dracula in the role of a vampire. The legend of vampirism is a commonly told tale in Romania, especially among the peasants in rural areas.

The Sheep Feast

This lively shepherd's folk feast, called *Sîmbra Oilor*, is an old custom of the sheep breeders associated with the organizing of grazing. Prefaced by a suggestive "Dance of the Girls," this festival takes place on a large clearing, usually in a picturesque natural landscape. It begins with a traditional "call to the *sîmbra*," shouted by the oldest shepherd. At his urging, the *sîmbroşi* groups, men and women, revive the ancient practices of the sheep milking of the "sheepfold" into wooden pails and a measuring of the milk. The festival, which takes place in an atmosphere of humor and song, continues with a large common meal composed of original local dishes (mutton steaks, cheese pies, flat cakes) together with the very strong *pălincă*, or plum brandy.

The climax of the feast is the popular artistic program performed by village groups made up of singers, dancers, *ţipuritori* (those who accompany the dances shouting short rhymes), pipers, and trumpeters singing and dancing old artistic creations such as "The Sewing of the Flag" and "The Wedding." As the feast is also an opportunity for organizing a folk art exhibition, the products for sale include hats, costumes, collars, shepherd's purses, embroidered towels, spindles, and wooden spoons. The sheep feast is also an occasion to display the creations by folk masters of their well-known ceramic art works.

Pottery

Archeological finds prove the existence of the burnt clay art on the whole Romanian territory since the New Stone Age. The early expressions (the Criş and lineary ceramics culture) have geometrical qualities that may be separated into three cultures, according to the evolution of their ways of adorning the pots.

The Boian (Wallachia) decoration was accomplished by excision in cylindrical forms and in the shape of a truncated cone with rectilinear direction and meanderlike ornamentation. It is stylized in angles. The Cucuteni (Moldavia) decoration was painted with white, red, and black in shapes with convex directions arched into attentuated angles and spiral-shaped ornamentation. Turdaş

(Transylvania) decoration was scratched in directions with sharp angles having arched sides and spiral shapes, tending to acquire geoid forms.

During the Bronze Age the black ceramics appeared in the Otomani, Pecica-Periam, Bucharest, and Sarata-Meonteoru cultures. Produced by suppressed burning, they usually have shining surfaces because they were rubbed with graphite.

After a relative stagnation at the beginning of the Iron Age (about 300 B.C.), the Dacian-Getic pottery developed by using a wheel operated with the foot while molding. The Romans brought to Dacia a new style in pottery art, developed by adapting the forms of the Greek art in a simplified version, a style that still lasts in some areas until the present. Later on, the influences of the Byzantine ceramics with enamel, as well as introduction to the European art, brought about the emergence of a local production (Curtea de Argeş) that, together with the old traditional Getic-Dacian and Roman art, cultivated a bright chromatism made with a brush or a horn arranged into original shapes. Clay, the modern material used in ceramics, is cleaned of impurities, cut, leavened, tempered, shaped by imprinting, molded by hand (on a wheel with a slow circular motion or on a wheel worked with the foot), casted, and burnt in a furnace.

Current potters follow the ancient Romanian art of making pottery by preserving the old traditions in the multitude and elegance of shapes, in the development of motifs and decorative compositions, maintaining its authenticity, and rendering it unique in artistic creation. Classified according to the burning system, Romanian ceramics include two groups presently: (a) the black ceramics of Dacian tradition; and (b) the red ceramics, whose development has been influenced by the assimilation of elements of Roman origins. The black ceramics have tall, slim, or conic shapes and generally show a simple, discreet decoration of classical distinction. The red unenameled ceramics show the elegance of their shapes and decorations usually in white or brown and assert an aesthetic vision of accuracy and consistency.

Still, the most refined standards of folk artistic creation are mirrored in the enameled ceramics that, by way of varied shapes, geometrical motifs, and chromatic structures, retain a distinctive quality. A technique specific to Romanian pottery, *jirăvirea cu gaiţă*, or a manner of scratching the clay that permits the colors painted on the pottery to intermingle without mixing, results in a pattern of intertwined delicate lines.

Romanian folk ceramics have a multitude of traditional methods and techniques, which are: (a) *angobare*—the covering of the surface of the pottery with very fine, usually white, clay in order to seal its porosity and hide its color; (b) glazing—the laying of a protective stratum resembling enamel but which is transparent; (c) *graphiting*—the coloring of the surface by rubbing it with fine coal or graphite; (d) *îmbrînare*—the sticking of thin clay rolls having ornamental functions on the surface of the unburnt pot by pressing them with the finger; (e) *incision*—a decoration system consisting in the scraping of the unburnt surface with simple drawings—usually linear, then spirals and meanders—taking care that the edges of the cut should not have lateral irregularities; (f) *inlay*—the filling of the excised parts on the surface of the pot with colored material; (g) *jirăvire*—a device characteristic only of Romanian ceramics, achieved with the help of a *goiţă* (a comb with hair cogs) which allows the painted colors to intermingle without mixing; (h) *polishing*—the rubbing of the surface of the pot, which is still unburnt, with a hard object in order to make the surface compact and thus lend it a black metallic shine; (i) *enameling*—the covering of the pot with an opaque layer of metallic oxides (sometimes tin or zinc) vitrified by baking; and (j) *zgrafitare*—the scraping of the unburnt part so that the clay background should appear, which has a darker color after burning.

Cula (Fortified House)

This is a special type of house citadel found beginning with the 16th century in Oltenia in the northwest of Wallachia. It functioned as a means of defense against the numerous raids of the Turks from the area south of the Danube, as well as against the increased intensity of local peasant uprisings and banditry. The most common form of *cula* is a prismatic building with a square or rectangular basis, with the side about 236 feet long at maximum and thick walls (2 to 3.3 feet) made of stone or brick masonry.

The rooms—located on two or three levels, of small height with floors made of large joists of oak or with arches—connect, by means of interior wooden ladders when they are on different floors. The ground floor, with only one or two narrow little windows, serves as a cellar and as a tool and food storage room.

The entrance door, built of oak joists, is equipped with strong bolting systems and very often flanked by battlements, or small holes, that permitted the defenders to shoot at the attackers. On the upper floor, beside the living quarters, is found a watchtower with columns and arches. Sometimes the upper floor is entirely occupied by a lookout tower. According to its building plan and the way the rooms are placed on the terrain, the *cula* may be divided into three categories, or three different functions: refuge, defense, or temporary dwelling; watch, signalization, and alarm; and permanent dwelling, also fulfilling signalization and defense functions.

Peasant Houses

Romanian peasant houses are picturesque. Many are whitewashed and are commonly decorated in blue trim. Their roofs are usually covered with red tiles or corrugated metal. Wood carvings and fretwork are distinguishing features of the trim. The houses are traditionally small, and outside stairs are usually built to connect with rooms on the second floor. Cooking may be done outdoors in a bake oven. One or more sheds or straw shacks may surround the house. Fences are ubiquitous, either surrounding the house or running across the front of the yard. The furniture and pottery in the homes are often handmade by the family, as are the curtains, rugs, and clothing.

Many houses are built with a porch. The eaves commonly overhang, and this makes it easy to add more rooms or a second story. Sheds may also be built underneath the eaves, or they may simply shelter tools or equipment. Few of the houses today have the old, traditional half underground floors. Peasant houses in Moldavia and Wallachia are usually white in color, whereas those in Transylvania and Maramureş are frequently multicolored. Wooden benches generally line the living room of the house, which usually contains a bed or two and a stove. Beds are usually made by the family out of wood.

Many peasant houses are located in the more than 13,000 villages. In cluster villages the houses are very close together, whereas in the compact villages the houses run wall to wall and open on a courtyard entered through big gates. In the mountain areas, villages are dispersed with pastures and hayfields separating the homesteads.

CHAPTER 2

Bucharest

Romania's 500-year-old capital lies on a wooded plain just 37 miles from the Danube River and 80 miles from the Carpathian peaks. The city has 2.3 million inhabitants. With its broad, cafe-lined boulevards, garden restaurants, parks, lakes, and monuments, it is a metropolis of unique beauty and Latin charm. It is a beautiful city and one of Europe's main capitals. Bucharest is the vibrant center of Romania's economic and cultural life. It is the major transportation hub of the country and the gateway to Romania for a number of foreign airlines as well as its own government-run airline, Tarom. Many of Romania's major highways focus on Bucharest and radiate from it like spokes on a wheel. The city is indeed the major starting point for visiting other areas of the country. Bucharest has dozens of museums with valuable and internationally recognized collections in the fields of art, history, science, and technology. The city features numerous theaters, opera, ballet, a circus, and concerts of the Bucharest Philharmonic Orchestra. It is also an important center for international meetings, congresses, conferences, symposia, and artistic events.

For the connoisseur in matters of taste there are a great many delicacies to excite the palate. You can feast on garnished grilled beef, pork, or chicken. The highly seasoned grilled meatballs are found in most restaurants. The city is well known for its luscious cakes and pastries. Romanians are especially fond of cream cakes, of which there is a wide selection.

At the end of the First World War, Bucharest had only 300,000 people; but in the period between the two world wars it grew rapidly and became known as "the little Paris of the East." Its sprouting cafes, clubs, restaurants, hotels, and foreign embassies made the city a center of one of Europe's cultural and political circles. One of the main boulevards of Bucharest is a long, wide avenue often referred to as "the little Champs Elysees." It is longer than the famous Parisian boulevard and is lined with trees in similar fashion. Where once richly decorated and ornate carriages, drawn by beautiful horses and driven by uniformed coachmen pulled finely dressed men and women along its thoroughfares, now the automobile moves in their place. In the spring, the trees along this Bucharest avenue (Şoseaua Kiseleff) blossom and help to dress the city much the same as those between the Place de la Concorde and the Arc de Triomphe in Paris. In the center of Şoseaua Kiseleff stands an Arc de Triomphe which is almost indistinguishable from its lookalike in the French capital. This gigantic structure was erected in Bucharest at the time of the coronation of King Ferdinand.

What strikes a visitor to Bucharest today is the new urbanistic growth of the past several decades. Notable is the architecture of some residential districts, such as Drumul Taberei, Militari, Tian, Băneasa, 1 Mai, N. Titulescu, Pantelimon, Stefan ce Mare, and Cgingasi. The new political administrative center, the systematization of the streets, the Dimbovita River arrangement as well as the Danube-Bucharest Canal (making Bucharest a port directly connected with the Black Sea) are some of the notable constructions of more recent decades.

The economic importance of Bucharest compared to the rest of Romania is attested to by the fact that about 14 percent of Romania's industrial production is achieved in the city. It has 158 research and design institutes employing 100,000 people; 20 theaters; 42 museums and memorial houses; 50 movie houses; 75 clubs and cultural centers; 12 higher education institutes with 47 faculties and more than 60,000 students; 2 national libraries (the Library of the Academy of the Socialist Republic of Romania and the Central State Library); an opera house; and the two largest airports in Romania (Otopeni and Băneasa). Eight major highways and railways lines center on the capital. Bucharest had the first underground subway in the country (5.53 miles were opened to traffic in 1979).

Bucharest has nearly 10 percent of the total population of the country spread over 1,053 square miles. The municipality of the city includes six urban districts and the Ilfov Agricultural Sector surrounding the metropolis. Bucharest turns out a variety of industrial goods: textiles, shoes, automobiles, machinery, food products, construction materials, and household items. About one-fifth of the country's metal products and machinery is built in the capital. In addition, the city refines petroleum products, produces pharmaceuticals, and tans leather.

Bucharest lies on the Wallachian plain at an altitude of 269 feet above sea level. January temperatures average 36° F during the day, while July and August average 86° F in the daytime. Two rivers, the Dimbovița and Colentina, flow through the city. The Dimbovița has been channeled to carry both sewage and clean water, while the Colentina consists of a chain of lakes (Băneasa, Floreasca, Grivita, Tei, Fundeni, Cernica, Străulesti, Plumbuita, Pantelimon, and Herăstrău).

The city developed on the site of a Dacian settlement but was first mentioned in documents only in 1459. Bucharest has many old churches, the oldest of which is the Curtea Veche (Old Church) built in 1545–59 by Prince Mircea Ciobanul. During the 17th and 18th centuries a number of other churches were built and several monasteries were established beyond the medieval boundaries of the city. In 1850 the College of Engineering was founded, and in 1863 the Old University was built. The beautiful Athenaeum, a concert hall on the Calea Victoriei, was constructed in 1888. The National Art Museum, formerly a royal palace, was built in 1935–37.

When Wallachia and Moldavia united in 1859, Bucharest became their capital, and in 1862 it became the capital of Romania. The city was occupied three times by the Russians between 1828 and 1855 and by the Austrians during the Crimean War (1854–56). The Germans marched into the city in 1916 and stayed until after the armistice in 1918. The Germans took control of the city again in September 1940 but departed in August 1944 when the Russian army entered it. Air raids heavily damaged the city during World War II.

What to See

History and Art Museum of the City of Bucharest, 2 Blvd. 1848. Originally a palace, this museum consists of more than twenty rooms of art and historical objects covering the ancient period of Romania through its modern history. Before World War I this former palace was the setting of formal parties, balls, and receptions attended by the elite and wealthy members of Romanian society. After World War I a number of banks operated in its rooms. It was made into a museum after World War II, and its collection of art and other objects began to grow in number, now totaling about 100,000 items. Included in its collection are frescoes, ceramics, embroideries, and works of sculpture. In addition there are old maps, parchments, items from the period of Roman occupation, and early Romanian newspapers. The former collections of the Bucharest Historical Museum were added to this museum after 1959.

Village and Folk Art Museum, 28 Şoseaua Kiseleff. The museum is open between May 1 and October 1, 10 A.M. to 6 P.M. (closed on Mondays). It was founded in 1936 by Professor Dimitrie Gusti after ten years of research and acquisitions. An open-air ethnographic museum, it is one of the most interesting ones in Romania. Its objects represent the main historical and geographic areas of the country and include seventy complete farms with more than three hundred buildings set up on a twenty-five acres of ground on the border of the Herăstrău Lake. Old-style architecture seen includes Zapodeni-Iasi (17th century), Straja-Suceava (18th century), and Berbesti-Maramureş (1775), dwelling types that no longer exist. There are earth huts from Oltenia, farms with fortified enclosures from Cimpul lui Neag-Hunedoara, pastoral aggregate from the Sebeş Mountains. Farming technical equipment includes old mill types with buckets, "tubs," Dobrudja windmills, fulling mills, and gold pestle stamps. Wooden churches include Dragomiersti-Maramureş (1772), Turea-Cluj (1770), and Rapciuni-Bacău (1773). Old roadside crosses are displayed. Inside the farms, the interiors were reconstructed with their furniture, fabrics, parts of folk costumes, household objects, icons, and pottery. The collections comprise over 50,000 art objects brought from all areas of the country: woven materials for the adorning of interiors, men's and women's folk costumes, painting on glass from different areas (Nicula, Maramureş, Bihor, Alba Iulia, Laz, Fagaras, and Scheii Brasovului), painted eggs, wooden objects, household objects, tools, architecture elements, ceramics, metal objects and a permanent exhibition on "Romanian Popular Carpets." The museum possesses extensive documentary archives about Romanian villages.

Brancoveanu Palace, Mogoşoaia, Bucharest municipality. This palace is representative of Romanian architecture of the time of Constantin Brancoveanu, ruler of Wallachia (1688–1714), and was built in 1702. The three-storied building is built symmetrically in relation to its main axis. At the main entrance, the palace has a front yard surrounded by a high wall and monumental gate and at the other facade a park descending to a lake by means of successive terraces. Its original ornamentation style of Renaissance and Baroque was adapted to the Romanian national style. Its artistically styled watchtower with ladder is a multitude of architectural elements carved into stone. The decorative details of the building are typified in its elegant "spathory" hall where the ruler's councils and trials used to take place. The palace was restored with additions according to its original style and became a museum of Brancoveanu art dating from 1957.

Arts Museum of the Socialist Republic of Romania, 1 Ştirbei Vodă St. The museum is open 11 A.M. to 7 P.M. and closed on Mondays. It was founded in 1948 by assimilation of the collections of the State Picture Gallery, the Municipal Museum, the Simu Museum, the Kalinderu Museum, the Toma Stelian Museum, and the former royal collection. Its present-day organization has been in the Palace of the Republic since 1962. The museum has seven sections with more than 70,000 exhibits.

The collection in the *Old Romanian Art Section,* brought together under the guidance of the historian and writer Al.I. Odobescu in the years 1862–64, is a genuine treasure: embroideries, costume parts, metalworks, icons, wooden and stone sculptures, mural painting fragments, and manuscripts from Wallachia, Moldavia, and Transylvania (10th to 13th centuries). The *Modern and Contemporary Romanian Art Section* was assembled in 1962, and its works illustrate the development of fine arts in Romania in the 19th and 20th centuries. A special hall is dedicated to Th. Aman

(1831–91), who, together with Gh. Tattarescu, founded the Romanian school of beaux arts (1864). Two halls shelter the largest N. Grigorescu collection (1838–1907).

The *European Art Section* is grouped according to national schools and chronology: the Italian school (Antonello da Messina, Domenico Veneziano, Lorenzo Lotto, Tintoretto, Tizian Palma Vechio, the Basano family, Bronzino, Corregio, Magneso), the Spanish school (Juan de Juanes, Alonsa Cario, El Greco, Zurbaran, Murillo); the German school (Lucas Grande the Old, Bartholome Zeitblom, Hans Meltscher, Adam Elsheimer); the Flemish-Dutch school (Jan van Eyck, Hans Memling, van Hemessen, Peter Breugel the Young, Jan I. Bruegel, Peter Paul Rubens, Jordaens, and others); the French school (Claude Lorrain, Jacques Courtois, N. Largilliers, H. Rigaud, Greuze, Delacroix, Daubingny, Millet, Daumier, Courbet, Monet, Renoir, Sisley, Pissaro, Signac); Russian and Soviet paintings: Repin, Aivazovski, Serov, Levitan, Joganson. The *Oriental and Far East Art Section* contains Chinese art collections, starting with the 3rd century B.C. to the 20th century, and Japanese and Persian art collections. The *Decorative Art Section* (1971) is comprised of furniture (German late Gothic pieces, Italian and French Renaissance pieces, Louis XV and Louis XVI drawing room sets, Biedermayer pieces); Flemish and French tapestries (16th to 18th centuries); silks, brocades, lace, ceramics, Murano and Bohemian glasswares, and others. The *Graphic Arts Section* (1950), divided into Romanian graphic art and world graphic art sections, exhibits engravings, drawings, aquarelles, pastels, posters, miniatures, and manuscripts. The *Section for Propaganda, Studies, and Documents* organizes dialogues with visitor's groups, lectures for school children, and conferences. The museum has a library consisting of records, tapes, and films; a card index; and collection of documents, as well as a restoration workshop (1952).

History Museum of the Socialist Republic of Romania, 12 Calea Victoriei. It is open Tuesday through Friday from 10 A.M. to 7 P.M.; on Saturdays, 10 A.M. to 2 P.M.; closed on Mondays. Founded in 1834. Since 1973 it has been in the Old Post Palace built between 1894 and 1900 (architectural monument). The main collection comes from the Museum of National Antiquities. By means of 50,000 original exhibits displayed in sixty halls, the museum presents the historical evolution of the Romanian people from Paleolithic times to the Socialist epoch.

The History of the Primitive Commune shows exhibits from the early Paleolithic to the 1st century B.C. *Old History* (1st century B.C.–3rd century A.D.) depicts outstanding events at the time of the Dacian state and Roman domination. Noteworthy are the pot with the inscription "Decebalus per Scorillo," Roman military diplomas, waxed slates, and epigraphic documents. *Medieval History* (A.D. 271 to 1820) points out the continuity of inhabitation in Romania, the origins of the Romanian people and language, the formation of feudal Romania, the anti-Ottoman struggle, and popular uprisings. *Modern History* (1821–1918) illustrates the most important events: the revolutionary movement in 1821, the revolution in 1848, the Union of the Principalities (1859), the obtaining of state independence (1877–78), the spreading of Socialist ideas in Romania, the First World War, and the influence of the October Socialist Revolution. Exhibits include the original text of the Pades Proclamation, manifestos and programs of the 1848 movement, and the 1892 Memorandum.

Contemporary History mirrors the period from the end of World War I to the present: the creation of the Romanian Communist Party, the 5th Party Congress, the struggles of the oil industry and railway workers in 1933, Romania's participation in World War II, and events in the history of the Romanian Communist party. *Historical Treasure* consists of 5,000 exhibits from Neolithic to contemporary times. This section includes the Moigrad, Ostrovul Mare, Cucuteni, and Baiceni treasures; a helmet found at Poiana Cotofeni; and the Pietroasa treasure ("The Hen with Golden Chickens"). The *Lapidarium* contains a replica of Trajan's Column and objects from former Greek colonies. The *Numismatic Cabinet* is a history of coin and monetary circulation in Romania. Exhibits include the archaic Bistrian drachma, Dacian and Roman coins, and emissions of the Romanian feudal states. The *Exhibition* was created to house testimonies of appreciation to Nicolae Ceauşescu, former secretary general and president of the Romanian Socialist Republic. Inaugurated in 1978, the the exhibit includes paintings, sculptures, tapestries, graphic art, decorative and folk art, carpets, and scale models of industrial objects.

Romanian Athenaeum, 1–3 Franklin St. This building was constructed by the initiative of Constantin Exarcu (a Romanian doctor, concerned with culture) according to the plans of French architect Albert Galleron, assisted by Romanian architect Constantin Baicoianu, between 1885 and 1888. Erected in the spirit of the French eclecticism school, the architectural ensemble is 134.5 feet high and has at the main entrance a portico with six Ionic columns and front part suggesting the facade of a Greek temple. The ground floor with rotunda comprises a ring with twelve masonry columns and four monumental staircases; a round concert hall (93.5 feet in diameter) with 600 seats at the ground floor and 60 boxes disposed on two levels; and a massive dome built in the Baroque style with rich interior decorations. A new wing of the building has been erected, according to the plans of architect Leonida Negrescu.

Central Exhibition Pavilion of Bucharest. This pavilion hosts fairs and exhibitions with international participation. The building was erected by Romanian architects Ascanio Damian and Mihai Emescu in 1962. Its edifice is 918.6 feet in diameter and is impressive due to the dimensions of the cupola (305 feet in diameter and 138 feet high at the keystone, without sustaining pillars) as well as its elegant and functional architectural style.

Library of the Academy of the Socialist Republic of Romania, 125 Calea Victoriei. Founded in 1867, it is the library of the Society of the Romanian Academy and serves as a national repository. It is the largest scientific library of the country and the national exchange center and repository for Romanian and U.N. publications in Romania. Its collections include approximately 85 percent of the national fund of manuscripts, printings, and special collections (engravings, pictures, drawings, maps, scores, numismatics, philately) issued in Romania or abroad by Romanians or dealing with problems concerning Romania. Since 1972, publications have been exchanged with more than 9,000 institutions in 92 countries. It possesses over 1.5 million books, approximately 3,000 periodicals, 360,000 loose leaves and booklets, 446,160 manuscripts and documents, 340,000 engravings, 14,000 maps, 32,500 scores, and 218,180 coins. Rarities in the *Manuscript Fund* (6,000 volumes) include the oldest texts in Romanian: from *The Votonet Manuscript, The Schei Psalt Book* (16th century) to the manuscripts of the Romanian classical writers (M. Eminescu, I. L. Caragiale, M. Sadoveanu, and others). The *Collection of Letters* contains letters by the classics of literature, science, and art (V. Alecsandri, I. L. Caragiale, N. Iorga, N. Grigorescu, G. Enescu) and letters by foreign personalities (Chateaubriand, R. Realigned, Paul Valéry, Th. Manu, Einstein). The *Collection of Rare Books* (2,014 works) consists of the greater part of the Romanian printings between 1508 and 1830 and those of the Romanian press beginning with the first periodicals in Romanian (*The Romanian Chrestomatic* [1820] and *The Roma-*

nian Courier [1829]). These include over 33,000 titles. Early scientific magazines include *Le Journal des Savants* and *Arta Eraditorum*. The library makes photocopy and microfilm exchanges.

Triumphal Arch, Şoseaua Kiseleff. This arch looks like a copy of the famed Arch de Triomphe in Paris. Built in 1935–36, it is constructed of concrete and stone. Its designer, Petru Antonescu, modeled his arch on the blueprints used to build the well-known arch on the Champs Elysees. At the time of its construction a number of gifted Romanian sculptors carved and decorated the arch.

Museum of Natural History, 1 Şoseaua Kiseleff. Another name for this building is the Grigore Antipa Museum. It honors the well-known Romanian marine biologist and ichthyologist who lived from 1867 to 1944. He founded the museum and was its director until his death. The displays in the museum trace the evolution of life on earth from minute organisms to the development of man. Also on display is one of the largest collections of butterflies and moths in the world.

Museum of Pottery and Glass, 107 Calea Victoriei. In 1954 this museum was organized around a large collection of folk art objects, now totaling more than 25,000 in number. Built in 1837 the structure was later restored. In the mid-19th century it served as the palace of a prince. Built in neoclassical style, the building itself is an architectural landmark. It became a museum in 1906 and has undergone several reorganizations since. After its reorganization in 1954 it became known as the Museum of Folk Art, housing folk art and ethnographic items from all areas of Romania. Its objects include wood and bone carvings, pottery, furniture, embroidery, ceramics, glass and wood on which paintings have been made by skilled artists, and carpets. The museum is near the Hotel Bucharest.

Churches

Curtea Veche (Old Court) Church, 31—30 Decembrie St. This was the old chapel of the palace of the princes of Wallachia from the 15th to 18th centuries. It was built by Prince M. Ciobanul from 1545–59. The church was constructed of marble and brick and is one of the important historical monuments of Bucharest. Its doorway and facade are ornately decorated. It has undergone several restorations.

Colţea Church, 1 Blvd. 1848. This old church was constructed at the end of the 17th century. Built by Michael Cantacuzino, the church is located in the courtyard of Colţa Hospital. His statue erected in 1869 stands nearby.

St. Gheorghe Nou Church, Piaţa 1848. Originally built in 1707, the old church was gutted by fire in 1847 and rebuilt in the 19th century. It was founded by Prince Constantin Brîncoveanu, whose statue stands in front of the church.

Stavropoleos Church, 6 Postei St. Built in 1730, this church is another example of outstanding old Romanian architecture. Ion Mincu (1852–1912), a noted architect, restored it at the beginning of the 20th century. The stone columns supporting its portico are uniquely carved.

Kreţulesscu Church, 47 Calea Victoriei. Constructed in 1722, this church is an interesting example of the Brîncovean style of architecture. The church is named after Iordache Kreţulesscu, a son-in-law of Prince Brîncoveanu, who had it built. It underwent restoration before World War II.

Church of the Patriarchate, 41 Aleea Patriarhiei. Built during the 1650s, this church incorporates many features of Byzantine architecture. It was the residence of the metropolitan of Wallachia and became the seat of the patriarchate in 1925. Its original features were restored in 1960.

Church of St. Antim, 29 Antim St. This church dates from the 17th century and is named after Antim Ivireano, a well-known metropolitan of that period. It has a beautiful iconostasis and is decorated in frescoes. Both Georgian and Persian styles of architecture were incorporated into its features.

Bucur Church, 12 Splaiul Unirii. According to legend, this church was founded by a shepherd who gave it his name. Built in the 18th century it attracts attention due to its tower which is constructed in the shape of a cap traditionally worn by shepherds.

Other Places of Interest

University of Bucharest, 13 Blvd. Republicii. The university is located on the Piaţa Universităţii where the Blvd. Republicii meets the square at that point. The old university was founded in 1863, but the main part of it was destroyed in 1944 by air raids. The large building on the north side of Blvd. Republicii houses the majority of the faculties of the university. The departments of history, physics, mathematics, geography, and foreign languages are located in it.

Cişmigiu Gardens. These lovely gardens border Ştirbei Vodă St. on the north, Blvd. Gheorghiu-Dej on the south, and Blvd. Schitu Măgureanu on the west. They are but a short walk from either the Bucureşti or Inter-Continental hotels. A large lake lies in the center of the gardens, which were laid out beginning in 1851. They are the oldest and regarded as the most beautiful public gardens in Bucharest. Many walkways and benches are found in the gardens.

History Museum of the Romanian Communist Party, 3 Şoseaua Kiseleff.

Numismatics Museum, 21 Ana Ipătescu Blvd.

Museum of Romanian Literature, 4 Fundatiei St.

Corneliu Medrea, 16 Budişteanu St.

Gh. Tattarescu Museum (art), 7 Domnita Anastasia St.

Museum of Art Collections, 111 Calea Victoriei.

Theodor Aman Museum (art), 8 C.A. Rosetti St.

Frederic Storck–Cecilia Cutescu-Storck Museum (art), 16 V. Alecsandri St.

D. Minovici Museum (art), 3 Dr. Minovici St.

George Bacovia Museum (history), 63 G. Bacovia St.

Cornel Medrea Museum (sculpture), 16 Gl. Budişteanu St.

Severeanu Museum (coins), 26 I.C. Frimu St.

Science Experiments and Astronomical Observatory, 21 Ana Ipătescu Blvd.

Palace of Justice, 4 Calea Rahovei.

Faculty of Medicine. 8 Dr. Petru Groza Blvd.

Palace of the Grand National Assembly, 5 Aleea Marii Nationale.

Statue of Michael the Brave. Piaţa Universităţii.

V.I. Lenin Statue. Piaţa Scinteii.

Ion Eliade Radulescu Statue. Piaţa Universităţii.

Gheorghe Lazăr Statue. Piaţa Universităţii.

Useful Addresses

Train Stations and Airports

Gara de Nord, Piaţa Gării de Nord.
Gara Basarab, 33 Rue Orhideelor.
Gara Băneasa. 1 Blvd. Poligrafiei.

Gara Obor, Blvd. Gării Obor.
Gara Routière Filaret, 1 Piaţa Gării Filaret.
Gara Titan, 2 Şoseaua Gării Cătelu.
Gara Routière Băneasa, 5 Rue I. Ionescu de la Brad.
Gara Routière Rahova, 164 Şoseaua Alexandriei.
Otopeni International Airport, Şoseaua Bucureşti-Ploieşti. 10 miles. Phone: 333137.
Băneasa Airport, 40 Şoseaua Bucureşti-Ploieşti. Phone: 330033.

Restaurants

Excellent restaurants are located in the major hotels, including the Bucureşti, Inter-Continental, Athenée Palace, Bulevard, Flora, Ambassador, Continental, Dorobanti, Lido, Nord, Capitol, Modern, Palas, Parc, Union, and Hanul Manuc. Other restaurants are:

Parcul Trandafirilor, 9 Piaţa Cosmonauţilor.
Mărul de Aur, 163 Calea Victoriei.
Pescăruş, Parc Herăstrău.
Cina, 1 C.A. Rosetti St.
Cişmigiu, 22 Blvd. Gh. Gheorghiu-Dej.
Berlin, 4 C. Mille St.
Tei. 5 Doamna Ghica-Tei St.
Dunărea, 3 Blvd. N. Bălcescu
Turn, 25—13 Decembrie St.
Miorita, 24 Şoseaua Kiseleff.
Capsa, 1 Edgar Quinet St.
Monte Carlo, Cişmigiu Gardens.
Chinois Nan Jing, 2 Lt. Lemnea St.
Herăstrău, Parc Herăstrău.
Budapest, 13 Blvd. Cantemir.

Restaurants with a typical Romanian atmosphere are:
Carul cu Bere, 3 Stavropoleos St.
Hanul Manuc, 62—30 Decembrie St.
Bucur, 2 Poenaru Bordea St.
Doina, 4 Şoseaua Kiseleff.
Crama Domneasca, 13 Şelari St.
Parcul Privighetorilor, Pădurea Băneasa.
Doi Cocosi, 6 Şoseaua Străuleşti.
Rapsodia, 2 Şelari St.

Nightclubs
Athenée Palace, 1–3 Episcopiei St.
Melody, 2 Pictor Verona St.
Doina, 4 Şoseaua Kisseleff.

Video-Disco Clubs
Athenée Palace, 1–3 Episcopiei St.
Nord, 143 Calea Grivitel.
Dorobanti, 1–3 Calea Dorobanti.
Flora, 1 Blvd. Poligrafiei.

Department Stores
Unirea, 1 Piaţa Unirii.
Victoria, 17 Calea Victoriei.
Cocorul, 33 Blvd. Année
Bucur Obor, 2, Şoseaua Colentina.
Bucureşti, 2 Bărăţiei St.
Tineretului, 10 Calea Dorobanţi.

Banks
Romanian Bank for Foreign Trade, 1–3 Eugen Carada St.
National Bank of the S.S.R., 25 Lipscani St.

Telephone Exchange
Local and international calls, 37 Calea Victoriei.

Libraries
Library of the Academy of S.S.R., 125 Calea Victoriei.
State Central Library, 4 Ion Ghica St.
University Central Library, 1 Oneşti St.

Exhibition Halls
Dalles, 18 N. Bălcescu Blvd.
Căminul Artei, 16 Biserica Enel St.
Simeza, 20 Magheru Blvd.
Orizont, 23 N. Bălcescu Blvd.
Galateea, 132 Calea Victoriei.
Tudor Arghezi, 2 N. Bălcescu Blvd.
Art Galleries of the City of Bucharest, 15 Academiei St.

Concert Halls

Romanian Athenaeum, 1 Franklin St.
Romanian Radio and Television, 62–64 Nuferilor St.
Hall of the Palace of the S.R. of Romania, 13 Decembrie St.

Theaters, Opera, Circus

I.L. Caragiale National Theater, 2 N. Bălcescu Blvd.
Lucia Sturdza Bulandra, 1 Schitu Măgureanu Blvd.
Constantin Nottara, 20 Magheru Blvd.
Mic Theater, 16 Constantin Mille St.
Foarte Mic Theater, 21 Republicii Blvd.
Ion Creangă (for children and youth), 13 Piaţa Amzei.
Comedy Theater, 2 Măndinesti St.
Giuleşti (Majestic Hall), 40–42 Calea Victoriei.
Constantin Tănase (musical theater), Victoria Hall, 174 Calea Victoriei.
Rapsodia Română (folklore theater), 53 Lipscani St.
Constantin Tănase (music hall), 33–35 Calea Victoriei.
Tandarica (puppets), 50 Calea Victoriei.
Tandarica (puppets), 3 Eremia Grigorescu St.
Patria Cinema, 12–14 Magheru Blvd.
Opera, 70 Gh. Gheorghiu-Dej Blvd.
Circus, 1 Aleea Circului.

Hotels

Inter-Continental (deluxe), 4–6 N. Bălcescu Blvd.; phone: 140400
Continental (deluxe), 56 Calea Victoriei; phone: 145349.
Bucureşti (deluxe), 63–81 Calea Victoriei; phone: 154580.
Athenée Palace (deluxe). 1–3 Episcopiei St.; phone: 140899.
Ambassador (deluxe), 5 Magheru Blvd.; phone: 110440.
Lido (deluxe), 5 Magheru Blvd.; phone: 143939.
Dorobanţi (deluxe), 1–3 Calea Dorobanţi; phone: 110860.
Flora (deluxe), 1 Poligrafiei Blvd.; phone: 184640.
Nord (deluxe), 143 Calea Griviţei; phone: 506181.
Bulevard (deluxe), 1 Gh. Gheorghiu-Dej Blvd.; phone: 153300.
National (deluxe), 33 Republicii Blvd.; phone: 130199.
Modern (first class), 46 Republicii Blvd.; phone: 156470.
Capitol (first class), 29 Calea Victoriei; phone: 140926.
Central (first class), 13 Brezoianu St.; phone: 155637.
Palas (first class), 24 Brezoianu St.; phone: 167099.
Negolu (first class), 16—13 Decembrie St.; phone: 155250.

Bucharest

Union (first class), 11—13 Decembrie St.; phone: 132640.
Majestic (first class), 11 Academiei St.; phone: 162174.
Manuc Inn (first class), 62—30 Decembrie St.; phone: 131415.
Astoria (first class), 27 Dinicu Golescu Blvd.; phone: 495210.
Parc (first class), 3 Poligrafiei Blvd.; phone: 180950.
Turist (first class), 5 Poligrafiei Blvd.; phone: 663020.
Carpati (second class), 16 Rue Matei Millo; phone: 157690.
Banat (second class), 5 Piaţa Rosetti; phone: 131057.
Bucegi (second class), 2 Witing St.; phone: 495100.
Cişmigiu (second class), 18 Gh. Gheorghiu-Dej Blvd.; phone: 147410.
Dimbovita (second class), 6 Blvd. Schitu Măgureanu; phone: 162069.

Geriatric Treatment

Otopeni Sanatorium, Flora Cure Hotel, 307 Blvd. R.S.R.; phone: 337220.

CHAPTER 3

Wallachia and Dobruja: Major Cities and Historic Sites

CONSTANŢA

Constanţa is the third largest city in Romania, with only Bucharest and Braşov exceeding it in population. The city numbers about 330,000 people. Constanţa is located on the Black Sea and lies almost due east of Bucharest. By highway, Constanța is about 165 miles from the capital. It is the county seat and administrative center of Constanța County. The city is linked by air with Bucharest and other Romanian cities. An east/west rail line, which crosses the Danube River, connects the port city with Bucharest.

Constanța is the major seaport of Romania. On the Black Sea, only the Russian seaport of Odessa exceeds it in importance of shipping. Its port facilities and docks are modernized and have been expanded with the growth of its shipping. An oil pipeline connects the port with the refineries at Ploești.

The coastline on which Constanța is located averages about three hundred hours of sunshine a month. The average annual temperature is 52° F. The summers average 70° F. The seacoast, both north and south of Constanța, is one of the principal spa and health resort areas in the country. A chain of modern hotels and beaches stretches along the coastline.

The site and locality of Constanța is rich in legend, mythology, and history. The foundations of the city were laid in the 6th century B.C. when Greek colonists built the city of Tomis on its site. Ancient Tomis is associated with the legend of Jason and the Argonauts. Jason, the leader of the Argonauts, embarked on a long voyage from Greece to the Asiatic country of Colchis on the Black Sea in search of the golden fleece. Jason and his illustrious companions (Hercules, Pollux, Theseus, Peleus, Castor, and Prithous) set sail in the *Argo*, a swift, 50-oared ship which gave its name to the participants (Argonauts) in the expedition. With the help of Medea, the daughter of the king of Colchis, Jason obtained the fleece and left Colchis with Medea. On their return voyage the Argonauts laid anchor at the site on which Tomis would be built. Jason then slew the son of King Aetes of Colchis. The legend continues by noting that ancient Tomis was founded by members of an expedition sent there by King Aetes, who remained and built the settlement.

Constanța is built on and around a promontory of land extending into the Black Sea. It helps to afford protection to ships from the strong winds that blow along the seacoast. Greek ships plied the coastal waters long before they established a trading post on the site of Tomis.

Burebista, a Dacian chieftain, occupied Tomis and the Greek cities along the coast in the 1st century B.C. and organized them into a strong Dacian state that extended to the Carpathians. The

Dacian state reached the height of its power under Decebalus (A.D. 87–106). Roman legions under Emperor Trajan occupied Dacia in A.D. 106; and the process of Romanization of the Dacians began, which lasted until A.D. 271. Gradually the Daco-Roman population became a Latin-speaking people. At Adamclisi, forty miles southwest of Constanţa, stands a huge column dedicated to the Emperor Trajan decorated with scenes of Roman victories in the area. The Romans gave the name Scythia Minor to the present region of Dobruja, including the Black Sea coast around Constanţa. In the 4th century A.D., Christianity spread into the Danubian provinces.

Under the Romans, Tomis became a prosperous city. The Romans transformed the old Greek city into a beautiful metropolis, gracing it with statues, temples, and monumental architecture. In modern times many of these have been unearthed or their ruins discovered by archeologists. The Archeology Museum in the city has a rich collection of ancient pottery, weapons, tools, and statues found in Constanţa and nearby areas.

With the spread of the influence of the Eastern Roman Empire headquartered in Constantinople into the Black Sea coastal area, Tomis was again modernized and changed in its features. Constantine the Great ordered the city rebuilt and changed its name to Constantiana (from which the present name of the city is derived) to honor his sister. Rebuilt in the 4th century A.D., the city was left in ruins by the migratory Avars in the 6th century. The city recovered little of its former importance after its destruction. For centuries it functioned as little more than a small fishing port and trading center. The Genoese built a lighthouse there in 13th century and improved its harbor, but these changes did little to enhance the fortunes of the city. Several centuries of Turkish rule that lasted until 1877 brought no improvements or changes in the status of the city. The tide of the city's misfortunes only began to turn in 1895, when a group of Romanian engineers led by Anghel Saligny (1854–1925) finished constructing the Cernavoda railway bridge over the Borcea branch of the Danube River. England had previously built a railway in 1860 between Constanţa and Cernavoda after the port of Constanţa had been granted to it in 1858. Subsequent improvements in the port of Constanţa in 1908 and the building of grain storage facilities there the following year helped to resuscitate the city and arouse its growth once again.

In the past twenty years or so the harbor of Constanţa has

become very busy with shipping, and its volume in tonnage has substantially increased. About 60 percent of all of Romania's exports pass through Constanţa. Most operations at the port are now mechanized, and the building of Constanţa South port has greatly enlarged the cargo-handling capacity of Constanţa. Ships of 150,000 tons can be received by the port. Between 1965 and 1985, port tonnage for Romania rose from 1.4 million tons to 25.7 million tons. In 1984 the Danube-Black Sea Canal (forty miles long) opened to navigation. This canal connects Constanţa on the Black Sea with Cernavoda on the Danube River.

Constanţa is also an important industrial center. Its industries include textiles, meat packing, flour and rice milling, food processing, shipbuilding and repair, brickmaking, processing of vegetable oils, and metallurgy. The city also makes the well-known Murfatlar wine. Fishing is an important activity in the Black Sea.

What to See

Archeology Museum, 23 Muzeelor St. The museum is open from 9 A.M. to 9 P.M.; closed on Mondays. It was founded in 1879 and reorganized and opened in the building it now occupies in 1957. It comprises exhibits from archeological diggings in Constanţa and Dobruja, chiefly at Adamclisi. Its archeology and numismatics collections are exhibited in twenty rooms. The exhibits begin with objects dating from prehistoric times until the early feudal period: tools, weapons, pottery, and remains of fauna from the Paleolithic and Neolithic eras; the menhir statue from Hamangia (oldest of its kind found in Romania, it depicts a female goddess); a bronze kettle of Scythian origin and Scythian coins; ceramic pots; architectural and town-planning elements; statues, sarcophagi, and gold jewels.

Outstanding are the statues of Fortuna and Pontos (divine gods who were the patron protectors of ancient Tomis; the Glykon serpent that depicts the body of a snake with human hair and ears; a bas-relief of a Thracian knight; Cybela; Dionysus; bronze figurines; and a pot with a Greek inscription including the name of the pottery master, Petre of Capidava. The statues are part of a collection of marble statues and bas-reliefs discovered under the old railway station in 1962.

A special hall is dedicated to the Latin poet Publius Ovidius Naso (43 B.C.–A.D. 18), who lived in exile in Tomis. The museum also has a valuable repository and a restoration workshop. Other important archeological treasures are exhibited in the park nearby or in the streets of the town, near the places where they have been found.

City Walls, intersection of the Blvd. Republicii and the Rascoala 1907 St. These are the ruins of a wall the Romans built in the 2nd century A.D. for the protection of the city on its north side. A noted part of the wall is the Butchers' Tower dating from the 6th century. Nearby is a map of ancient Dobruja depicting the locations of Greek and Roman settlements.

Piaţa Independentei (Independence Square). This huge square is separated from the sea by Marcus Aurelius St. The square lies on the north side of the large promontory of land jutting into the Black Sea. In ancient Greek times the square was the *agora,* or marketplace, of old Tomis. In the center of the square is a statue showing the Roman poet Publius Ovidius Naso (Ovid) in a meditation pose. Ovid was exiled to Tomis by Emperor Augustus in A.D. 8. While in Tomis, Ovid finished several projects of his, the *Metamorphoses* ("Transfigurations") and *Fasti* ("Calendar"), and wrote the poems *Tristia* ("Sorrows") and *Epistulae ex Ponto* ("Letters from the Black Sea") as an endless form of pleas to the emperor and his friends to have his banishment lifted. The latter two works express Ovid's melancholy and self-pity and his descriptions of the climate, inhabitants, and battles with the barbarians along the Danube. Near the Roman frontier with the barbarian world, Tomis was a far cry from Rome and its amenities; and Ovid complained of the lack of pleasures and civilized friends. He even had to do sentry duty. Ovid was a great poet and even described as a genius and influenced all Latin poets from his time. He enjoyed tremendous popularity in his lifetime and influenced medieval literature to the extent that the 12th and 13th centuries have often been referred to as "the age of Ovid." When he died in A.D. 18 the inhabitants of Tomis buried him in a ceremony befitting an emperor.

On the south side of Piaţa Independentei is the Town Hall built in 1921 and now used as the People's Council of Constanţa. Its architecture is Romanian of that period, and it is situated among newer structures built since its erection. In its vicinity, a large commercial building was unearthed in 1959 whose edifice was decorated with a superb multicolored mosaic of 13th-century origin.

Plastic Art Museum, 12 Muzeelor St. This museum contains an assemblage of art work (drawings, paintings, and sculpture) by 19th- and 20th-century Romanian artists.

Greek Orthodox Church, located at the end of V. Alecsandri St. along the seacoast. Constructed in the mid-1860s during Turkish rule, this interesting church is built on a plot of land donated by Sultan Abdul Aziz. The sultan ordered that the height of the church could not exceed that of the mosques of the city.

Catholic Church, Muzeelor St. near the Archeology Museum. This church is built in a Romanesque style of architecture and is constructed of colored bricks. Built by the architect Romano de Simon in 1885, it has an imposing high tower.

Mosque, located near the southeast corner of Piața Independentei. This mosque was constructed in the first decade of the 1900s and is visible from a distance owing to its 160-foot-high minaret. It is built in a typical Moorish style of architecture.

Hebrew Temple of the Spanish Rite. This synagogue is situated near the coast and adjacent to the Greek Church. Marcus Aurelius and V. Alecsandri streets meet in the vicinity of the two churches. The Hebrew Temple is built in a Gothic style of architecture and dates from the early 1900s.

Aquarium, located on the 16 February Blvd. running along the seacoast on the land promontory jutting into the sea. It contains marine life from the Black and Mediterranean seas and the area of the Danube delta. A small tropical collection is included. The aquarium is connected with a marine zoological station that conducts research on the marine biology of the Black Sea.

Casino. This building is situated opposite the aquarium and faces the 16 February Blvd. It is built on a platform of land extending into the sea and dates from the beginning of the 20th century.

Genoese Lighthouse. This structure stands at the end of the land promontory jutting into the sea. The Genoese built it in the 13th century at the time they made improvements to the harbor of the city. In the mid-1800s it underwent restoration. It is 315 feet in height.

Palace of Sports. This large structure is located in the Park of Culture along the seacoast and terraces leading down to beaches. It contains a large hall that can seat 2,500 persons and includes facilities for various sports. Its facade is ornamented with bas-reliefs from the time of the construction of the building in the 1950s.

Railway Station. This large structure is located on the west side of the city and contains facilities for handling several thousand passengers. Completed in 1960, it includes a restaurant, bar, waiting rooms, and other public facilities.

Other places to see include the **Planetarium,** 267 Lenin Blvd.; and the **Delphinarium** (flora and fauna), 265 Lenin Blvd.

Useful Addresses

Tourist Office, 69 Blvd. Tomis; phone: 12342.

Theaters
Drama and Comedy Theater, 97 Mircea cel Bătrin St.
Revue Theater, 11 Blvd. Republicii.
Puppet Theater, 16 A. Caratzali St.
Republic Theater, 54 Blvd. Republicii.
Progresul Theater, 53 Ştefan cel Mare St.
Tomis Theater, 11 Blvd. Republicii.
Popular Theater, 48 Blvd. Tomis.
Dacia Theater, 153 Blvd. Tomis.

Hotels
Continental (first class), 20 Blvd. Republicii; phone: 12343.
Palas (first class), 11 R. Opreanu St.; phone: 17784.

BRĂILA

Brăila is located on the left (west) bank of the Danube River in the southeastern part of Romania. The city lies 21 miles south of Galaţi and 130 miles northeast from Bucharest by road. Brăila is one of Romania's 10 largest cities and has a population of 238,000 people. At Brăila the two northward flowing arms of the Danube join after the river bifurcates more than 50 miles south of the city. It is the county seat of Brăila County and, along with Galaţi, is one of the two leading ports on the Danube. By the Danube the distance from Brăila to the Black Sea at Sulina is 106 miles. Brăila is an important fishing center, with most of its catch coming from the Danube.

Brăila is an important industrial center for the country. It handles and processes large quantities of wood and manufactures pulp and paper. A large cellulose plant produces artificial fibers. Other significant enterprises include iron and steel, shipbuilding, textiles, construction materials, shoes, clothing, food processing, and the manufacture of rolling stock for railroads. The city stores and ships large quantities of grain. Along the Danube are docking and port facilities, and many ocean-going ships can reach it from the Black Sea. Brăila has rail connections to Galaţi, Bucharest, and Ploieşti. The streets of the city radiate away from the harbor, and as they extend outward they are crossed by other streets which are semicircular in shape. Streetcars run by electricity move through the city and extend and carry passengers about six miles to Lake Sărat (saltwater) on the southwest side of the town.

The first document to mention the city was originated in 1368 by a Wallachian prince. By his authority goods were permitted to be shipped into and out of Brăila by traders from the city of Braşov. The Turks captured the city in 1554 and built five walls around it running in semicircles which match the layout of the present-day streets. Afterward the Turks lost and recaptured the city several times in wars with Russia and Austria during the 18th century. The Russians and Turks fought fiercely for control of Brăila, with the Russian forces taking the city on several occasions. Fires devastated the city during the fighting. At the end of the Russo-Turkish War of 1828–29, Turkey relinquished its claim to the town; and it returned to Wallachian control. Rebuilt after World War II, the town has a contemporary look to it.

The city's best known structure is the **Cathedral of St. Michael and Gavril,** an Orthodox Church that was founded in 1829 when Brăila's only mosque lost its Turkish worshipers and the Orthodox Wallachians converted it into a church of their belief. Another interesting old church is the **Greek Church** dating from the 19th century. On the Piaţa Lenin is the **town hall,** next to which is the **Art and Historical Museum.** A bust of the Emperor Trajan can be seen in the Central Park. On the Danube just north of the city there are the ruins of an ancient bridge which tradition says was built by Darius I, the Persian king who invaded the area of Wallachia in 514 B.C. Neither Brăila nor its sister city to the north, Galaţi, are regarded as important tourist sites when compared to those of Bucharest, the Black Sea coast, or the mountainous resorts of the Carpathians.

Useful Addresses

Tourist Office, 20 Republicii St.

Hotels
Traian (first class), 1 Piaţa Lenin.
Delta (second class), 58 Republicii St.

PLOIEŞTI

Ploieşti (also spelled Ploeşti) is the tenth largest city in Romania. It has a population of 236,000 people and is the capital of Prahova County. Ploieşti is located 37 miles north of Bucharest on Highway 1. It is situated on the Wallachian Plain between the Prahova and Teleajen River valleys, and its topography is relatively flat. The city lies on the rail line connecting Bucharest and Braşov, and the Orient Express passes through it.

Ploieşti is not regarded as a major tourist center, although many tourists pass through it on their way to the mountain resorts that lie to the north of the city. Along the highway leading into the city from Bucharest are a number of small villages and towns. They are rustic in appearance, interesting, but drab and without much color. Most of their inhabitants are peasants and till the nearby fields. About 60 percent of Romanians are employed in agriculture. Carts and wagons pulled by oxen are common on the roads. On the outskirts of Ploieşti, the oil refineries and distillation towers soon come into view.

Ploieşti was a small city until the middle of the 19th century before it began to experience much growth. Its development has paralleled the exploitation of petroleum in the area and the refining industry related to it. The first refinery was built near the city in 1857, which was one of the first refineries built in the world. Romania was producing 80,000 metric tons of petroleum by 1895, and by the time of the First World War production had surged to nearly 9 million metric tons. Most of this oil came from the Southern Carpathian foothills in the region around Ploieşti. During the 1920s Romania held sixth place among the world's oil producers. Prior to 1930 more than one hundred oil companies operated in Romania, the largest of which was Standard Oil.

During World War II the Germans maintained oil production and refining in Romania on a high level to feed their war machine.

In 1944 production had dropped to only 3.5 million metric tons due to Allied bombing of the production facilities and refineries. Romania fought on the side of Germany in World War II and was then Europe's second largest oil producer, with only the Soviet Union exceeding it in production. So vital was Romanian oil to Germany that the Americans and British determined that the Ploieşti refineries and derricks must be destroyed. The first major raid was mounted on Ploieşti in June 1942 when a dozen B-24 Liberator bombers hit the area. A heavy raid was carried out on August 1, 1943, in which 177 B-24s bombed the refineries. The Germans had the city ringed with heavy antiaircraft guns. The attacking bombers came in at low elevation, so low in fact that if one was hit it had to try to gain altitude to give its crew sufficient height for their parachutes to open when they bailed out. Nearly one-third of the attacking aircraft were shot down, with one plummeting into a prison for women. Operation "Tidal Wave," the code name for the mission, left the refineries, oil tanks, and related facilities in ruins and flames. The attack lasted less than thirty minutes but crippled Romania's refining capacity.

After World War II, production began to rise again and passed 10 million metric tons in 1955, 13 million tons in 1968, and then fell to under 11 million by 1986. Romania even imports oil now and has built its first nuclear power plant to keep up with growing demands for energy.

Ploieşti is a center of one of Romania's main industrial regions. A large petrochemical complex has grown up at Brazi on the southern side of the city. Other important industries in Ploieşti include the making of heavy equipment for the oil industry and mining, textiles, agricultural machinery, turbines and engines, and the processing of food.

Excavations at the site of Ploieşti have turned up artifacts dating from the Bronze Age, while in the vicinity of the city traces of settlement have been found dating back to the Paleolithic period. The medieval origins of the town are rooted in a legend concerning Father Ploaie, who after escaping from Transylvania founded a settlement on the site of Ploieşti. According to the earliest record about the settlement (1503), his descendants still lived there. Michael the Brave and his army camped at the town at the end of the 16th century, prior to his achieving the unification of Wallachia, Moldavia, and Transylvania.

After 1476 the rulers of Wallachia were selected by the Turkish

Wallachia 51

sultan. At times, however, they revolted against the Turks (as Michael the Brave did in 1595), which led them to select Greek princes from the Phanar quarter of Constantinople (resulting in the Greeks being called Phanariots) to rule Wallachia beginning in 1716. In the late 1700s, Greek boyars (the ruling class) took control of Ploieşti and exacted heavy taxes from its people. The Romanians revolted against the Phanariots in 1821, and during the Russo-Turkish War of 1828–29 the Russians marched in and controlled Wallachia until 1834. The Romanians revolted again for their freedom in 1848, but the revolution was crushed by the Turks.

What to See

Oil Museum. This museum recognizes Ploieşti as the center of the Romanian petroleum industry. Its exhibits, photographs, and models trace the evolution of the oil industry in Romania. It was opened in 1960. Located in the center of the city, the museum is situated at the meeting point of Diligentei and Karl streets.

Caragiale Museum. The building which houses this museum was built 1710 and is located on Kutuzov Street within a few steps of the main post office. The building is old Romanian in style, and the museum inside is dedicated to Costache Caragiale (1815–77), a well-known Romanian dramatist who promoted the theatrical movement in Wallachia and Moldavia. He attended school in Ploieşti and lived in the city for several years.

Historical Museum. This museum is located in a large building which formerly housed the law courts of the city. The museum has a large section on Romanian folk art and exhibits on the historical development of the country's culture.

The same building houses the Museum of Natural Science. The collections of the two museums are located in what is known as the Palace of Culture, built around 1900. It stands on a corner of Karl Street near the Oil Museum.

Other noted sights are the **Art Museum, Town Hall, Church of St. George** (1831), and **Church of St. Basil** (1857).

Useful Addresses

Tourist Office, 6—16 February St.

Hotels

Piatra-Neamț, Ceahlăul (deluxe), 1 Piața Karl Marx.
Berbec (first class), 1 Republicii St.

CRAIOVA

Less than four hours after leaving Bucharest, Romania's beautiful capital, after having passed fertile fields and dense forests, hills covered with orchards laden with fruit trees, and rivers crossed by concrete and steel bridges, one can see on the horizon the outlines of the silver or multicolored buildings of this old, as well as modern, city. This is Craiova, the county seat of Dolj County, the heart of Oltenia, which "has been beating" for over five centuries. Craiova was first mentioned in a document on June 1, 1475; less than twenty years later another document specified that the headquarters of the *bania,* an important feudal, political, and military institution, was moved from Strehaia to Craiova and that its authority was extended over the whole Oltenian territory. Several ruling princes of Wallachia came to power from among the Oltenian *bani* (governors).

Archeological discoveries in various parts of the city prove that there was human life in this area as early as the New Stone Age. The Geto-Dacians had a settlement here called Plendava; the Romans erected a *castrum;* and the traces of the defense wall crossing Oltenia from the west to the east, known as Trajan's Wall, can still be seen in Craiova.

Located at an important crossroads and in a fertile area with vast stretches of wheat fields, vineyards, and orchards, Craiova developed through the centuries into an important trading center in the middle ages. Merchants came from the county and abroad to sell their wares in spite of such calamities as the fires that burnt it to the ground on several occasions during the anti-Ottoman Wars. In the 19th century, this "town with many beautiful houses" (as the foreign travelers called it), as well as historical and architectural monuments, and a flourishing cultural life became a center of much social and political unrest. Here occurred the revolutionary movement led by Tudor Valdimirescu (1821); the Revolution of 1848; the movement for the unification of the Romanian Principalities in 1859 (the supporters of the union danced here the first Union Round Dance [1857], which was rendered on canvas by the Romanian painter Theodor Aman); the peasant uprising of 1907; and the working people's movements since the end of the 19th century.

The years of Socialist construction, in particular, the last twenty years, have turned Craiova into one of the major industrial and cultural centers of Romania. Industries in Craiova include thirty-three industrial units of national importance in which over 150,000 laborers, engineers, and technicians work. Their products are continually being exported to over fifty countries on all continents. Mention should be made of some of the enterprises making Craiova well known abroad: Electroputere, a model of the Romanian electro-technical industry; the plane plant which manufactures the IAR-93 plane, the first bi-engine transsonic jet plane to be made in Romania; the chemical complex plant—one of the largest in the country; and the Oltcit car factory. The city also contains textile plants, food-processing industries, and woodworking enterprises. It has a population of 180,000 people. Several large housing projects have been built in recent years.

Craiova is also an important cultural center, with about two hundred educational establishments of all kinds; a university housing eight departments attended by over 10,000 Romanian and foreign students; the National Theater; museums; art collections; exhibitions and memorial houses; a publishing house; scientific societies; literary and art clubs; and libraries.

Noted artistic events include the Festival of the Historical Theater; the "I. L. Caragiale" Cultural Days (Caragiale was a great Roman dramatist); the Maria Tănase Folk Music Festival; and the Fair of Folk Artisans in Oltenia, which has become part of Craiova's cultural tradition and draws large audiences.

Contemporary buildings have become an integral part of the old town. Yet the town's architects have carefully preserved the "jewels" of old Oltenian architecture which display the long history of the city.

What to See

Museum of Oltenia, 44 Maxim Gorki St., established in 1915 and expanded after 1948, has three sections—history, natural sciences, and ethnography—in which over 250,000 exhibits are displayed. The history department mirrors the evolution of human society in Oltenia from the remote times to the contemporary age. Some exhibits of particular note include a richly ornamented

Stone Age painted pot in perfect condition which is nearly 7,000 years old; the well-known "Thraco-Getic Treasure in Craiova," including silver horse saddles and other objects from the 4th century B.C.; the collection of small Roman statues found in Cioroiu Nou (ancient Aquae) which are made of white marble and represent such ancient gods as Apollo, Jupiter, and Bacchus; and documents referring to important events in Romania's history.

Ethnography Department of Oltenia's Museum, 14 Matei Basarab St., is housed in Bănia House, the oldest public building in the town, dating from the time of Constantin Brancoveanu's reign. The building, which served as the headquarters of the *bănia* was built on the site where in the 15th century were located the houses of the Craioveşti boyar family. The exhibition mirrors the rich folk heritage of Oltenia. Its collection of traditional folk costumes specific to the area represents objects of old trades such as Oboga, Horezu, Vlădeşti, and Siseşti pottery, pieces of peasant furniture, and household utensils.

Art Museum, 15 Calea Unirii, is arranged in a building built between 1900 and 1907 in an architectural style combining Renaissance with late Baroque. Its Romanian Art Gallery contains paintings by Nicolae Grigorescu, I. Andreescu, St. Luchian, C. Lecca, Theodor Aman, Gheorghe Tattarescu, N. Tonitza, Ch. Petraşcu, Th. Palady, D. Ghiţă, D. Paciurea, Gheorghe Anghel, and others. The works of the sculptor Constantin Brancuşi hold a place of special importance within the gallery. Its World Art Gallery displays works of artists of Dutch, Flemish, French, and Italian schools.

Department of Collections of the Art Museum, 10 Calea Unirii, opened in 1979 and contains collections of works by artists born in Oltenia. On the ground floor is a comprehensive collection of paintings and graphics by Ion Tuculescu, while works on the first floor include those by Eustaţiu Stoenescu, N. Furduescu, D. Stoica, and others.

Standing Exhibition "The Trial of the Railway and Oil Workers in June–July 1934," 7 N. Titulescu Blvd., is located in the building where the war council of the Army First Corps operated in 1934 and where the trial of revolutionary leaders in 1933 was conducted. The objects and documents on display show events of the revolutionary struggle waged in 1929–33, as well as from the time of the trials in Bucharest in 1933 and those in Craiova in 1934.

Standing History Exhibition of Medicine and Pharmacy, 104

Calea Unirii, houses exhibits honoring the scientist Victor Gomoiu, an innovator in surgery techniques (1882–1960).

Exhibition of "History of Printing and Books in Oltenia," 7 N. Titulescu Blvd.

Traian Demetrescu Memorial House, 13 Silozului St., displays manuscripts, books, and personal objects which belonged to the Craiovean poet who lived and worked here.

Historical, Architectural, and Art Monuments

Administrative Palace, Calea Unirii, built from 1907–10 in Romanian style from the plans of architect Petru Antonescu, is the headquarters of the Dolj County Committee of the Romanian Communist Party and of the County People's Council.

Building of the Municipal People's Council, 7 Al.I. Cuza St., is a beautiful architectural monument displaying national art styles. It was erected between 1902 and 1908 on the design of architects Ion Mincu and C. Lotzu.

Nicolae Balcescu Secondary School, 6 T. Maiorescu St., was built in 1893–95 by architect Toma Dobrescu on the site where in 1826 a well-known educational establishment, the Science School in Romania, was set up. Important personalities who were students at this school included Theodor Aman, Alexandru Macedonski, Traian Demetrescu, Nicolae Titulescu, Gheorghe Țițeica, Nicolae Coculescu, Gogu Constantinescu, Ion Tuculescu, Corneliu Baba, and Ion Vasilescu.

National Theater, 11 Al.I. Cuza St., opened in 1973 and built on the plans of architect Al. Lotzu, is remarkable for its modern architecture. The artists of the theater continue the traditions of acting begun in 1849 by Costache Caragiale and the theater troupe of that time.

Metropolitan Cathedral in the Garden of Roses is one of the oldest buildings in the city. It is a remarkable monument of medieval architecture, located near Bănia House. Built by Matei Basarb in 1651, the church stands on the site of a building erected by ban Barbu Basarab (16th century). Nicknamed Craioveanu, the building was restored in 1690 by Petru Obedeanu and rebuilt in 1889 by French architect Lecomte de Nouy.

Obedeanu Fountain at the Severin Barrier, on the road to Filiași, was built in the 18th century by Constantin Obedeanu and became well known for its fresh and cold water.

Glogoveanu House, 14 Brestei St., is a Romanian-style architectural monument built in 1783.

Public Gardens and Parks

People's Park, Calea Unirii, was laid out in 1901–02 on the plans of French landscape architect Edmont Redont. It is one of the largest (2,400 acres) and most beautiful parks in Romania. Located in the park is a romantic lake surrounded by tree-lined alleys, a cozy restaurant, numerous waterfalls; rocks, a suspended bridge, an imitation of a medieval citadel, and statues of well-known Romanians—M. Eminescu, C. Brancusi, and T. Arghezi. The park is an ideal place for relaxation and recreation.

Botanical Gardens, Iancu Jianu St., was laid out in 1955 on a 425-acre area containing over 6,000 plant species from all the continents. Inside the garden one can admire the Jianu Fountain where tradition says that the outlaw Captain Iancu Jianu stopped and drank water in the 18th century.

The 1 May Garden, Al.I. Cuza St., laid out at the beginning of the 20th century in front of the Municipal People's Council, contains a small square with the Statue of Ruling Prince Al.I. Cuza, by Italian sculptor E. Romanelli.

Useful Addresses

Headquarters of the Dolj County Tourist Office, 2 Calea Bucureşti; phone: 941-18169 or 18076.

Branch of the Romanian Automobile Club, Bucureşti St., block A 8; phone: 941-46166. Technical assistance, 171 Prelungirea Severinului.

CFR Travel Office, 2 Calea Bucureşti; phone: 941-11049.

Tarom Agency, 9 Al.I. Cuza St.; phone: 941-11049.

Hotels

Jiul (first class, 404 beds, restaurant, snack bar, swimming pool), 1 Calea Bucureşti; phone: 941-10611.

Minerva (first class, 86 beds, restaurant, brasserie, wine cellar, cafe, summer garden), 1 M. Kogălniceanu St.; phone: 941-33532.

Palace (first class, 101 beds, restaurant, cafe), Al.I. Cuza St.; phone: 941-16932 or 16548.

Doctorului Inn (first class, 82 beds in the hotel, 75 beds in the bungalows, restaurant, summer garden, lake), Calea Bucureşti; phone: 941-44031.

Wallachia

Restaurants, Cafes
Oltenia (restaurant, brasserie), 13—20 Decembrie St.; phone: 941-15571.
Perinita (restaurant), 94 Calea Unirii; phone: 941-32620.
Rotonda (restaurant, cafe), Calea Bucureşti; phone: 941-44585.
Femia (cafe), Al.I. Cuza St.; phone: 941-16352.
Unirea (cafe), 2 Calea Bucureşti.

Shops
Mercur (department store), Griviţa Roşie St.; phone: 941-19413 or 19696.
Unirea (department store), 2 Calea Bucureşti; phone: 941-18236.
Femina (handicrafts), Al.I. Cuza St.; phone: 941-16624.

Theaters and Cinemas
National Theater, 11 Al.I. Cuza St.; phone: 941-13577 or 11726.
Oltenia's State Philharmonic, Calea Unirii; phone: 941-12324.
Puppet Theater, 32 Al.I. Cuza St.; phone: 941-12473.
Lyrical Theater, 6 T. Maiorescu St.; phone: 941-13427.
Patria Cinema, 37 Al.I. Cuza St.; phone: 941-43850.
Central Cinema, 3 Al.I. Cuza St.; phone: 941-14029.
30 Decembrie Cinema, 2 M. Kogălniceanu St.; phone: 941-33236.

Sports Hall, Stadiums
Sports Hall, 23 August Blvd.; phone: 941-32544.
Central Stadium, 23 August Blvd.; phone: 941-33004 or 34578.
Tineretului Stadium, 23 August Blvd.; phone: 941-33716.

Post Office, Savings Bank
Main Post Office, 69 Calea Unirii; phone: 941-53171.
Savings Bank, 16 Calea Unirii; phone: 941-12548.

Railway and Bus Stations
Railway Station, Republicii Blvd.; phone: 941-10111.
Nord Bus Station, 13 Argeş St.; phone: 941-45405.
Sud Bus Station, Poporului St.; phone: 941-23064.

Medical Assistance
Pharmacy No. 2 (24 hours), 9 Al.I. Cuza St., block 1A; phone: 941-11308.

Pharmacy No. 7 (24 hours), Piaţa Unirii, block L.; phone: 941-12716.

Hospital No. 1, Emergency Section, 60—1 Mai Blvd.; phone: 941-32498.

First-Aid Station, 60—1 Mai Blvd.; phone 06.

Petrol Stations, Car Service

Petrol Stations (Peco), 260 Calea Severinului, phone: 941-11082; 70 Caracal St., phone: 941-46000; Calea Bucureşti, phone: 941-45624; Calea Dunării, phone: 941-23062; 2 Ştefan cel Mare St., phone: 941-12890.

Car Sevices, Calea Severinului, phone: 941-14032; Dacia Car Service, Lăpuşului St., phone: 941-44634.

Nearby Places of Interest

Jiul Valley, a natural park of about 1,500 acres, located 1.9 miles southwest of the town on highway DJ 522. It has tourist camping, swimming pool, and restaurant.

Bucovăţ Village, 3 miles southwest of Craiova on highway DJ 522. It has tourist camping and a medieval monument (16th century) built with materials from the Roman Castrum in Pelendava.

Coşoveni Village, about 6 miles from Craiova on highway DN 6. It includes a forest containing deer and pheasants and a historical monument dating from the 18th century.

Beharca Tourist Inn, about 10 miles from the city on highway E 79, on the way to Drobeta-Turnu Severin; phone: 941-64471.

Preajba Tourist Inn, about 5 miles south of Craiova on highway DN 55; phone: 941-33426.

Victoria Recreation Center, about 17 miles from Craiova on highway DN 56. It has lake swimming, a pool, sauna, and deer and pheasants in its forest.

BUZĂU

Buzău is located 68 miles northeast of Bucharest on the south bank of the Buzău River. The Buzău River is a tributary of the Siret, which enters the Danube near Galaţi. Buzău is the county seat of Buzău County and has a population of 138,000 people. The city is a crossroads for several major highways and railroads. Buzău is 44 miles distant from Ploieşti and 65 miles from Brăila.

Wallachia

The city lies between the Subcarpathian hills to the northwest and the more fertile plains to the south and east of it. The growing of cereals and raising of livestock are important activities in the vicinity of the city. Grape growing is prominent to the west of it. Industries in Buzău include those of metalworking, food processing, textiles, alcohol, woodworking, plastics, building materials, and winemaking.

Remains of both Thracian and Gothic settlements have been unearthed in the surroundings of the city. A document dated in 1431 is the earliest recorded evidence of a town existing on the site of Buzău. The document refers to a medieval fair held in the city. The city has grown fast in recent decades with the addition of new apartment buildings. The remains of an old cathedral (fifteenth century) were restored in 1640. The seventeenth-century Bishop's Palace was reconstructed in the eighteenth century. Buzău is not an important tourist center.

Useful Addresses

Tourist Office, 176 Unirii St.

PITEŞTI

Piteşti is located 70 miles northwest of Bucharest by highway. It also lies on a direct rail line from the capital. Piteşti is a crossroads city, with several major highways and lesser roads running into and out of it. It is the county seat of Argeş County and has a population of 155,000 people. The city lies on the west bank of the Argeş River in an agricultural area where livestock raising and fruit growing are important activities. Grape growing is also practiced nearby, and wine making has long been an enterprise in the city. Large stands of trees are found in the vicinity of Piteşti.

Excavations at the town have turned up objects dating back to the Neolithic Age. Roman and Dacian artifacts have also been found on its site. First mention of the city in documents discloses that it existed in the 16th century. It originated as a trading center lying along several major trade routes. The city has grown substantially in the last several decades and ranks as one of Romania's important industrial centers. Its industries include machinery, woodworking, chemicals, textiles, leather, automobiles, shoes, food processing, structural steel, and machine tools. Nearby oil wells are connected to Ploieşti by pipeline to its refineries. About one-quarter of Romania's domestic oil supply is produced in the area around Piteşti. Natural gas is also produced. Tourist sights in the city include the **Art Museum** with its large collection of Romanian art noted for its simplicity and lack of sophistication; the old **Prince's Church** (1656); and the **Historical Museum**. Several interesting parks add to the city's features. The cultural life of the city is lacking when compared to a number of Romania's other cities and resorts.

Useful Addresses

Tourist Office, 2 Plevnei St.
Arges Hotel (first class for the city), 19—7 November Blvd.

DROBETA-TURNU SEVERIN

Located on the Danube River in southwest Romania, Drobeta-Turnu Severin is situated on the northern bank of the river where it forms a large bend in its course after exiting the Iron Gates. The city lies 215 miles west of Bucharest by highway. It is also connected by rail with the capital. Drobeta-Turnu Severin is the county seat of Mededinti County. The city has about 70,000 inhabitants, and its altitude is 129 feet above sea level.

Downstream from the city the banks of the Danube begin to flatten out as the river flows toward the Black Sea. Drobeta-Turnu Severin is an important river port on the Danube. The city depends heavily on trade and commerce. It builds and repairs ships, has a railway car manufacturing company and a metalworking complex, mills flour, brews beer, makes furniture, distills alcohol, produces textiles and plywood, and processes food. The area around the city grows grapes and produces a white wine of good vintage.

Drobeta-Turnu Severin was founded on the site of a former Dacian settlement known as Drobeta. The Romans knew the town as Drobetae or Drubetis. Some ruins of the first century settlement still exist. In the third century A.D. the Roman Emperor Severus built a tower there to commemorate a local victory. The tower was called Turris Severi (Tower of Severus) and contributed its name to that of the present-day city. Between A.D. 28 and 102 the Emperor Trajan had a narrow road chiseled out of stone on the nearby Yugoslav side of the Danube through the Iron Gates. This road, cut six feet into the rock, ran a distance of 12 miles. The ancient Roman road was connected with the Romanian side of the Danube by Trajan's Bridge (built between A.D. 103 and 105). At low water the piles of this ancient bridge can still be seen in the river. It was the longest bridge ever built by the Romans in their empire.

The town became the capital of the Banat of Severin in the twelfth century. A medieval citadel that protected it was destroyed in the sixteenth century by the Turks, and its remains can still be seen. The present-day town developed according to a plan that was carried out in 1836. The port was built in 1851. One of the city's features is the Rose Park, and many roses bloom around the city, prompting its inhabitants to call it the "City of Roses."

Five miles upstream from the city is the Iron Gates dam, built jointly by Romania and Yugoslavia, which backs up a 95-mile-long lake. The dam was built in 1965 to 1971 and raised the level of the river by more than 100 feet. The dam stands 98 feet above the water level. Some of the ancient ruins and islands in the river were covered by the lake. A road crosses the dam connecting the Romanian and Yugoslavian sides of the river. Locks are located at either end of the dam to allow ships to go around the dam, which produces hydroelectric power.

Upstream (15 miles) from Drobeta-Turnu Severin is the small city of Orsova, built at the time of construction of the Iron Gates dam. A former town by the same name lies covered by the reservoir created by the dam. The strategic location of the old town made it a scene of repeated fighting in bygone centuries.

Useful Addresses

Tourist Office, 64 Traian St.

Hotels
Parc (first class), 2 Republicii Blvd.
Traian (second class), 1 Karl Marx St.

TÎRGOVISTE

Tîrgoviste is located 51 miles northwest of Bucharest in the valley of the Ialomiţa River, a tributary of the Danube. It is the county seat of Dimboviţa County and has a population of about 45,000 inhabitants. Between the 14th and 17th centuries, Tîrgoviste was the capital of Wallachia. The modern city has grown up largely around its oil-related industries, producing oil field and mining equipment, machinery, and engineering products. The city lies where the Wallachian Plain meets the foothills of the Carpathians.

The city is full of history with its old buildings, churches, monastery, and the ruins of the old palace. The palace was founded by Mircea the Old, ruler of Wallachia from 1386–18. The palace is mentioned in a document dated in 1396. Some of its walls, made of river stones set irregularly, have been preserved. The palace was a large building with rooms grouped around a hall for ceremonies. The cellar, supported by sturdy pillars, covered an area of 95 feet by 105 feet. Above it was built the ground floor of the palace and the foundations of a chapel on the northeastern side. Although it burnt down in 1462 during the battles of Vlad Ţepeş (the Impaler) with the Turks, the palace has represented the main cultural center of the country ever since the time of the ruler Radu the Great (1495–1508). Here the monk Macarie issued the first printed book in Wallachia on November 10, 1508. Extended by Petru Cercel in 1584 and by Matei Basarab subsequently, the palace was restored and amplified by Constantin Brîncoveanu in the 17th century. Combining Renaissance elements, the palace has spacious halls supported by arches and powerful central pillars. Its bathrooms were heated, and a park and a greenhouse for Mediterranean plants were built on the bank of the Ialomita River. After Brîncoveanu was killed, the palace was destroyed and subsequent rulers were obliged by the Ottoman Porte to live in Bucharest.

Rebuilt by Constantin Mavrocordat in 1731–33, it was later burnt during the war between the Turks and Austrians. The palace was rearranged by Grigore Ghica in 1768–69, after which it was abandoned. Although a ruin, the present-day appearance of the palace, due to efforts to preserve it, lends identification of certain building elements and stages of the evolution of its original architecture.

Near the ruins, the **Chindia Tower** (16th century) was built as a watchtower. The **Prince's Church** (16th century) contains beautiful frescoes from the 17th and 18th centuries. Even older is the **Dealul Monastery** (15th and 16th centuries), which is believed to have been the site of Macarie's printing press. The head of Michael the Brave is said to have been sent to the monastery following his death. Another example of interesting architecture is the **Stelea Church** (17th century) built of a combination of Moldavian and Wallachian designs by the Moldavian voivode, Vasile Lupu.

Tîrgoviste has a thick smell of Romanian history about it, and a trip there will be a rewarding experience.

SLATINA

Slatina is located 114 miles west of Bucharest on the Olt River. It is the county seat of Olt County and has a population of about 50,000 people. Several highways and a railroad run through the city. Slatina is primarily an industrial center, with aluminum making as its main industry. Bauxite ore, used to make aluminum, is mined in the Western Carpathians. Power lines bring in electricity from Oradea to make the aluminum. Built in the 14th century, there is little tourist trade in the city.

RÎMNICU VÎLCEA

Rîmnicu Vîlcea is a city of about 30,000 people located in Vîlcea County, of which it is the county seat. The city lies 108 miles northwest of Bucharest along both banks of the Olt River. The city lies in the foothills of the Subcarpathians surrounded by orchards. North of the city the Olt cuts a path through the Carpathians, which is followed by a major highway through the mountains. A north-south railway connects the city with Slatina to the south and Sibiu to the north. The town has many old wooden buildings and is located in an area rich in folk art and ethnography. It is mentioned in documents of the 14th century and was an important trading center during the Middle Ages. The city has several industries making shoes and leather products, chemicals, and machinery. It also makes *ţuica*, a noted Romanian plum brandy. Its main tourist attractions are its old churches: the **Annunciation** and **St. Parasceva** both date from the 16th century; the **All Saints Church** built in the 18th century; and the **Citadel Church** constructed in the 15th century. The local museum is devoted to the history, art, and ethnography of the surrounding area. There is also the **mansion-museum of Anton Pann,** a noted 19th-century writer; the **Monument of Independence** (1913); and a memorial to the independence fighters of 1877–78.

Useful Addresses

Tourist Office, 30 Arges St.
Alutus Hotel (first class), Piaţa Maxim Gorki.

HISTRIA

Histria is located in Constanţa County, approximately 41 miles north of Constanţa. The city is full of ancient historical remains. It was the oldest Greek colony in Dacia, founded in 657 B.C. by Mileus navigators. In Greek times the city sat on the seacoast, but over the centuries its harbor silted up. Its settlers carried on a prosperous trade with Greece, Asia Minor, and other areas. Before the Romans came, its flourishing trade had largely ceased. The Romans revived the town, building temples, baths, and commercial buildings in it. In the 3rd century the Goths ravaged it, but it was rebuilt a short time later and then declined again in the 7th century. Histria reveals remains of buildings constructed at different times: precinct walls (7th and 6th centuries B.C.); the district with three levels of inhabitation (7th century B.C.); the sacred area, with the temple of Aphrodite (5th century B.C.); fragments of the temple of the "great god" made of Thason marble (3rd century B.C.); Roman camps and thermal baths; the economic district (4th–6th centuries A.D.); basilicas (4th–6th centuries); and the residential district "Domus," with public and private edifices (5th–6th centuries).

CHAPTER 4

Transylvania: Major Cities and Historic Sites

BRAŞOV

This ancient city in Transylvania preserves much of its medieval charm. There were settlements on its site during both the Neolithic and Bronze Ages. Later, the Geto-Dacians settled in the area during the Iron Age. The Romans also occupied the site and left behind evidence of their presence to be discovered by archeologists. Other invaders, including the Turks, Germans, and Austrians, have marched and fought on its soil.

Braşov is a city of some tourist importance, but it is more noted as a gateway to the important Romanian resorts of Poiana Braşov, Predeal, Sinaia, and others which lie largely to the south of it and in its nearby vicinity. In spite of the fact that Braşov is the second largest city in the country (353,000 population), it has little in the way of the attractions of the capital, Bucharest. Nevertheless, many tourists pass through the city, and sufficient numbers of these spend some time there to see its sights.

Braşov lies 106 miles north of Bucharest via Highway 1, which generally parallels the Prahova River north of the capital, following it as it flows off the slopes of the Carpathians. The Prohova valley separates the Eastern and Southern Carpathians. When Highway 1 leaves behind the Prahova valley, it follows the Timiş valley until it reaches Braşov. The Orient Express also follows this route between Bucharest and Braşov. Braşov is also connected by air with Bucharest and other Romanian cities.

Braşov is located in the central part of Romania and lies in the major gateway leading through the central part of the Carpathians. The city is the administrative center and county seat of Braşov County. Braşov is also an important transportation center. Neaby mountain passes lead to Wallachia and Moldavia. From Braşov, Highway 11 runs northeast through the Carpathians to Gheorghe Gheorghiu-Dej, while Highway 1 turns west to Sibiu, and Highway 13 heads northwest to Tirgu Mureş.

The city lies in the largest depression of the Transylvanian tableland. Around it are large forested areas, with resinous species (fir and spruce) being the most common types. An extreme temperature of $-37°$ F has been recorded in the Braşov depression in winter.

Braşov lies adjacent to the main mountain resort area in Romania. This resort area stretches along the Prahova and Timiş valleys and over the surrounding mountains (Postavarul, Cristianu Mare, and the Bucegi). Poiana Braşov, six miles south of the city, is the major winter sports resort in Romania.

Present-day Braşov is an industrial center which produces textiles, ball bearings, trucks, food products, chemicals, tractors, building materials, sawn timber, and electrical equipment. It is one of the major industrial centers of the country and has traditionally been a hub of trade. Nearby deposits of lignite help to provide a source of power for the city's industries.

Braşov was known as Orasul Stalin (the city of Stalin) during the 1950s. In 1960 the name Braşov replaced that of Stalin. The Hungarian name for the city is Brassó. Transylvania was part of Hungary from the 11th century until 1918, at which time it joined with Wallachia and Moldavia to form today's Romania.

In 1211 the Teutonic Order of Knights settled on the site of Braşov; German settlers poured into the area and gave the name

Kronstadt to their settlement, which expanded over the centuries into the modern city at that location. The district around Kronstadt was called Burzenland by the Germans. Kronstadt was one of seven major fortified towns which the Germans founded in Transylvania. In 1224 King Andrew of Hungary granted the Saxons, descendants of the original German settlers, a large degree of autonomy which they were vigilant in maintaining for centuries. The Saxons believed their autonomy helped to preserve their cultural and ethnic identity and attempted to keep the Romanians and Magyars out of important positions in their towns or from owning property in them. The traditional rights and privileges of the Saxon "nation" continued even after Transylvania passed into the hands of the Habsburgs. In 1699 the Ottoman Empire ceded Transylvania to Austria. As late as the 1930s, over 30 percent of the inhabitants of Braşov were of German descent. Germans are still the major minority group in the area of Braşov today.

Johannes Honterus (1498–1549) was the leader of the Protestant Reformation in Kronstadt, his birthplace and site of burial. His religious activities led to him being called "the apostle of Transylvania." He also founded the first printing press in Transylvania. It was in Kronstadt that the first book printed in Romania was published in the mid-1500s by Coresi, a local deacon.

The city was attacked by the Turks on several occasions, who successfully took it in 1421 before its citadel was completed. In 1434 the Turks again attacked it, but this time they were repulsed by the heavy fortifications. The Austrians attacked the city in 1689, and amidst the fighting a fire swept through it. During the First World War, the Romanian army marched into the city but retreated in the face of German pressure in 1916. When the war ended, Braşov passed into Romanian hands.

On the northeast, Braşov runs into a valley opening overlooked by Tampa Mountain (3,160 feet in elevation). This part of the city is the site of the old town with its medieval walls, Town Hall, several churches dating from the 14th through 18th centuries, and the ruins of the old citadel. The elevation of Braşov varies, with much of the city ranging between 1,900 and 2,300 feet.

What to See

Black Church (1425), or Gothic Protestant Church. This church acquired its name when a fire in 1689 smoked and damaged its walls. It was restored in the early 1700s and is an excellent example of late Gothic architecture. Measuring 290 feet long and 75 feet in width, it is Romania's largest church. Inside is a huge organ constructed in 1859 which resounds through 4,000 pipes. The church also has a beautiful collection of Oriental carpets dating from the 16th century. The Black Church is located on Piața 23 August, which is the largest square of Brașov. On the east side of the square is Republicii Street, while on the north side the 7 November Street leads into the square.

Old Town Hall, or Casa Sfatului (the Council House). Also located on Piața 23 August, this building is now a regional museum. It dates from the 15th century, while the Trumpeters' Tower standing beside it was constructed in the 16th century for use as a watchtower and for announcements of special events. The Town Hall was restored in 1777.

Merchants' Hall. It is located on the same end of the square as the Old Town Hall. It was built in 1542 in Renaissance style and restored in the early 1960s after a fire damaged it in 1957. During the Middle Ages its three floors housed guilds engaged in trading their wares. Several inner courtyards and a wine cellar were built into it. Over the centuries its layout changed several times as alterations were made to it. The well-known *Cerbul Carpatin Restaurant* is presently located in part of the building.

St. Nicholas Orthodox Church. This old church is located in the Șchei district of the city, or Romanian quarter. In the Middle Ages the Romanians were excluded from entering the old town except at stated times during the day. In 1392 a wooden church was built on the site of the present church; a stone cross currently marks its location. In the late 1400s a stone church was constructed, with work on it continuing until 1700. In 1751 some restoration was done to the church, and a clock tower was added to it. To Orthodox Romanians, the church was a symbol of their resistance to the Habsburg monarchy and its efforts to force Catholicism on them. The Orthodox Romanians were supported by Russia (also Orthodox) and its ruler, Empress Elizabeth.

Church of St. Bartholomew. A 13th-century Saxon church, it is located on Lunga Street, which runs north from Blvd. Gheorghiu-Dej. The church is built in a Gothic and Romanesque style of architecture.

Cetățuia (Citadel Hill). On this hill is a group of fortifications built during the 14th through 16th centuries. The citadel, which is well preserved, is made of bricks and overlooks the wooded slopes below. Its coat of arms can be seen on Catherine's Tower, which dates from the mid-1500s. The old archives of the town are located in Blacksmiths' Bastion. Also dating from the 15th century is the Weavers' Bastion, which houses a historical museum.

Other major sights include the state theater, polytechnic institute, the opera, puppet theater, and state philharmonic orchestra.

Useful Addresses

Tourist Agency *ONT Carpati.* 15—7 November St.; phone: 921-42849.

Hotels
Carpati (deluxe) 9 Carpati Blvd.
Postavarul (first class) 2 Grigorescu St.

Restaurants
Cerbul Carpatin (Carpathian Stag) is located in the old Merchants' Hall. Its architecture and interior decoration recall a medieval atmosphere. Romanian dishes and drinks are its specialty. It provides a program of folk music and dances. There is a bar and wine bar.

Cetăţea Braşov has as its setting the old citadel. Its atmosphere is medieval style. It has a program of preclassic music and folk dances. There is a wine cellar, beer hall, bar, and confectionery.

TIMIŞOARA

Set amidst a rich plain, crossed by the Bega River, the city of Timişoara is one of the main economic, scientific, and cultural centers in Romania. Its population numbers about 325,000 people. Timişoara is situated near the Yugoslavian frontier, 39 miles from the Moraviţa border crossing, and 27 miles from the Jimbolia crossing. Timişoara lies 352 miles from Bucharest, 32 miles from Arad, and 106 miles from Oradea. Timişoara is the capital of the Banat region.

Timişoara is an ancient settlement. Archeological diggings have provided evidence of man's presence here since the Neolithic Age. The former Castrum Temesiensis was mentioned in documents dating as far back as 1212. The Tartars sacked the city in the 13th century.

During the 15th century the city was rebuilt and enlarged by Lancu of Hunedoara, who was a count of Timiş at that time (1441). Old documents also mention the name of Gheorghe Doja, the leader of the Peasant's War in 1514, who died as a martyr at the gates of the city. The Turks captured the city in 1522. Timişoara grew rapidly after sewerage and damming works of the Bega River were carried out in 1728, in order to drain the surrounding swamps which had become a hindrance to the growth of the town.

Public lighting with illuminating gas was introduced in 1857. Timişoara is one of the first cities in Europe where horse-driven tramways were used as a means of conveyance in 1869 and where electrical lighting was used in 1884.

The first electrical tramways were used in 1899. The famous French engineer Gustave Eiffel built a bridge here over the Bega River. In spite of the many architectural styles which have put their stamp on the city, an harmonious atmosphere greets the newcomer. In 1918, Timişoara was returned to Romania.

The city has a variety of industries including engineering, metal works, textiles, food processing, and chemicals. Timişoara is noted for electrical engineering; Romania's first electronic calculating machine was manufactured here.

One of the greatest charms of the town is the Bega River, flowing slowly through the weeping, "thoughtful" willows and under magnificent stone bridges. Timişoara, "the garden town," is renowned for its parks and gardens blossoming with exquisite flowers and rare species of trees. A former medieval city surrounded by outer walls, Timişoara has become a modern center of science and culture. Its monuments and sights have been drawing ever larger numbers of tourists.

Timiş County covers a very wide region. In area it is one of the largest counties in Romania (3,351 square miles). The Banat region, where it is located, is one of great variety and beauty.

The towns and villages are each a feast to the eye. They have preserved their traditional charm and peaceful atmosphere. The local people are pleasant, cheerful, and hard working. They enjoy folk songs and dances and are always happy to welcome guests. One should come here if one really wants to get to know them. The surroundings of Timişoara are rich in tourist sights. Special

Transylvania

mention must be made of the museums in Timişoara, Lugoj, Sinnicolau Mare, Jimbolia, Lenauheim, Giarmata, Ortisoara, Teremia Mare, and Buziaş. Folk art masterpieces are displayed alongside other items.

Sixteen miles from Timişoara, at Bazosul Nou, a splendid arboretum can be visited. Lovers of nature can admire vegetation species from all over the world. At Izvin, 11 miles from Timişoara, the Republican Riding and Horse Breeding Center is found. A folk architecture open-air exhibition is set in the outskirts of this town.

Another place well worth seeing is the Buziaş Spa, located 19 miles from Timişoara. It provides treatment all year round and is rich in mineral water sources effective in the treatment of heart diseases. Therapeutical methods include the use of a well-known Romanian drug, Boicil Forte.

The thermal mineral waters (100–104°F) of the Călacea Spa, located 16 miles distant from Timişoara, are used both in the treatment of locomotory apparatus affections and peripheral nervous system diseases.

What to See

Huniad Castle, 1 Piaţa Huniade, was built on the site of the former city which was a seat of the Romanian ruling princes for centuries. It was erected by Carol Robert d'Anjou in 1316 and redecorated and enlarged by Lancu of Hunedoara (15th century). Restored in 1856, it plays host at present to the history department of the Timis Museum.

City Bastion, 4 Popa Sapca St., was built in the 18th century. The technical and ethnography department of the Banatului Museum is found here. It has an outstanding collection of Romanian folk art.

Folk Architecture, Banat area, in Pădurea Verde park, is open daily from 10 A.M. to 6 P.M. Closed on Mondays.

Residence of Ruling Prince Eugeniu, 24 Ceahlău St., was built in 1817. The fresco at the entrance depicting the Forforoza Gate shows that it was through here that Prince Eugeniu of Savoia entered the city after it was freed from a Turkish siege.

Old Town Hall, 1 Piaţa Libertăţii is the oldest building in town (18th century) built in the Renaissance and Baroque style. It is erected on the site of a former Turkish public bath, built in 1675, according to the stone inscription written in Arabic.

Romanian Soldier's Memorial, located in Central Park. It is a white marble monument erected in honor of the soldiers who died for the freedom of this country against Nazi domination.

Union Square, one of the old parts of the town, is well worth visiting.

Old Chief Commissioner's Office, in Piaţa Unirii. Built in 1754 in the Renaissance and Baroque style, this magnificent building is remarkable for its carved wooden gates set in stone portals and for its richly adorned walls.

Fountain of the Cardinal Points, in Piaţa Dr. Russel, was erected by the architect St. Iojică.

Iron Tree House, 2 Eminescu St., is an iron-circled tree stuck into the side of a house.

Dicasterial Palace, 2 Popa Şapcă and Ceahlău St., Its building began in 1847 and ended in 1861. Neo-Renaissance style.

Statue of Decebalus, set in Piaţa Libertăţii, is a sculpture by Pavel Mercea (1977).

Opera House and the **National Theater,** both set in Piaţa Operei, were erected in the 18th century and rebuilt in the 20th century. They are richly adorned and decorated.

Romulus and Remus Memorial, 30 Decembrie Blvd., is a replica of the Capitoline statue offered as a gift by the city of Rome.

Workers' House, 7 April 1929 St., played host to the Trade Unions Congress in 1929.

Polytechnical Institute, Politehnicii Blvd., is an impressive building, architectural style.

Banat Village Museum, in the Green Wood Park. Founded in 1971 on an area of 43 acres, it contains 21 monuments and 30 peasant dwellings (19th century) with all of their implements, brought from different areas of Banat: a farmhouse from Capilnas, water mills, a windmill, and old farm equipment. The museum is structured on the model of a village with all its institutions: a mayor's office, school, club, and church. Open 10 A.M. to 6 P.M; closed on Mondays.

Useful Addresses

Timis County Tourist Office, 8 Republicii Blvd.; phone: 961-36072, 36451, or 36421; telex: 71317.

Home Tourist Agency, 6 Republicii Blvd., books holidays, visits

Transylvania

to treatment facilities, and inland tours; phone: 961-36532. For trips abroad, phone: 961-36462.
 Tarom Agency, 3–5—23 August Blvd.; phone: 961-36855.
 Railway Travel Agency, 2—23 August Blvd.; phone: 961-13350.
 International Tourism Agency, 3 Piatra Craiului St.; phone: 961-36012; telex: 71242.
 Tourist Office, 72 Gh. Lazăr St.; phone: 961-43945.
 Tourist Office, 15 Ştefan cel Mare St.; phone: 961-33885.
 ACR (Romanian Auto Club) Branch, 1 Hector St.; phone: 961-33333.
 Technical Assistance Branch—ACR, 2 Calea Aradului, Intrarea Doninei; phone: 961-12345.

Hotels, Camping

 Continental Hotel Complex, 2—23 August Blvd.; phone: 961-34145; telex: 71266.
 Timişoara, 2—1 Mai St.; phone: 961-37815.
 Central, 6 Leanu St.; phone: 961-17670.
 Banatul, 5 Republicii Blvd.; phone: 961-37762 or 37855.
 Nord, 17—13 Decembrie St.; phone: 961-12308.
 Bega, 12 N. Titulescu St.; phone: 961-11496.
 Timiş Inn, 94 Calea Dorobantilor; phone: 961-32202.
 Camping, Padurea Verde St.; phone: 961-33925.

Restaurants

 Continental, 2—23 August Blvd.; phone: 961-34145.
 Timişoara, 2—1 Mai St.; phone: 961-37815.
 Central, 6 Leanu St.; phone: 961-17672.
 Cina, 4 Piatra Craiului St.; phone: 961-37977.
 Tourist Inn, 94 Calea Dorobantilor; phone: 961-33140.
 Bastion Wine Cellar, 2 Hector St.; phone: 961-33172.

Sweet Shops

 Flora, 9 T. Vladimirescu St.; phone: 961-15142.
 Violeta, 6—30 Decembrie Blvd.; phone: 961-36085.
 Trandafirul, 5 M. Eminescu St.; phone: 961-33707.
 Mercur, Piaţa Operei; phone: 961-30674.
 Fashion Center, 2 Piaţa Huniade; phone: 961-37750.
 Bega General Shop, 2 Bocşa St.; phone: 961-32741.
 Motor Car Spare Parts Store, Ceahlău St.; phone: 961-36447.

Drug Stores and Hospitals
Chemist's Shop No. 2, 1 Măciesilor St.; phone: 961-30384.
Chemist's Shop No. 3, 11—23 August Blvd.; phone: 961-33991.
General Hospital, 9—23 August Blvd.; phone: 961-36696.
County Hospital, 152 Stefan Plavăţ St.; phone: 961-63000.

Transportation
Northern Railway Station, 3 Gării St.; Information Office, phone: 961-12552.
Eastern Railway Station, 1 CFR St.; phone: 961-32151.
The *Airport* is set in the outskirts of the town on the road leading to Lugoj; phone: 961-16732 or 14099.
Bus Station, 54 Reşiţa St.; phone: 961-13630.

Post Office, Telephones
Central Post Office, 2—23 August Blvd.; phone: 961-12012.
Telephone Center, 4 Lenin St.; phone: 961-12557.

Opera House, Theaters, Cinemas
National Opera House, 2 Mărăşeşti St.; phone: 961-34660.
National Theater, 2 Mărăşeşti St.; phone: 961-34643.
German Theater, phone: 961-34638.
Magyar Theater, 2 Alba Iulia St.; phone: 961-34814.
Puppet Theater, 3 Tinereţii Blvd., phone: 961-17431.
Banatul Philharmonic Orchestra, 3 Tinareţii Blvd.; phone: 961-17431.
Banatul Philharmonic Orchestra, 2 Victoriei Blvd.; phone: 961-12521.
Capitol Cinema, 2 Victoriei Blvd.; phone: 961-14528 or 12521.
Timis Cinema, 30 Decembrie Blvd.; phone: 961-34744.

Sports and Entertainment Centers
Olympia Sports Hall, Eroilor Blvd.; phone: 961-25286.
1 Mai Stadium, phone: 961-62851.
Thermal Swimming Pool, V. Pîrvan Blvd.; phone: 961-15508.
Tineretului (Youth's) Swimming Pool, 93 Calea Dorobantilor; phone: 961-30051.

Peco Filling Stations, Car Service
Filling Station, Calea Aradului; phone: 961-41026.
Filling Station, Calea Dorobanţilor; phone: 961-32051, 32729.

Filling Station, Calea Şagului; phone: 961-55350.
Filling Station, Eroilor Blvd.; phone: 961-32381.
Car Service, Calea Aradului; phone: 961-43292.
Car Service, Calea Dorobanţilor; phone: 961-37663.

Parks and Gardens
City Park.
Central Park, Polithenicii Blvd.
Poporului Park, 12 Aprilie St.
Pădureau Verde, (The Green Wood), set in the northeastern part of the town.
Rozelor Park, Trandafirilor St.
Pioneers' Park, 23 August Blvd.
Alpinet Park, T. Vladimirescu St.
Doina Park, Gh. Doja St.
Botanical Gardens, Calea Aradului.

CLUJ-NAPOCA

This city is located on the Transylvania plateau at the foot of the eastern slopes of the Western Carpathians. It lies 277 miles from Bucharest via Braşov and Tîrgu Mureş. Cluj-Napoca is the county seat of Cluj County and has a population of 311,000 people. The city is one of Romania's largest industrial and cultural centers. It has comfortable hotels, appetizing restaurants, and interesting stores and shops. Cluj-Napoca is the sixth largest city in Romania. The city lies in the valley of the Someşu-Mic River, which divides it into a northern and southern sector. Several rail lines connect it with other parts of Romania. A large area of suburban horticulture surrounds the city.

The major ethnic minority in the city is Hungarian (including Szekler). The Szeklers originally settled in the eastern part of Transylvania in its mountainous and hill areas. Their ancestors were non-Hungarian speaking, but the present-day Szeklers living mainly in eastern and central Transylvania speak the Hungarian tongue. Today, the Szeklers identify themselves as Hungarians in language and culture, although they are aware of their once distinct non-Hungarian culture. They were Magyar colonists but not descendants of the Huns and Atilla.

The ancient history of the town dates back to the Stone Age. Artifacts from that age and the Bronze and Iron Ages have been discovered at the site of the city. Transylvania's earliest recorded inhabitants (according to Herodotus) were the Agathyrses during the 6th to 4th centuries B.C. The Celts occupied the area in the 3rd and 2nd centuries B.C., and in the 2nd century B.C. the Dacians appeared in the area. In A.D. 106 the Romans conquered Transylvania and controlled it until A.D. 275, after which German tribes, Sarmatians, and barbarians moved into the area.

The first recorded town on the site of the present city was a settlement named Napoca, which existed in the 2nd century B.C., according to Ptolemy. This Dacian town was occupied by the Romans and became a military garrison and a center of trade. The city's present name was first recorded in the 11th century.

Transylvania, including Cluj, was for centuries the center of efforts to impose Magyarization on the area. Transylvania was part of Hungary from the 11th century until 1918. Hungarian rulers invited many Germans to settle the lands of Transylvania during the 12th and 13th centuries. On the present site of Cluj-Napoca, the Germans founded the city of Klausenburg, which was one of the seven major towns founded by German settlers in Transylvania. The Germans, or Saxons, called Translyvania's lands *Siebenburgen,* a name generally believed to refer to the seven castled towns they built there. Some historians believe the name might refer or be derived from that of the old castled town of Sibiu, one of the seven fortified cities.

In 1405, Klausenburg was granted the status of a free town by the Hungarian king. Then in 1437, Transylvania was grouped into three nations (Magyars, Szeklers, and Saxons or Germans), each with its own political and cultural privileges which were jealously guarded. By the mid 1400s, the Saxons and Magyars came to govern Klausenberg jointly, and about a century later the Magyars came to control it. The Hungarians called the city Kolozsvár.

By the middle of the 16th century most of the Magyar nobility and their families had deserted the Catholic faith and turned to Protestantism, with Calvinism being their favorite choice. Klausenburg or Kolozsvár became a center of Calvinism, and David, a court minister, its main organizer in the city. However, in 1556 he shed his Calvinist beliefs and founded the Unitarian Church in Klausenburg. In 1551 the Hungarian Diet recognized equal status for four religions in Transylvania: Lutheran, Roman Catholic, Unitarian, and Reformed or Calvinist. Catholicism did not return in strength or importance in Transylvania until the 18th century. Following the murder of Michael the Brave in 1601, the Jesuits took over the old town church in the city.

The Austro-Germans invaded the area in World War I, at the end of which Transylvania became part of Romania. Later, Cluj and the northern part of Transylvania were handed over to Hungary (1940) by demand of Hitler. Northern Transylvania was transferred back to Romania at the close of World War II.

The present-day city of Clug-Napoca is an important industrial center which produces ball bearings and machine tools, textiles, shoes and leather, chemicals, glass, ceramics, sawn timber, machinery, and foodstuffs. Engineering industries are especially important in the city.

What to See

Matthias Corvinus House. This house is located on Matei Corvin St., which runs into the northern end of Piaţa Libertăţii Square. Matthias I. Corvinus, who became king of Hungary, was born in this house in 1440. He was the son of Ioan of Hunedora.

Ethnographical Museum of Transylvania. A short walk west of the Piaţa Libertăţii along 30 Decembrie St. will bring one to an early 19th-century building known as the Redoute. Here in 1846, Franz Liszt (1811–86), a magnetic piano player born in Hungary, performed to the delight of audiences. Famous for his *Hungarian Rhapsodies* and *Transcendental Études*, Liszt was a brilliant performer who broke the heart of many women, one of whom was a countess who deserted her husband to live with him. In the same building the "Memorandists," well-known cultural, literary, and political personages of Romanian society, were placed on trial in 1894 for their endeavors on behalf of the suppressed nationalities of people living under Habsburg rule. The building was converted into a museum in the early 1920s, and ethnographic material and objects were reposited in it. Enlarged in recent years, the museum houses a vast collection of traditional clothing and textiles, household objects, pottery, photographs and old prints, tools, a library, and old documents.

Gothic Church of St. Michael. Work on this church began in 1321 and continued through the years until 1444. It is one of the largest churches in Romania, with its 19th-century tower standing 260 feet high. A fire damaged it at the end of the 17th century, and since then its features have been altered several times. The longitudinal area of the nave is 160 feet long. Renaissance and Baroque elements are used in its decorative features. A 15th-century figure of St. Michael is located inside the main entrance of the church, which stands on the north side of Piaţa Libertăţii.

Mînăştur Church. This church erected in 1061 was reconstructed in Gothic style during the 15th and 16th centuries. Peasant revolts during the Middle Ages destroyed parts of it. To reach it follow Motilor St. off 30 Decembrie St. on the west side of Piaţa Libertăţii.

Art Museum. Located on the east side of Piaţa Libertăţii, this museum occupies a former palace dating from the 18th century. This beautiful structure done in Baroque style contains collected art works by several schools of painters and sculptors, with much of it dating from the time of the Middle Ages. Many of the works were done by local artists from the area of Cluj-Napoca, while other works represent artists from various areas of the country.

Botanical Gardens. These lovely gardens are located at 42 Republicii St. They are open from 9 A.M. to 7 P.M. during the summer and from 9 A.M. until 5 P.M. during the winter. They were founded in 1923 and completed by Al. Borza in 1930. The gardens stretch over three hills and cover thirty-five acres. The gardens contain plants from all over the world, with the exotic ones grown inside greenhouses. The open-air sections contain Romanian flora, desert flora from Africa and Mexico, American flora, Mediterranean and Chinese flora, and a Japanese Garden. The old greenhouses contain the large aquarium that shelters the lily from the Amazon *(Victoria Amazonica);* a special section 59 feet high for palm trees; the greenhouse for subtropical plants; the greenhouse for succulent flowers; and the greenhouse for epiphyteous and carnivorous species. The Botanical Museum shelters fossil plant collections and a berberium with over 500,000 leaves of plants from all over the world. The greenhouses are automatically watered and heated.

The **University** is located south and east of Piaţa Libertăţii along Kogălniceanu St. Another name for it is Babeş and Bolyai University, names honoring two well-known scholars who were natives of the city. The faculties of medicine and science are located along Miko St.

The **Citadel.** The ruins of the walls of its fortifications stand on the north bank of the Someş River, rising over 200 feet above its waters. Construction of the citadel began in the 16th century with other parts of it built in the 18th century.

Statues in the city include the **Equestrian Statue** depicting St. George and the Dragon, which stands in front of the small Evangelical Church near the eastern end of Kogălniceanu St. in the vicinity of the university. The statue was completed by two local sculptors in 1373 and is a copy or duplicate of the statue in the old Hradčany Palace overlooking the city of Prague, Czechoslovakia. Another well-known local statue is that of the **Equestrian Statue of Matthias Corvinus,** which stands in the center of Piaţa Libertăţii.

Piaţa Libertăţii is an old square located in the center of the southern half of the city that lies south of the Someş River. In the square and around it are many of the city's old buildings and historic places of interest. Several of the major hotels in the city also stand around the square. Major streets which lead into the square are Dr. P. Groza St., V. I. Lenin Blvd., 30 Decembrie St., and Napoca St.

Other sights to see include the **Collection on the History of Pharmacy,** 28 Piaţa Libertăţii; **Evangelical Church,** Kogălniceanu St., constructed in the 15th and 16th centuries in Gothic styles; **Tailors' Bastion,** Piaţa Ştefan cel Mare, the remains of 15th-century fortifications; **National Theater and State Opera House; Hungarian State Theatre;** and **Historical Museum.**

Useful Addresses

Tourist Office, 2 Gh. Sincai St.

Hotels
Continental (first class), 1 Napoca St.
Napoca (first class), 1 Iosza Bela.
Astoria (second class), 3 Horia St.
Central (second class), 29 Piaţa Libertăţii.

Restaurants
Bucureşti.
Someşul.
Clujul.
Gambrinus.

ORADEA

The tenth largest town in Romania, Oradea is located in the northwestern part of the country 9 miles from the frontier post of Borş on the border with Hungary. Oradea is situated on both the northern and southern banks of the Crişul Repede River in the historic province known as Crişana. The city is the county seat of Oradea County and lies at the gateway to the Tiza Plain. The population of the city is 215,000 inhabitants. By highway, Oradea is 369 miles from Bucharest, 72 miles north of Arad, and 97 miles west of Cluj-Napoca. The city is connected by several major rail lines, one of which crosses the Hungarian frontier and continues on to Budapest.

Archeological findings at Oradea date the remains of its ancient settlements back to the Neolithic Age. Later, both Scythian and Dacian tribes occupied its site. Roman ruins are present although the area of Oradea was not included as part of Roman Dacia. Roman soldiers marched on the roads passing through ancient Oradea. After the Romans departed, barbarian invaders swept across the area. The ruins of a citadel built by the migratory Slavs have been uncovered on a hill in the vicinity. Around A.D. 1080, St. Ladislaus established a Roman Catholic bishopric on the site of the town. A medieval state with its headquarters at Bihara citadel, a few miles northwest of Oradea, existed at the time that the Hungarians moved into the area. During the Middle Ages the 11th-century monastery stood where the citadel of Oradea was built in the 12th century. The citadel was destroyed by the Tartars when they swept into the old Hungarian town in 1241–42. It was rebuilt more than three centuries later. The town was rebuilt in the 14th century and gained in trade and population on into the 15th century when it came under the rule of Matthias Corvinus. In 1660 the Turks attacked the town but were twice repulsed by its citadel before they finally took it. The town was destroyed in the fighting but was rebuilt under Turkish rule that lasted until 1692.

The Hungarian name for the city is Nagy-Várad. Hungarians still constitute the largest national minority group in the city today. Germans know the town by the name of Grosswardein.

Present-day Oradea is a major industrial center in the country. The city produces aluminum (manufactured from ores on the slopes of the Western Carpathians), machine tools, ball bearings, chemicals, and machinery, and processes food. The growing of cereals and raising of livestock are important activities in the agricultural region around the city. Suburban horticulture is also practiced. Temperatures at Oradea average 29° F for January and 70° F for July.

What to See

Church of St. Ladislaus was originally built in the 12th century, then was reconstructed in the 18th century. The remains of St. Ladislaus repose inside the church.

Moon Church was built in the late 1700s and exhibits a number of beautiful frescoes on its interior. Its structure is a combination of Baroque and neoclassical styles of architecture. The church takes it name from a huge sphere located on its tower which displays a sort of exhibition of the different phases through which the moon passes.

Roman Catholic Cathedral was built during the last half of the 18th century and resembles the Baroque architecture found on churches and buildings in the northern part of Italy. The church was built from funds raised through the imposition of taxes on the serfs who toiled on lands owned by it.

Oradea Citadel occupies the site of a former monastery and was originally built in the 12th century. Destroyed by the Tartars in 1242, it was rebuilt in the 16th and 17th centuries. It fell to the Turks in 1660, who heavily damaged it when they withdrew from it in 1692. A moat was dug around it and filled with water that emanated from several springs.

Bishop's Palace was built in the last half of the 18th century. Its architects used as their model the lovely Belvedere Palace in the Habsburg city of Vienna. The Baroque-styled palace stands in a large park in which grow some of the large Sequoia trees from California. Inside the palace is the exquisite Tare Crişurilor Museum which contains a wealth of objects of art, history, and specimens of scientific value. There is an exquisite collection of works by Albrecht Dürer (1471–1528), a famed German printer and engraver. Included in the museum is a fanciful collection of thousands of bird eggs and an ornithology section exhibiting many rare and unusual bird species.

Other interesting features of Oradea include the **State Theater** (1900), the **Puppet Theater,** and the **Zoological Garden.** There are also several museums dedicated to Romanian artists.

Useful Addresses

Tourist Office: 1 Aleea Strandului.

Hotels

Transylvania (first class), 2 Teatrului St.
Dacia (first class), 1 Aleea Strandului.
Park (second class), 3 Republicii St.

ARAD

The town of Arad, the seat of Arad county, is located on the right bank of the Mureş River in western Romania at an altitude of 360 feet. The county is a wine- and grain-producing area. The town is built on an alluvial plain. Documents indicate Arad has a past rich in historical events, with its beginnings dating from the Neolithic Age.

Arad is the first major Romanian town seen by the tourist entering Romania from Hungary through the border points of Nădlac (31 miles by road from Arad), Curtici (11 miles by railroad from Arad), or Vărşand (42 miles by road). Arad is located 32 miles from Sibiu and 342 miles from Bucharest on highway DN 7. It has a population of about 190,000.

The presence of the Dacians and later of the Romans is confirmed by archeological diggings and written records. The great number of discoveries, both within the town and in the county (Vladimirescu, Felnar, Zătrani, Cladova, Lipova, Chişineu Criş), is evidence of the settlement in this area after Dacia's conquest by the Romans (A.D. 106) of the Daco-Romans and then the Romanian population. Arad was first mentioned in 1028, in the medieval chronicle *The Legend of Saint Gerard*, in the context of struggles waged by the native population against invading troops of the Hungarian kingdom. The Vienna Chronicle and others offer much the same information about the town. At the height of feudalism (13th–17th centuries) as well as during its decline (18th–19th centuries), the Arad area underwent important changes, although the foreign domination was an obstacle to its progress. Beginning in the 19th century, Arad became an important industrial center (food, wood-processing, textile, chemical, and machine industries) and a commercial town.

The development of capitalism in the latter half of the 19th century spurred Arad to become a center of the workers' movement and their struggle for social and national liberation in Transylvania. Numerous events were held expressing the determination of the people that Transylvania should unite with Romania. Thus, on November 2–December 1, 1918, Arad became the administrative and organizational center of the struggle for national liberation and unity. It was here, on the initiative of the Central Romanian National Council (set up on October 30, 1918), that was fostered the idea of the Plebiscite National Assembly in Alba Iulia on December 1, 1918, which was to implement the age-old dream of the Romanian people, that of a united Romanian national state. Arad became part of the Romanian state, and its development proceeded into all fields of activity. Arad boasts a rich cultural and articstic tradition, as its name is connected to famous scholars and artists, both Romanian and foreign, such as M. Eminescu, I. Salvici, G. Enescu, Johann and Richard Strauss, F. Liszt, B. Bartok. In 1812 the first Romanian teachers' college in Banat and Crisana was set up here, and in 1833 Arad established a music school that was followed in 1890 by a symphony orchestra.

Today Arad is one of the main industrial, cultural, and tourist centers in Romania. The city and its surroundings offer tourists the opportunity to admire landscapes of rare beauty, picturesque places and customs, museums, and art and history monuments. Some of the most attractive places are: the Dezna valley, the Mureş Pass, and the Cladova valley. The vineyards in the county, in Miniş and Baraţca, are charming and tempting.

In the area of Arad interesting dances have been transmitted from one generation to another, such as: Tîrgul Sărutului (Hălmagiu), Jocul Felegll (Văsoaia-Cuied), Vergelul (Cărand), and Paparuda (Diecil). Other interesting customs are the Feasts at Vintage Time (in the wine-growing areas), weddings, and the Lay Winter Customs (Pluguşorul and Capra). In the Apuseni Mountains (Western Carpathians), gates, alpenhorns, and household objects are carved in wood. The wooden churches, some of them built in the 18th and 19th centuries (Vidra and Tisa), have remarkable architecture. The folk costumes of great artistic value have been preserved in the Ineu, Gurahonţ, and Mureşu de Jos valleys.

What to See

Palace of Culture, 1 Enescu Square, built in a mixture of styles (in which the Romantic and Renaissance are predominant) between 1911 and 1913, is outstanding for its frontispiece built with Corinthian columns and its wide, monumental stairs. The Palace of Culture has hosted renowned Romanian and foreign artists such as George Enescu and Bela Bartok. Such personalities as Dr. Petru Groza, Lucreţiu Pătrăşanu, and Nicolae Lorga have delivered lectures here. The Palace of Culutre also houses the County Museum with sections of history, ethnography, and folklore.

County People's Council Building, 75 Republicii Blvd., an architectural monument, was built at the end of the 19th century in the style of a castle.

Casa cu Lacăt (The House with the Lock), 7 Tribunul Dobra St., was named after the tree trunk encircled with a locked metal ring in a recess in the wall.

Ardealul Hotel, 98 Republicii Blvd., built in the neoclassic style, dates from the 19th century. It served as an inn and stagecoach depot on the road from Vienna to Sibiu through Budapest. Franz Liszt, Johann Brahms, and Johann Strauss, Jr., played in the concert hall of this inn.

Serbian Orthodox Church, Sirbească Sq., is an 18th-century Baroque architectural monument. The small, main entrance looks like a triumphal arch. The oldest banners of the guilds in Arad and some of the pennants of the Mureş Border Guards are kept in this church.

Roman-Catholic Church, Republicii Blvd., a monumental Renaissance building erected at the beginning of the 20th century has a column-ornated facade. Noteworthy are the sculptures and stained glass inside the church.

State Theater, 103 Republicii Blvd., was built in the neoclassic style between the years of 1872 and 1874. The ornaments in the foyer and in the hall are exquisite.

Romanian Soldiers' Memorial, Avram Lancu Sq., was erected in 1960 in the memory of those who died for the liberation from Nazi domination.

Obelisk, erected in the memory of the Soviet soldiers who fell while liberating the town, is found in Vasile Roaită Park.

In western Arad, 1.2 miles from the airport you can find the forest of Ceala and Mureş Island, a picturesque and pleasant entertainment and resting spot. Nearby the restaurant *Zori De Zi* serves local dishes.

Romanian Orthodox Cathedral, Filimon Sirbu Sq., was built between 1862 and 1865 in predominantly Baroque style. Inside are remarkable sculptural and painting works; especially outstanding is the iconostasis.

Ioan Slavici High School, General Draglina Blvd., with the bust of the writer, a former student of this high school, in front of the building, was built between 1869 and 1872 in Renaissance style. It is noteworthy for its facade with its red marble stairs. The statues on the frontispiece are dominated by an allegorical figure which beckons students to study; decorative applications adorn the hallway and the festival hall.

Monument of St. Ioan Nepomuk, 7 Noiembrie St., the oldest art monument in Arad, was erected in 1729. Made of stone, the monument is in Baroque style.

Biserica Rosie (Red Church), 61 Republicii Blvd., was built at the beginning of the 20th century in the neo-Gothic style.

Memorial to the Păuliş Heroes, 17 miles from Arad to Lipova on highway DN 7.

Useful Addresses

County Tourist Office, 12 Decembrie 1918 St.; phone: 966-14334; telex: 046245 OJTR.

International Tourism Agency (exchange office), 79–81 Republicii Blvd.; phone: 966-13428; telex: 46212.

Romanian Automobile Club, 2—1 Decembrie 1918 St.; phone: 966-12345.

Tarom, 1 Unirii St.; phone: 966-11567.

Railroad Travel Agency CFR, 1 Unirii St.; phone: 966-12177.

Theater Office, 103 Republicii Blvd.; phone: 966-12188.

Post and Telephone Office, 48 Republicii Blvd.; phone: 966-17770.

Milliţia, Virful Cu Dor St.; phone: 966-16570.

Airport, Railway Station, Bus Terminal

Railway Station, 2–4 Aural Vlaico St.; phone: 966-12816.

Bus Terminal, 2–6 Vinători St.; phone: 966-30067.

Airport, Calea Bodrogului; phone: 966-12083.

Hotels

Astoria (first class), 79–81 Republicii Blvd.; phone: 966-15551; telex: 076212.

Arad (first class), 9 Armata Poporului St.; phone: 966-13380 or 15101.

Parc (first class), 25 Dragalina Blvd.; phone: 966-12628; telex: 046333.

Mureşul (second class), 88 Republicii Blvd.; phone: 966-11540.
Ardealul (first class), 98 Republicii Blvd.; phone: 966-11840.

Restaurants, Confectioners

Astoria (with disco), 79–81 Republicii Blvd.; phone: 966-16651; telex: 076212.
Parc, 25 Dragalina Blvd.; phone: 966-12628; telex: 46333 F 5.
Muresui, 1 Horia St.; phone: 966-163666.
Peria Mureşului (on the banks of the Mureş River); phone: 966-37739.
Zarandul (serving local dishes), 89 Republicii Blvd.; phone: 966-11283.
Ardealul (bar), 98 Republicii Blvd.; phone: 966-11840.
Cazino, 25 Dragalina Blvd.

Theaters, Video Clubs

State Theater, 103 Republicii Blvd.; phone: 966-15801.
State Philharmonic, 1 G. Enescu Sq.; phone: 966-16349.
Puppet Shows, 15—7 Noiembrie St.; phone: 966-12974.
Dacia Movie Theater, 49–53 Republicii Blvd.; phone: 966-31131.
Astoria Hotel, 79–81 Republicii Blvd.; phone: 966-16651; telex: 076212.

Stores

Ziridava Department Store, 39–41 Republicii Blvd.; phone: 966-36200.
Aradul Department Store, 2–4 M. Constantinescu St.; phone: 966-16058.
Romarta, 80 Republicii Blvd.; phone: 966-15978.
Turist. (handicrafts), 78 Republicii Blvd.; phone: 966-11105.
Porţelanul, 83 Republicii Blvd.; phone: 966-13161.
Fine Arts Galleries, 90 Republicii Blvd.; phone: 966-16071.

Polyclinic, Pharmacy

Polyclinic, 45 Republicii Blvd.; phone: 966-30001 or 30441.
Pharmacy, open 24 hours, 80 Republicii Blvd.; phone: 966-72450.

Peco (Filling Stations), Service Stations

Peco, V. Roaita Sq.; phone: 966-32947.
Peco, K. Marx St.; phone: 966-16422.
Peco, A. Vlaicu Rd.; phone: 966-30533.

Service Station, UTA Sq.; phone: 966-46750
Service Station, Armatel Roşii Rd.; phone: 966-30598.
Technical Assistance, 8 Unirii St.; phone: 966-12345.

Sports Grounds, Swimming Places
UTA Stadium, UTA Sq.; phone: 966-13915.
Gloria Stadium, Dacilor St.
The Swimming Place, on the banks of River Mureş.

Parks
George Enescu, on the banks of the Mureş River.
Children's Park, on the banks of the Mureş River.
Pădurice (grove), Republicii Blvd.

Camping
Arad (bungalows, camping sites), on the left bank of the Mureş River; phone: 966-11314.

SIBIU

Sibiu is located in the southern part of the Transylvanian plateau where the slopes of the Southern Carpathians drop off between 1,360 to 1,420 feet in elevation above sea level. By highway, Sibiu lies 170 miles northwest from Bucharest. It is also located on a rail line to the capital, from which trains arrive at the station situated on the large Piaţa Gării. Sibiu has about 180,000 population. It is the capital and administrative center of Sibiu County and one of Romania's largest cities. The city lies astride the banks of the Cibin River, a tributary of the Olt. Nearby cities are Sebeş, (34 miles) and Făgaraş (38 miles).

Ancient Sibiu was the site of a Bronze Age culture. Later the Romans were here and built a settlement (Cibinium) to guard one of their principal roads leading into Transylvania. The city's proximity to the Turnu Roşu pass made it an important transportation and communication artery.

Sibiu is one of Romania's most romantic cities which still preserves the character of its medieval past. It is a blend of old and new, which accounts for its charm and mystique. There are high brick walls, towers, narrow alleys, old steeples, and a varied assortment of architecture. The Cibin River divides the city into a lower and upper part connected by flights of steps. Sibiu is an important cultural, ethnographic, and folk art center. It lies in the vicinity of a number of resorts.

The site of the old city is mentioned in documents as being founded in 1191, when settlers from Saxony arrived on its location. Many Germans settled in the area and the town became known as Hermannstadt. Germans are still an important minority group in the city and surrounding area. Hungarians comprise another large ethnic minority in the city, which when it was part of the Austrian empire was known as Nagyszeben. It became part of Austria in 1699.

Medieval Sibiu was the site of a fortress built in the 13th century, which was destroyed by the Tartars in 1241 and rebuilt a century later. During the 14th and 15th centuries, the town became wealthy as a merchant and trading center. Its walls and fortifications were expanded and strenghtened and withstood three assaults by the Turks during the 1400s. At nearby Selimbar, Michael the Brave won a victory over the nobles of Transylvania in 1599. Today's Sibiu has a number of industrial enterprises: food processing, textiles, leather and shoemaking plants, ink and chemical works, metal fabrication; it also manufactures machinery and building materials used in construction.

What to See

Brukenthal Museum, 4 Republicii St. Its 18th-century architecture is representative of the Austrian Baroque style of that period which was constructed in Transylvania. The building was originally built as the residence of the governor of Transylvania and served as a palace. Constructed between 1778 and 1785, it houses the largest art collection in Transylvania and large displays on ethnography, natural sciences, and history. Samuel Brukenthal was an avid art collector and amassed a large collection of paintings by Flemish, Dutch, and German masters. There are also many works by well-known Romanian artists. The museum was greatly expanded after World War II when a rich collection of folk art was added to it. Romanian folk art differs from region to region but is noted for its harmony in color and decorative patterns. The museum's library contains several hundred thousand books, manuscripts, and documents.

Old Town Hall, 2—1 Mai St. It is an important ensemble of Gothic architecture constructed from 1470–91.

Orthodox Cathedral, 33—1 Mai St. Built in 1902–06 in Byzantine style, it served as the residence of the metropolitan of Transylvania. Sibiu is still the seat of the Romanian Orthodox metropolitan.

Evangelical Cathedral, Grivada Pl. This monument of Gothic architecture was constructed in 1370 and added to until 1520. It contains an ancient crypt and burial vaults.

Museum of Natural History, 1 Cetății St. Established in 1849, it is the foundation of the Natural Science Society of Transylvania.

Exhibition of Hunting Weapons and Trophies, 4 Scoala de Inot St. It contains a collection of trophies and medallions exemplifying the sport of hunting.

Exhibition of the History of Pharmacy, 26—6 Martie Pl. Opened in 1972, it is an exhibition of pharmaceutical items and their history.

Passage of Steps, 6 Martie Pl. These picturesque, old stairways lead from the old to the newer parts of the city.

Astra Palace, 3 G. Baritiu St. An initiative of the Association of Culture, it houses 600,000 volumes.

The Arsenal, 1 Armelar Pl., is mentioned in documents dating to 1427.

Ancient Romanian School, 35 Reconstructiei St., is an old school of which Gheorghe Lazăr was the director from 1811–16.

Ancient Summer House of Brukenthal, 48 Moscova St., was founded in the 18th century amidst the gardens.

Bridge of Iron, 6 Martie Pl., was constructed in 1859.

State Archives, 3 Arhivelor St. Built 1913–14, it has a manuscript from the 1500s describing the techniques of small rockets.

Useful Addresses

Theaters
State Theater, 2—23 August Blvd.
Puppet Theater, 4 Al. Odobescu St.
State Philharmonic Theater, 2 Filarmonicii St.
School of Popular Art, 2 Al. Odobescu St.
Pacea Cinema, 29 N. Bălcescu St.
Arts Cinema, 6 Tribunei St.

Parks and Gardens
Astra Park, founded in 1879.
Dumbrava Park, founded in the 18th century.
Zoological Gardens, established in 1929.

Department Stores
Dumbrava, 4 Unirii Pl.
Central, 15 N. Bălcescu St.
Auto-Motor Store, Mihai Viteazu Blvd.
Sports Store, 24—9 Mai St.
Photo Shop, 17 N. Bălcescu St.

Places of Public Service
Tourist Agency, 53 N. Bălcescu St.; phone: 12559.
Tarom Airlines, 10 N. Bălcescu St.; phone: 11157.
Pharmacy, 53 N. Bălcescu St.
Postage-Telephone, 14—1 Mai St.
Service Stations (Peco), 2 de Medias and d'Alba Iulia.

Hotels
Bulevard (first class), 10 Unirii Pl.
Continental (first class), 2-4 Calea Dumbravei.
Imparatul Romanilor (first class), 4 Nicolae Bălcescu Blvd.

Nearby Places of Interest

Dumbrava Forest has a zoo, campsite, restaurant, and bar.

Cisnădie is a village located 8 miles south of Sibiu. It has a textile industry, a 13th-century church, and a citadel and fortifications built in the 15th century.

Cisnădioara is a village situated near Cisnădie (1.5 miles distant). Its attractions are an old Romanesque-style church, medieval walls, and citadel. It is set amidst orchards around a hill.

Selimbăr is located 3 miles southeast of Sibiu on a plain where Michael the Brave won a victory in 1599 over the governor of Transylvania. Remains of tombs, an old cemetery, and an obelisk stand on its site.

Cristian is a village located about 7 miles west of Sibiu. It has an ethnographical museum containing art objects related to the lives of its citizens of the 17th and 18th centuries. An old citadel and fortifications built in the 13th through 16th centuries surround it.

Răşinari is a village lying 8 miles south of Sibiu and was the home of the poet Octavian Goga. Its ethnographic museum contains over 1,500 objects of art illustrating the lives of the local inhabitants.

Păltiniş is a small resort located about 22 miles southwest of Sibiu at an altitude of 4,731 feet in the forested, mountainous area of Cindrel. Many streams and several lakes lie in the area. There are ski lifts and a sports complex at the resort.

Ocna Sibiului is a small resort which treats a variety of ailments and is described in the chapter on health resorts. It lies near Sibiu.

TÎRGU MUREŞ

This city is the county seat of Mureş County located on the Transylvanian plateau. It lies in the valley of the Mureş River, which flows south, then west, and into Hungary where it joins the Tisa. Tîrgu Mureş is 214 miles by highway from Bucharest and lies northwest of the capital. Located on a terrace overlooking the Mureş, the city has a population of 160,000 people.

Tîrgu Mureş is an industrial center whose main industries include textiles, chemicals, woodworking, machinery, food processing, and metal products. Around the city are several natural gas deposits. The gas is largely methane, and Tîrgu Mureş is the center of the natural gas industry in the country.

The city is surrounded by a region where livestock raising and cereals are important. Tîrgu Mureş averages about 25 inches of rainfall a year, compared to 15 inches for Constanţa. The area around the city has large forests, especially beech and oak.

The province of Transylvania and Tîrgu Mureş were part of Hungary from the 11th century until 1918. Hungarians are still the major national minority group in the area and total more than 2 million of Transylvania's population. The Romanian government has used both violent and nonviolent means to control this large minority population within its borders.

The first document to mention Tîrgu Mureş was dated in the 14th century, although there were settlements in the area for many centuries before then. A large cemetery nearby dates to the 4th century. During the 14th century, documents mention the town both as Agriopolis and Novum Forum Siculorum. The present name of Tîrgu Mureş was recorded in the early 1600s. The Diet of Transylvania met in the town during the 15th century and continued to meet there until 1707. During the 14th century, schools in the town began the use of Latin as their language of instruction. A number of Romania's well-known cultural leaders of the 19th century studied in these schools, including the mathematician Ianos Bolyai, who was fascinated by non-Euclidean geometry and helped to found its principles.

What to See

The Citadel was built in the 14th century and reconstructed in the 17th century. Its ruins contain the Evangelical Church built in the 15th century.

Palace of Culture is a large structure built in the early 1900s. It showcases the Museum of Art and the exquisite Hall of Mirrors whose windows are decorated in stained glass, which add to the composition and uniqueness of the palace. The palace also contains a school for training artists, and their union is headquartered in the building.

Other interesting features of Tîrgu Mureş include the **Museum of History and Ethnography** and the **Bolyai Museum,** which also houses the **Teleki Library** with its many rare manuscripts.

Useful Addresses

Tourist Office, 31 Piaţa Trandafirilor.
Transylvania Hotel (first class), 43 Piaţa Trandafirilor.

BAIA MARE

This city is located in the northwestern part of Romania in Maramureş County, of which it is the county seat. The city lies 369 miles by road from Bucharest. It has rail connections with other parts of Romania. Nearby Satu Mare is 42 miles distant. The city has a population of 140,000 people. It has grown fast in the last several decades, adding blocks of new apartments and office buildings. Mountains overlook the city, which lies 41 miles south of the Soviet border.

Baia Mare was founded in the 12th century but would not be recorded in documents until the 14th century. At the time of its founding by Saxon immigrants (converted to Lutheranism during the Reformation) it was named Neustadt. During the centuries, gold mining lured new immigrants to the city. Copper, lead, and zinc ores are also found in the vicinity of Baia Mare, which is the largest processer of nonferrous ores in the country.

The city was part of Hungarian territory prior to World War I, at the end of which it became the possession of Romania. The Hungarian name for the town is Nagybánya. During World War II, the Hungarians again took possession of it, and following that war it reverted to Romania again. Under Communist planning, Baia Mare received attention to foster the growth of its industries, which in addition to the nonferrous metals industry, include machine building, food processing, the making of chemicals and sulfuric acid, and the production of artificial fertilizers.

The city's cultural features include its **Historical Museum, School of Painting,** and its medieval towers and walls, the most well known of which is **St. Stephen's Tower** (14th century). The old towers and walls are located in the central part of the city, which has a medieval look and charm to it.

Useful Addresses

Tourist Office, 9 Pietrosului St.
Bucureşti Hotel (first class), Piaţa Victoriei.

SATU MARE

Satu Mare is located in the northwest corner of Romania next to the border with Hungary. The city lies 386 miles by highway from Bucharest. It is the county seat of Sate Mare County and has a population of 132,000 people. The city lies on both banks of the Someş River, which flows into Hungary. Satu Mare is an important crossroads of several highways and railroads.

Its foundations were laid by boatmen floating cargoes of salt down the Someş from salt mines further upriver. In 1241 the Mongols attacked the town and destroyed its 13th-century fortress. The town was an important trade center during medieval times, with much of its produce coming from the bountiful agricultural lands surrounding it. Today, the growing of grain, raising of livestock, and the harvesting of fruits, vegetables, and grapes are important activities. Industries have increased in the city in recent decades and include woodworking, textiles, machine building, and food processing. Rolling stock for the railroads is also produced.

The city's main tourist features include the **Historical and Ethnographical Museum** founded in 1891 and located in a building constructed in the 1700s; the **Roman Catholic Cathedral** built in the 18th century; the **Episcopal Palace** (1828). Hungarians are the principal national minority group.

Useful Addresses

Tourist Office, 14 Eliberării Blvd.
Dacia Hotel (first class), 12 Piața Libertății.

RESIȚA

Resița is located in southwestern Romania at the foot of the slopes of the Southern Carpathians on their western flank. It is situated 317 miles by road from Bucharest. Resița is the county seat of Caraș-Severin County and has a population of 107,000 inhabitants. Several highways and a rail line link the city with other parts of Romania. Resița lies less than 20 miles from the border with Yugoslavia.

The city is a major industrial center, lying in an area of coal and iron mining. The coal and iron ore are hauled into Resița to be used in its iron and steel mills. The city builds locomotives and machinery and manufactures textiles. The first blast furnace in the city began operating in 1771. Resița is one of the major iron and steel centers in the country. Around the city, grain growing and livestock production are important. An increasing amount of its coal and iron are being imported. Resița is not noted as a tourist center.

Useful Addresses

Tourist Office, 2 Lenin Blvd.
Semenic Hotel (first class), 2 Lenin Blvd.

ALBA IULIA

Located at the juncture of highly traveled ancient roads, Alba Iulia is recognized not only as a major stopover on a tour of the country but also as a place rich in unique historical and art possessions. As Dacian land coveted and conquered by the Romans some 2,000 years ago, Alba Iulia is located in the middle of the country at the confluence of the Ampoi and Mureș rivers in the eastern part of the Western Mountains (866–924 feet in altitude) in Alba County. The city is 213 miles from Bucharest on Highway 1.

The major Neolithic district of the city is the New World. Other historical sites include the Hallstattian settlement (5th century B.C.), an early Dacian settlement (Teleac-Jidovina), the fortress of the 13th Gemima Legion of the Romans, the Roman colonies of Nova Apulensis and Aurelia Apulensis in the vicinity of the Mureș River (the ancient navigable Maris River according to Herodotus). Alba Iulia was a municipality at the time of Septimius Severus (2nd–3rd centuries A.D.); and the town, then the capital of the province of Dacia Aqulensis, was well known. Its name was usually accompanied by the term "Chrysopolis," designating its richness in gold.

Under the name of Bălgrad (White Fortress) during the 8th–13th centuries, it became a local Romanian political center (probably governed by Voivode Geiu). It survived the Tartar invasion (13th century) and was the capital of Transylvania (1548–1685) and even the land of the Romanians (Wallachia). It was part of the union of Romania (Wallachia, Transylvania, and Moldavia) under Michael the Brave (1599–1600). After the devastating plunders committed by the Turks in 1658 against the old city, a medieval fortress was built on its ancient precincts which at present is one of the largest and best preserved Transylvanian fortresses.

Over the years, Alba Iulia has also been a cultural and artistic center: The People's Academy was founded here in 1622; the first book was printed here in 1639; and here in 1648 Bishop Simeon Ștefan advocated the necessity of a literary language understandable by all Romanians. Yet the town's memory is also full of many painful historical events: the martyrdom of Gheorghe Doja, leader of the Peasant War in 1514; the execution of Horea and Cloșca, leaders of the People's Uprising in 1784–85; and the imprisonment of representative leaders of the 1847–48 revolutionary movements, such as Ecaterins Varga and Avram Iancu. In Alba Iulia was also signed the historical document officially certifying the constitution of the Romanian National Unitary State on December 1, 1918. In that year, Transylvania became part of Romania.

The modern city is the result of several decades of economic and urban development which triggered an increase in the number of inhabitants from 16,000 to 65,000. The industrial area is the northeast section of town and comprises such industries as Refractara, the Mechanical Enterprises, the Equipment Works, and the impressive halls of the Porcelain Works. Several other industrial enterprises are located in the north sector of the city. The Ampoi and Mureş rivers, often subject to flooding, were dammed off and utilized for hydroelectric development. These enterprises led to the growth of a new town with nearly 10,000 flats, elegant shops, and cinemas. A House of Culture and hotels have grown up on the ancient Romans' plateau around the city. Alba Iulia is rejuvenating after three hundred years.

What to See

Museums

Union Museum, 12–14 Mihai Viteazul St., is housed in the Babylon building (1853). Founded in 1887, it was one of the first Romanian museums scientifically reorganized during recent years. It exhibits over 130,000 objects in its prehistoric, Roman antiquity, medieval, modern, and contemporary sections. It also possesses precious stones and valuable stone inscriptions.

Union Hall, part of the above museum, is a building which dates from 1906. The document certifying the union of Transylvania and Romania was signed here on December 1, 1918 (there are original documents, bas-reliefs, and frescoes).

Batthyanaeum Documentary Library, 1 Bibliotecii St., was established in 1794 inside the Baroque edifice of an ancient monastery built in 1719. This renowned institution set up in 1784 has over 1,600 rare manuscripts, 600 incunabula (the largest Romanian collection), tens of thousands of printed works and documents dating back to the 16th–19th centuries, medieval art pieces, coins, and mineral collections. It also housed the first astronomic observatory in Romania (1792). The oldest translation of the Bible in Romania

Transylvania

(the *Palia of Orostie,* published in 1582) and the *Codex Aurens,* a 9th-century manuscript, are found in the library.

Horea's Cell (inside the basement of the Third Gate's Statue of the Fortress) is where the popular uprising leader from 1784–85 was imprisoned.

Historical, Architectural, and Art Monuments

Medieval Fortress, of Vauban type, was built over the period 1714–38 by Giovanni Visconti, an Italian architect, and the painful toil of 20,000 serfs. It consists of seven large bastions, and its walls are 7.4 miles in length. The medieval fortress includes most of the tourist sites of the city.

The First Gate is a monumental triumphed-arch-shaped construction fully decorated with Baroque bas-reliefs featuring ancient characters in various scenes.

The Third Gate is a double-triumphed arch adorned with Baroque bas-reliefs and stone sculptures. It supports the equestrian statue of Carol the Sixth, the emperor who defeated the Turkish armies. A panoramic view of the city and the Mureş River can be seen from its terrace.

The Fourth Gate is remarkable because of the two Baroque Athlas statues and bas-reliefs showing military trophies.

The Roman Camp and the ancient city are relics of the fortifications built between the 2nd–17th centuries.

Roman Catholic Cathedral (inside the fortress) is one of the oldest and most historic monuments in the country. It was built over the period 1200–1500 and replaced older religious dwellings dating back to the 9th–12th centuries. A combination of several architectural styles (Roman, Gothic, Baroque, and Renaissance), the cathedral possesses some unique art pieces. The lateral naves shelter the sarcophagi of Iancu of Hunedoara and the Zapolya and Sigismund royal families. The Bishop's Palace is located near the entrance to the cathedral.

Royal Palace (inside the fortress) was built in the 15th–17th centuries in Gothic style. Famous for its art pieces, it was also the residence of Voivode Mihai Viteazul.

University College (inside the fortress), built in the 17th century, sheltered the high school founded by Prince Bethlen during the period 1619–62.

Episcopal Palace (inside the fortress) is a Renaissance and Baroque building constructed during the 17th–19th centuries.

Apor Palace (inside the fortress) is an edifice with Renaissance elements, built over the period 1670–90; its inside portals are adorned with trophies resembling those on the fortress gates.

Reunion Cathedral (inside the fortress) is an architectural gem displaying old Romanian stylistic elements, ancient book and art collections, valuable stones, sarcophagi, Roman inscriptions, tombstones, and statues.

Horea, Cloşca and Crişan Memorial (inside the fortress, on the Third Gate terrace), dedicated in 1937, is 91 feet high. It is depicted in a bas-relief featuring the three serf leaders and the Winged Victory statue on the obelisk.

Equestrian Statue of Mihai Veteazul (inside the fortress) is 21 feet high. Unveiled in 1968, it features the voivode in an impressive pose with his scepter raised in triumph.

Mihai Viteazul's Coronation (inside the fortress), is a bronze cast bas-relief, 19.7 feet long, 13 feet high, showing the voivode's triumphal entrance into Alba Iulia.

Custozza Memorial (inside the fortress) was raised in 1906 in the memory of the 50th Infantry Regiment which perished in 1866 during the Austro-Italian War.

Obelisk Dedicated to Horea and Cloşca, 53–55—6 Martie St., was raised in 1926 on the place called "la Furci" (the Pitchforks). It stands on the site of the ancient town of Apulum, an execution place during the Middle Ages.

Maieri Church, 69 Iaşi St., built in 1715, bears the mark of traditional Romanian architecture with brick milled edges.

Useful Addresses

Alba County Tourist Office, 22 Piaţa 1 Mai; phone: 968-12547; telex: 36230 OJTRK.

Romanian Automobile Club, 5 Ardealului St.; phone: 968-12345.

Railway Tourist Agency, 5 Ardealului St., phone: 968-11744.

Post and Telephone Office, 2 Eroilor St.

Railway Station, Republicii St.

ITA Bus Terminal, Republicii St.; phone: 968-12748.

Gas Station, Clujului St.

Auto Service Station, 1 Clujului St.; phone: 968-12847.

Hotels, Camping

Transylvania, 22, Piaţa 1 Mai; phone: 968-12547; telex: 36230 OJTR.

Apulum, 1, Piaţa 1 Mai; phone: 968-12126.

Cetate, 41, Horea Blvd.; phone: 968-23804.
Între Salcii Camping, on DN 1 (2.7 miles south of Alba Iulia).

Nearby Places of Interest

Teleac Village, in Mureş River valley, 3 miles northeast of Alba Iulia. Jidova Fortress, dating from the 5th century B.C., is an early Dacian settlement covering 75 acres and is the largest one in the country. It is surrounded by ditches and walls (traces of which remain).

Sîntimbru Village, in Mureş River valley (6.7 miles northeast of Alba Iulia). Iancu of Hunedoara fought one of his first battles here against the Turkish armies. The church, built in 1442 by the Transylvania voivode, is a Gothic monument with Roman influences (mural painting fragments dating back to the 15th–16th centuries).

Teiuş Village, in the Homonymous River valley near its confluence with the Mureş River, 10.7 miles northeast of Alba Iulia. Architectural monuments in different styles include Romanic (13th century) and Gothic (its foundation was laid by Iancu of Hunedoara in 1449, bearing the family's coat of arms). Traditional Romanian influences, particularly on wood (1606), and valuable mural paintings (1790), can be seen.

Valea Mănăstirii Village, in Homonymous River valley inTrascău Mountains, 21 miles northwest of Alba Iulia. An old architectural monument dating from the 14th century features picturesque inscriptions. The nearby mountain gorge (natural monument) and a mountain chalet are located at 1,398 feet in altitude.

The Wine Country (Tara Vinului) is a general description of this famous wine-growing district. Sard, Ighiu, Bucerdea Vinoasă, and Cricău villages, 12 miles northwest of Alba Iulia, have century-old wine cellars. Historical and architectural monuments, dating back to the 13th–18th centuries, are surrounded by various natural monuments and reserves.

Craiva Village, of the Wine Country, is located at the bottom of Piatra Craivii Mountain, 3,553 feet in altitude, 13 miles northwest of Alba Iulia. The Dacian fortress, (2nd century B.C.–1st century A.D.), stretching across the high plateau and several artificial terraces, is the remains of ancient Apulon mentioned by Ptolomy (A.D. 90–168) in his *Geography*. In the Middle Ages it was a medieval fortress from 1250 to 1667.

Galda de Jos—Intregalde, a tourist site in the Wine Country in Galda River valley, 27 miles northwest of Alba Iulia, has architectural monuments (18th century), a mountain gorge, natural reserves (Edelweiss, Narcissus), and a mountain chalet. The valley lies at 1,968 feet in altitude.

Fenes Village, at the confluence of the Homonyous valley with the Ampoi River, lies 19 miles west of Alba Iulia. It is a traditional area of folklore and folk art, natural reserves (fossil deposits, calcereous clipps), a mountain gorge, and caves.

Vinţu de Jos Village, in the Mureş Valley, 7 miles southwest of Alba Iulia. It has a palace in old Transylvania style (1550), architectural monuments from the 13th–18th centuries, and old ruins.

Pianu Village, in the Homonymous River valley at the bottom of the Sebeş Mountains, 20 miles southwest of Alba Iulia. It was the site of ancient gold mines, a peasant fortress (15th-century traces), and architectural monuments from the 13th–17th centuries.

Sebeş, a town at the confluence of the Secaş and Sebeş rivers, 11 miles south of Alba Iulia. Settled in the 12th–13th centuries, it became an important center of government in 1345 and a powerful trade center during the Middle Ages. Its old fortress dates from the 14th–15th centuries and consists of precinct walls, towers, ditches, and a recreation lake. There is a museum of history, ethnography, natural sciences, and fine arts. The Voivode's Palace dates from the 15th century; the church (an artistic monument) is the most valuable Gothic achievement in Transylvania (1240–1382). The Guild Hall (17th century) and the Red Precipice in Rîpa Roşie Natural Park are other interesting sites. The city is well known for its leather and textiles.

Petreşti, a component part of Sebeş, located in the Sebeş River valley, 14 miles south of Alba Iulia. It is an ancient site of the Petreşti culture, a general term for the Neolithic material culture discovered in this area. Its major characteristic is the linear painted motifs applied on pottery before burning. There is a medieval fortification from the 13th century set amidst an area rich in folklore.

Săsciror Village, in the Sebeş River valley, 16.7 miles south of Alba Iulia. Its feudal fortification, built in the 12th–13th centuries, possibly stands on ancient Dacian precincts. A traditional pottery (red ceramics) is well known in this area, which is noted for its folklore and ethnography.

Cîlnic Village, in the Homonymous Brook valley, 20 miles southeast of Alba Iulia, contains a donjon fortification, built in 1272, and a rural fortress built in 1450, one of the oldest, strongest, and well-preserved constructions in Transylvania.

MEDIAŞ

Mediaş is located in the heart of the Transylvania plateau 34 miles north of Sibiu. The city has a population of about 50,000 people and is situated along the banks of the Tîrnava Mare River. It is the crossroads of several highways and is connected by rail with Braşov. Vineyards grow in the vicinity and wine making is important. The city is part of the Transylvanian industrial region and contains engineering works, textile plants, food-processing facilities, and chemical and leather-working plants. It is also an important center for the production of natural gas. The city has a long history of settlement. An ancient Geto-Dacian village existed on its site, and the Romans also founded a town there to guard one of their main routes through the area. During the Middle Ages the town grew as a trade center and a citadel was built to protect it. The city largely developed after World War I when gas-well drilling and pipelines were laid in the area. Besides the ruins of the old citadel, its 14th-century **Evangelical Church** with a 250-foot belfry is of interest. An added feature is the town's historical museum.

Useful Addresses

Central Hotel (first class), Rosmarinului St.

DEVA

Deva, the chief town of Hunedoara County (in the west-central part of Romania) is located south of the Mureş River, at the foot of the last branches of the Poiana-Ruscăi Mountains, at an altitude of 614 feet. Deva has a population of about 47,000 people. It lies at a distance of 245 miles from Bucharest.

The ancient history of the town is the same as that of Hunedoara lands. Though the first documentary record of the area dates from 1269, the territory was inhabited as early as the Neolithic Age (4000–1800 B.C.), as confirmed by archeological findings of the Cotofeni and Sighişoara cultures.

After a period of disorganization created by the death of the great king of the Dacians, Burebista (44 B.C.), who achieved the first centralized Dacian state, the area was reorganized under the leadership of the brave and wise king of all Dacians, Decebalus (A.D. 87–106). In this process, the area surrounding the capital of the state, Sarmizeqetusa, became quite important. The traces of the Roman rule in Dacia, following their victory in A.D. 106 under the Emperor Trajan, are numerous throughout the county.

Archeological findings in this area point to intense and permanent settlement by the Daco-Roman population after the withdrawal of Roman legions from Dacia (A.D. 271). The homogeneous Romanian population organized its ranks while keeping in close contact with the Romanians beyond the Carpathians and made strong opposition to the expansion and exploitation of their area by the Magyar nobility. This resistance materialized in the Middle Ages in the Peasants' War in 1514, led by Gheorghe Doja, and culminated in the Revolution of 1784, headed by Horea, Cloşca, and Crişan. In the years of the revolution of 1848–49, it was in this region that revolutionary struggles were led by Avram Lancu for the social and national rights of the people.

Hunedoara County is closely linked to the economy of Socialist Romania, ranking first in the output of pit coal, iron ore, and electric energy; second in coke, pig iron, steel, rolled metals, and complex ores; and third in silk tissues. The current industrial output of Hunedoara County is seventeen times larger than that of 1950.

The county is a rich agricultural area farmed with tractors and agricultural equipment and set amidst pastures and hayfields.

Deva has become a large economic center as well as a valuable cultural center of research and education. Deva's industries include building materials, electric energy output, food processing, light, and handicraft operations. The people have transformed their town into one with wide avenues and blocks of houses erected in architectural styles with personalities of their own.

Hunedoara County has a population of some 560,000 inhabitants, 75 percent of which are employed in twelve towns.

What to See

Deva Citadel. It was erected on the top of a conical hill (1,217 feet) at the end of the 13th century with a system of outer defenses modernized in the 17th century. Built of rough stone from nearby areas, it is surrounded by three enclosures. The entrance to the citadel is through the gate on the western side, sheltered by a corridor with a cylindrical valuted shape. During the 1784 revolution, the citadel was besieged by hostile peasants who were defeated and withdrew. In 1849 the citadel walls were destroyed by the explosion of the fort's powder house. The citadel is now an important tourist attraction. From the top of the citadel, a splendid view is afforded of the Mureş valley and of the town.

Magna Curia. This castle is located in the vicinity of the hillock of the Deva Citadel and was built in the 16th century in the style of the Renaissance and later with Baroque features. In the 17th and 18th centuries the castle underwent some changes. It now houses the county museum with its departments of archeology and natural sciences.

Statue of King Decebalus, at the foot of the citadel hillock. It is the creation of sculptor Radu Moga (1936) as a homage to the great king who had achieved a strong centralized Dacian state (87–106) and offered strong resistance to the Roman Empire in the wars of 101–2 and 105–6.

Statue of Dr. Petru Groza (1884–1958), located in Piaţa Unirii. It was created by sculptor C. Baraschi (1963) to the memory of the politician, statesman, and president of the first Socialist government in Romania's history, established on March 6, 1945.

Decebalus' Equestrian Statue. This statue stands in the center of the town and is the work of sculptor Ion Jalea (1976). It is 14 feet high and made of bronze.

Useful Addresses

County Tourist Office, 11 Dr. Petru Groza St.; phone: 956-14730 or 12026.

Romanian Automobile Club and Federation, 16 Dr. Petru Groza St.; phone: 956-12822.

Railways Agency, Post Office, 2 V.I. Lenin St.; phone: 956-12527.

Savings Bank, 12 Dr. Petru Groza St.; phone: 956-11551.

Hotels:

Sarmis (first class, 124 rooms, restaurant, and shop), 9 Piaţa Unirii; phone: 956-14730.

Dacia (first class, 51 rooms), 11 Piaţa Unirii; phone: 956-14730.

Deva (first class, 122 rooms, restaurant, and shop), 110—23 August St.; phone: 956-17515.
Bulevard (third class, 38 rooms), 16 Dr. Petru Groza St.; phone: 956-14730.

Restaurants
Turist, 11 Piaţa Unirii; phone: 956-14730.
Transylvania, 1 Piaţa Victoriei; phone: 956-12518.
Bachus, 8 Piaţa Unirii; phone: 956-14083.
Astoria, Mihail Eminescu St.; phone: 956-21762.
Peria Cetatil, Cetatil Park; phone: 956-11920.
Cafe-bar, 16 Dr. Petru Groza St.

Services
Hospital, 58—23 August St.; phone: 956-13020 or 15050.
Pharmacy (24 hours), 9 Piaţa Victoriei; phone: 956-11616.
Patria Cinema, 5 Dr. Petru Groza St.; phone: 956-11987.
Arta Cinema, 17 Dr. Petru Groza St., phone: 956-15260.
House of Culture, Piaţa Victoriei; phone: 956-16882.
Peco Filling Station (town entrance from Sibiu), 24 hours; phone: 956-15303.
Dacia Service, 23 August St.; phone: 956-23941.
Service, 273—23 August St.; phone: 956-13446.

Nearby Places of Interest

Geoagiu-Băi is a spa located at 1,148 feet altitude in a small depression on the last branches of the Apuseni Mountains. It has been known since the Roman times and is 30 miles from Deva. It is characterized by landscape embracing a climate with fine therapeutic effects, abundant mineral waters, and an annual average temperature of 46–49°F in winter and 68°F in summer. Thus the winters are mild and the summers are pleasant.

The natural cure factors include mineral waters that are mesothermal, bicarbonated, calcic, magnesian (with traces of iron and hydrogen sulfide), hypotonic, and slightly carbogaseous. Mineralization varies from 1355 to 1490 milligrams per liter; water temperature at the spring is 68–91°F. Peat mud is available.

Therapeutical indications for the resort include those for: rheumatismal afflictions (chronic and degenerative), polyarthrosis, spondylitis, abarticular rheumatism, diseases of the peripheral nervous system (neuritis and polyneuritis), peripheral circulatory troubles, hyperstress neurosis; postrheumatic conditions, convalescences, asthenias; cardiovascular afflictions; women's diseases. Other cure indications are those for gastroduodenal afflictions (gastritis, colitis, ulcer), hepatobiliary troubles, and afflictions of the renal system.

Treatment facilities include baths with warm mineral water in pools or tubs, hydrokinetotherapy, thermotherapy, plant baths, mud poultices, medical gymnastics, massage, underwater shower, phytotherapy, *mofettes*. In summer, a prophylactic cure is available beside thermal swimming pools in the open air. Accommodations: first-class hotels (*Germisala* and *Diana*), villas, and camping site.

Recreational activities include: House of Culture, cinema, sports grounds, mountaineering, trips by motorcoach in the Hunedoara County and neighboring counties (one day), and excursions to Hungary (one–two days).

Vata-Băi is a spa and health resort located on national highway DN 76, about 36 miles from Deva. It is famous for its thermal waters used in the treatment of rheumatic diseases, troubles of the peripheral nervous system, and women's diseases. Treatment by acupuncture is also available. The climate is healthy in any season. Springs with thermal water are 96–99° F in temperature. The water is calcic, hypotonic, magnesian, and slightly radioactive. Accommodation is in a rest home (first class). It also has a restaurant. For leisure there are sports grounds and excursions.

Dacian Citadel at Costeşti lies 11 miles from Orăştie, in the Costeşti village of Orăştioara de Sus commune. The development of the citadel coincides with the reign of the two great Dacian kings, Burebista and Decebalus (1st century B.C. and 1st century A.D., respectively). It was a castle fortified with pallisades, or walls with defense towers. Diggings have unearthed military buildings and dwellings, religious sites, and storerooms.

Blidaru Citadel is 2.5 miles from Costeşti village. It is a fortified complex located on the top of the Blidaru—an extensive plateau protected by massive stone walls. The functional characteristics of this place, its strategic importance as well as the numerous watchtowers, both in the citadel and in its surroundings, are evidence of the military role of the citadel.

Archeological Complex Ulpia Traina Sarmizegetusa is a tourist site frequently visited by both Romanian and foreign tourists. It is located in Sarmizegetusa commune about thirty-eight miles from Deva. The citadel was founded after the conquest of Dacia by the Romans (A.D. 106), on order of Emperor Trajan, and soon became an important political, religious, and cultural center. Archeological excavations have unearthed parts of the citadel walls, the palace of Augustus, a forum and amphitheater, and several buildings.

Medieval Monument of Densuş. On the road leading from the town of Haţeg to the Cerna meadow, in the Densuş village (a place in the Poiana-Ruscă Mountains), there stands a building of beauty and quaintness which is perhaps the best-known Romanian medieval monument. This building has a nonhomogeneous planimetric layout because of many subsequent additions to it. It is made of quarry stone, bricks, and Roman stones with inscriptions, coming from the ruins of Ulpia Traina Augusta Sarmizegetusa, found in its vicinity.

Its origin gave birth to several hypotheses. Research, which preceded recent restoration, led to the discovery of elements pointing to a period prior to the occupation of Transylvania by the Magyar kingdom (11th–13th centuries) and to the penetration of forms of Western architecture in a time coinciding with the process of Romanian national formation on this territory (10th century). Rearrangements and extensions of the building occurred in the 13th century in forms peculiar to the Romanesque style. Starting with the 14th century, the knyazs Mănjina of Densuş are recorded in documents, and they are credited with achievement of the pictorial decoration of the present monument.

Corvin Castle of Hunedoara was probably erected on the site of a Roman construction at the end of the 14th century. In 1421, Lancu of Hunedoara strengthened the citadel, updating it to the contemporary military technique. After 1446 the citadel underwent extensive reconstruction aimed at making it a sumptuous castle. By sacrificing the defense system of the citadel, these works resulted in the west wing with the Knights' Hall and Diet Hall, transforming the construction in a building resembling the castles of the Loire valley in France. It largely reflects the spirit of the Renaissance, despite the Gothic architecture embracing the building. After the death of Lancu of Hunedoara (1456), work continued on the northern wing, the so-called Mattias Corvinus wing. The eastern wing, dating from the 17th century, was built at the same time as the white bastion and the citadel on the left bank of the Zlasti River, of which little is left nowadays. Restoration begun in 1956 restored the castle to its original appearance. An interesting museum of history is housed in it.

Complex of Monuments at Ţebea. On the Brad-Oradea Highway, DN 76, a short distance from Brad town, is located the Mesteacăn village, the place where in 1784 rebelling peasants under the leadership of Horea, Cloşca, and Crişan had their first meeting. Three miles further is the locality of Ţebea, a historic spot. Here is Horea's Oak, a tree under which Horea addressed passionate appeals to the Motzi in 1784, urging them to struggle against social injustice. Here is also Avram Iancu's Grave, the tomb of the "mountain's king," together with those of other heads of the 1848 revolution in Transylvania. The tomb is a symbol of resistance for all who know it.

Oak Planted by Nicolae Ceauşescu. On the occasion of a visit made in the Hunedoara area (1966), it is a token of high esteem for the past sacrifices of the Romanian people and for the continuity of traditions of revolutionary and democratic struggle. It was also here that in December 1935 the Agreement of Antifascist Unity was concluded by initiative of the Romanian Communist Party. The agreement was signed under Horea's Oak, near Avram Iancu's grave, as a homage to those fighting for freedom and a better life.

Monument of Sîntamaria-Orlea stands in the commune with the same name, in the vicinity of the town of Haţeg, and seems to be the foundation of the Cinde knyazs of Riu De Mori. It represents the transition from Romanesque to Gothic, characteristic of Transylvania in the second half of the 13th century. The four layers of mural paintings are extremely valuable and represent the oldest group of Orthodox paintings in Romania.

National Retezat Park is a natural reserve, with an area of 52,500 acres, created in 1935 in the Retezat Glacial Massif to protect the numerous rare species of plants and animals. It is a genuine museum of natural history, providing a great variety of landscapes, a natural botanical garden, and source for researchers. Here at an altitude ranging between 6,535 and 6,791 feet, there are 82 lakes, one of which, Bucura, is the largest lake of the Carpathians (37 square miles) and another, Zănoaga, the deepest (95 feet). In winter the Retezat becomes a paradise for skiers. At an altitude of 4,593 feet, in the vicinity of the Riuşor River, favorable conditions exist to meet the exact requirements for skiers. The necessary equipment may be rented at a special center, while accommodation and meals are provided by the *Alpin Complex* (first class).

Aurel Vlaicu Memorial Museum is located about nine miles from the locality of Orăştie and recalls moments from the life and activity of Aurel Vlaicu (1882–1913), an engineer who built airplanes, as a Romanian inventor and pilot; he was one of the pioneers of early aviation. One can see plans of his inventions, types of planes, correspondence, photos, and the inventor's workroom.

Orăştie Museum of Folk Art presents the folk customs of the Mureş meadow and the area of the Dacian citadels.

Storage Lake Cinciş. Unforgetable moments may be spent here in this area of 625 acres. It is a genuine paradise for lovers of rowing and angling. Entertaining trips on board a ship are also available, as is water skiing.

SIGHIŞOARA

Sighişoara is an ancient town whose beginnings date back into the Bronze Age. It has a medieval-looking appearance with a large citadel overlooking the city. It is located in Transylvania along the banks of the Tirnava Mare River. The city is situated 74 miles northwest from Braşov and has a population of about 40,000 people. A settlement existed on its site in the 1st century, and the Romans occupied it. During the Middle Ages it was a busy trade center and was referred to as *Castrum sex* in documents of that period. A citadel stood on its site during the 13th century and was expanded in the 14th century. During the 17th century the city suffered both a major fire and an earthquake. Interesting tourist sights in Sighişoara include the old citadel, its walls and towers (in particular the Clock Tower which stands 200 feet high and has a tall figure inside it which comes into view to mark the beginning of each day), and several churches dating from medieval times. Vlad Dracula, the legendary Count Dracula, was born here. His birthplace is now a restaurant sought out by tourists. The city was one of the seven major fortified towns founded by German colonists in Transylvania. The Germans named it Schässburg, and later the Hungarians called it Segesvár.

Useful Addresses

Steana Hotel (first-class), 12 Gh. Gheorghiu-Dej Blvd.

SFÎNTU GHEORGHE

This city is located 126 miles north of Bucharest and 20 miles north of Braşov. It is the county seat of Covasna County. It is sometimes confused with the city by the same name in the Danube delta. A Daco-Roman settlement once occupied the site of this small city. It has a small local museum with an interesting collection of Dacian silver, ancient pottery and a pottery workshop, and an ethnographical section. During the Middle Ages the town was settled by Szeklers, a Hungarian-speaking people. They once had a language and culture of their own but eventually became Magyarized, although in the Middle Ages they were a distinct people apart from the Magyars (Hungarians). The local museum contains some of their interesting wood carvings. Lying on the Olt River, Sfîntu Gheorghe is currently an industrial town which processes wood and lumber and manufactures textiles. It contains one of the old fortified type of churches commonly found in the surrounding area. Its tourist trade is small, with most tourists passing through it to Braşov, the resorts in its vicinity, or perhaps going to Bukovina.

Useful Addresses

Tourist Office, 2 Ciucului St.
Sfîntu Gheorghe Hotel (first class).

SARMIZEGETHUSA (DACIAN)

This village, located in Hunedoara County in the western part of the country, was the capital of ancient Dacia. It lies near the town of Orăştie, a lumbering center in the Orăştie Mountains. Sarmizegethusa lies at an altitude of 3,937 feet in a place called "La Tau." A railway goes to within a short distance of its site. Founded in the 2nd century B.C., it was the economic, military, political, and religious center of the Dacian state. Located in mountains difficult to reach by an attacker, its bastion had the form of an irregular quadrilateral (787 by 499 feet) comprising, on five terraces, an area of 11.5 square miles. The walls, without towers, were provided with gates on the east and west sides. In the old precincts, destroyed when the city was conquered by the Roman imperial armies, only traces of wooden buildings are preserved. Outside the precincts one can distinguish the traces of a civil

Dacian settlement and of a sacred area made up of seven quadrilateral sanctuaries, an andesite altar representing the sun (evidence of the Urano-solar feature of the Dacian's religion), and two round sanctuaries, with andesite pillars set into a circle. These last two sanctuaries are of exceptional value; they signify the old Dacian calendar, according to which the year was divided into three periods (having the following duration and sequence: 13-21-13 weeks), in 13-year cycles adding up to 4,748 days each. The small circular sanctuary includes 13 separate slabs and 101 pillars—set into 8 groups of 8 each, one group of 7, 3 groups of 8, and one group of 6. The big circular sanctuary is made up of three concentric circles (A, B, C) and a central apse having the shape of a closed hoof; the outer circle (A) is made up of 104 andesite blocks; the next (B) of 30 separate slabs and 30 groups of 6 pillars each; and the third circle (C) is comprised of 14 slabs and 68 pillars set as follows: 17 pillars/4 slabs/18 pillars/3 slabs/16 pillars/4 slabs and 17 pillars/3 slabs. The central apse has the following setting: 13 pillars/2 slabs and 21 pillars/2 slabs. Calculations made by several scientists led to the registering of 365.29 days in a Dacian year, a fact that makes the sanctuary-calendar at Sarmizegethusa one of the most accurate calendars of the ancient world.

Rebuilt by the Romans after the conquest of Dacia (A.D. 106), Sarmizegethusa became the headquarters of a detachment of the 4th Legion Flavia Felix, who erected in the southeast part of the precincts a stone building (the only building whose traces may still be distinguished). From this citadel of the brave Decebalus, the Dacians' king (A.D. 87–106), significant archeological finds were discovered that demonstrate the stage of civilization of the Dacian people at that time: pipelines, made of burnt clay processed on the wheel; developed tools (tongs, hammers, anvils, ploughs, scythes, compasses); and water storage tanks.

SARMIZEGETHUSA (ROMAN)

Founded in A.D. 110 by the Romans, this town lies to the west of the Dacian city by the same name. After conquering the old Dacian capital, the Romans founded its counterpart on a plain whose site they preferred to that of the mountainous capital. They built a large citadel, an amphitheater, and other buildings at their town, which they called Colonia Ulpia Traiana Augusta Dacia Sarmizegethusa. Its amphitheater represented the largest building of the capital of Roman Dacia in the 2nd century. Built entirely of stone, the building has an elliptical shape (the main axis is 295 feet long and its secondary one is 230 feet in length) with four entrances and a capacity of 5,000 seats on marble and chiseled stone.

MICIA (RUINS)

The ruins of this Roman town are located in the Mureş River valley near the city of Deva in Hunedoara County. The ruins date from the 2nd and 3rd centuries, when a large Roman fortress and settlement were founded on its site. Archeological research has revealed the famous "radiator of antiquity"—the hypocaustum—based on the heating of the floor of a room by a stream of air brought from a furnace outside the building and connected to it by means of burnt clay pipes. The high degree of civilization reached in the Roman settlement at Micia is also demonstrated by the magnificent thermal complex, made up of baths on a sizeable area considered to be the largest complex of its kind that has been discovered in a Dacian settlement. The basins, tubs, and the whole system has been preserved undamaged.

CHAPTER 5

Moldavia:
Major Cities and Historic Sites

IAŞI

"It is not the town that makes the roads, but the roads that make a town," wrote the well-known Romanian historian Nicolae Lorga. A telling example is Iaşi (Jassy), the capital city of Iaşi County, an urban settlement developed at an important crossroad of old trade routes in the northeastern part of an historical area of Romania called Moldavia. The city has a population of 315,000 people.
    The city is an old cultural center with Carpo-Dacian and Paleo-

lithic vestiges and is located amidst meadows on the terraces of Bahlui River. It was first mentioned in documents of the period 1387–92. It became a customs point after 1400, a princely residence in 1492, and the capital of Moldavia between 1565 and 1862 when its function was usurped by Bucharest.

The city became a cultural and artistic center at the time of the founding of many institutions there: the Vasiliană Academy in the 17th century; the Mihăileană Academy in 1835; the first Romanian polytechnic school in 1814; *Albina,* Moldavia's first newspaper printed in Romanian (1829); the Philharmonic and Drama Conservatoire in 1836; and Romania's first university in 1860. Iași was a strong nucleus of the 1848 revolutionary movement and of the national movement which was to lead to the Union of the Romanian Principalities in 1859. It also housed Romania's first Socialist circles and became one of the centers of the working-class movement in the period immediately following the First World War.

Beginning in 1902, the bases of a tourism department were established in Iași, which later took the initiative of marking the first mountain itineraries in the Mount Ceahlău where the chalet called "Dochia" was built.

Numerous foreign travelers have praised and admired the city of Iași. The Italian missionary Marcus Bandinus (17th century) considered it "the metropolis of the entire province" and mentioned that Iași had 15,000 houses, 60 churches, 11 monasteries, as well as 20 schools. Outstanding Romanian writers and poets such as Ion Creangă, Mihail Eminescu, Vasile Alecsandri, Mihail Sadoveanu, Nicolae Iorga, and George Călinescu spoke nostalgically about Iași and mentioned it in their works. Today, Iași is an important chemical center, a main producer of raw materials for machine-building, food, and light industries; and a traditional focal point of Romania's cultural and university life.

The relief of Iași's surroundings has no spectacular heights or gorges but attracts visitors by its scenic lakes, legendary woods, and interesting monuments of nature such as those of Valea Lui David and Bîrnova on Repedea Hill and Lazul Chirița. The hands of many anonymous craftsmen have left behind the imprint of their creations on the landscape, pottery, and anthropomorphous statuettes at Cucuteni (Cucuteni culture, one of the most prominent Neolithic European cultures, 3rd millenium B.C.; the settlement was called Cucuteni) and a Dacian fortification in the 4th-3rd centuries B.C.; another Neolithic settlement—Ruginoasa—with a

Moldavia

great many anthropomorphous and zoomorphous statuettes; the Neolithic settlement rebuilt by the Dacians at Dumbrava (1st-2nd centuries A.D.); and an important gold Thracian-Getic treasure (4th century B.C.) at Băiceni. Important buildings created during the Middle Ages included: Princely Courts; remarkable architectural monuments at Hîlău (14th century); Cotnari and Tîrgu Frumos (15th century); Deleni (17th century); as well as many monasteries and churches at Hîrlău (1492), Dobrovăţ (1504), Hlincea (1587), Bîrnova (1629), Paşcani (1664), and Deleni (1669).

The architectural ensemble of the area was also enriched with houses and palaces (some of them are currently museums) at Paşcani (1695); Deleni (1730); Miclăuşeni (1752); and Ruginoasa (1811; palace of Prince Alexandru Ioan Cuza). One can also visit the memorial houses devoted to poet Vasile Alecsandri at Mirceşti, prose writer Mihail Sadoveanu at Paşcani, and poet Dimitrie Nghel at Corneşti.

The old habitat of Moldavian Lains invites you to its traditional pottery centers at Lespezi and Poiana Deleni, where makers of pots still use the potter's wheel; to the locality of Tătărusi where furriers have still preserved their guild; and to the Tansa locality where there live stone dressers and carvers of wood. Peasant architecture, folk costumes and dances, as well as old traditional customs, can be admired at Şipote and Bivolari. The village of Cotnari, a famous medieval market town renowned for its vineyards, is also an enticing spot. The Cotnari wine was highly appreciated by Prince Stephen the Great (15th century) and Prince Dimitrie Cantemir, who said in 1700: "I dare say that the Cotnari is a select wine, more savory than other European wines and even more savory than Tokay wine."

What to See

Museums

Palace of Culture, 1 Palatului St., an imposing neo-Gothic edifice built between 1906 and 1925 on the site of the old palace of Prince Alexandru Moruzi (1804–06), was erected on the ruins of a 15th-century princely court. The palace, with tens of rooms, houses fine arts, ethnography, history, and polytechnic museums as well as an original collection of old instruments for sound recording and emission. Visiting hours are 10 A.M. - 6 P.M.

Museum of the History of Old Romanian Literature, 69 A.

Panu St., is a rich depository of manuscripts and printings, many of them signed by well-known men of letters who lived in Iaşi. The museum is located in "The House with Archways" where Metropolitan Dosoftei (1624–93) set up his printing press and brought out in 1673 the *Psalter,* the first large-scale work in verse printed in Romanian. Visiting hours are 10 A.M. - 6 P.M.

Museum of Moldavia's Literature, 4 I.C. Frimu St., with modern and contemporary departments, is set up in the V. Pogor House, the former headquarters of the Junimea Literary Society (1863–85). Important cultural events are organized in the museum. Visiting hours are 10 A.M. - 6 P.M.

Union Museum, 14 Al. Lăpuşneanu St., exhibits original documents and personal belongings of the fighters for the union of the Romanian Principalities, sculptures, and other items related to the 1859 union. The museum was inaugurated in 1959 in the former residence of Prince Alexandru Ioan Cuza (1859–62), an empire building with daryatids built in 1806. Visiting hours are 10 A.M. - 6 P.M.

Museum of Natural History, 16 Independence Blvd., inaugurated in 1834, was one of the first such museums in Romania. It has rich collections of rocks, minerals, fossils, and species of flora and fauna. The museum is housed in "The Ruset House," the former headquarters of the Society of Physicians and Naturalists, an edifice built in the 18th century. The election of Alexandru Ioan Cuza as prince of Moldavia on January 3, 1859, took place in this building. Visiting hours are 10 A.M. - 6 P.M.

Museum of the Theatre, 3 V. Alecsandri St., houses a large-scale retrospective of the theatrical activity of Iaşi. Documents on display attest to the beginnings of the Romanian theater in 1816. The building housing the museum was erected around 1800 and belonged to Alecsandri's family. Visiting hours are 10 A.M. - 6 P.M.

Museum of the University, 11—23 August St., housed in a few rooms of the Al. I. Cuza University, is a neoclassic edifice built between 1893 and 1897. Visiting hours 10 A.M. - 6 P.M.

Architectural Monuments

St. Nicolae Domnesc Church, 65 A. Anu St., the city's oldest monument, was built in the style of the epoch by Prince Stephen the Great in 1492. It was restored by the French architect Lecomte de Nouy in 1904.

Galata Monastery (Galata District) was built by Prince Petru

The Presidential Palace, Bucharest. *(Photo by author)*

Ploesti Orthodox Church. *(Photo by author)*

National Theatre, Bucharest. *(Photo by author)*

The Athenaeum, Bucharest. *(Photo by author)*

Baile Herculane Spa in the Southern Carpathians. *(Courtesy Romanian National Tourist Office)*

Mount Postavaru winter ski scene. *(Courtesy Romanian National Tourist Office)*

Voronet Monastery in northern Moldavia. *(Courtesy Romanian National Tourist Office)*

Rarau—Pietrele Doamnei in the Northern Carpathians. *(Courtesy Romanian National Tourist Office)*

Şchiopu in 1584 and fortified in 1733. A stately house was added to the church in 1800. The style recalls Wallachia's characteristic architecture. The church houses the tomb of its founder and of his daughter Despina (1588).

Trei Ierarhi Church (Three Hierarchs Church), 62 Ştefan cel Mare St., the most beautiful foundation of Prince Vasile Lupu (1639), is Iaşi's most famous monument. This unique piece of old Romanian architecture displays a rich, beautifully chiseled ornamentation covering the entire facade. This building's construction, attributed to the Armenian masterbuilder Ianache Etisi, is in fact a successful synthesis of Moldavian and Wallachian architecture. It was restored by the architect Lecomte de Nouy between 1882 and 1890. The church houses the tombs of Princes Vasile Lupu, Dimitrie Cantemir and Al. I. Cuza. Nearby is a museum of religious art.

Golia Monastery, 51 Cuza Vodă St., was built by Prince Vasile Lupu in 1660 on the site of a monastery erected by chancellor Ioan Golia in 1564. Its enclosure walls were erected in the 17th century, and dwellings were added to it in the 18th century.

Cetăţuia Monastery on Cetăţuia Hill was built in 1672 during the reign of Prince Gheorghe Duca. The church, an unassuming replica of the Trei Ierarhi, has enclosure walls, a gate tower, house of Father Superior, and a main dwelling—valuable monuments of Iaic architecture, all dating from the same epoch.

St. Gheorghe Church, 46 Ştefan cel Mare St., an old metropolitan church, was built in 1761. The stone-chiseled ornamentation on the facades reminds one of the 18th century post-Brancovan style of Wallachia. Nearby stands the new Metropolitan Church and the Metropolitan Palace (1833–1907).

Catholic Bishopric, 60 Ştefan cel Mare St., was erected in 1785 on the site of a 17th-century wooden church.

Great Synagogue, 7 Sinagoglior St., is a building dating from the 18th century.

Frumoasa Monastery, 1 Radu Vodă St., was built by Prince Grigore Ghica in 1733 on the site of the old Balica Monastery (1587). The beautiful palace (1819) and the church (1836) in the precincts of the monastery are built in an architectural style with neoclassic influences.

Memorial and Historical Houses

Creanga's Mud House, 11 S. Bărnutiu St., is an unassuming peasant house in Ţicău district where the great storyteller Ion

Creangă (1839–99), the author of the well-known *Childhood Recollections,* spent the last years of his life.

Otilia Cazimir Memorial House, 3 Bucşinescu St., exhibits many documents and personal belongings of poetess Alexandra Gavrilescu (pen name Otilia Cazimir)—1894–1967. She was awarded the national prize for literature in 1937.

Mihail Kogălniceanu Memorial House, 15 M. Kogălniceanu St., evokes the personality of historian, writer, journalist, orator, statesman, and academician M. Kogălniceanu (1817–91). He was one of the main promoters and leaders of the Union of the Romanian Principalities (1859).

Mihail Codreanu Memorial House, 5 Rece St., also called "Vila Sonet" (Sonet Villa), evokes the personality of poet M. Codreanu (1876–1957), well known for his sonnets describing landscapes and human feelings.

Mihail Sadoveanu Memorial House, 12 Aleea Sadoveanu, was the temporary home of the great prose writer M. Sadoveanu (1880–1961). He was awarded the national prize for literature in 1924 and won numerous other national and international awards.

Ilie Pintilie Memorial House, Soseaua Iasi-Ciurea 62, is the house where Communist supporter Ilie Pintilie (1903–40) spent part of his life. Documents relating to the history of the local working-class movement are on display.

Cantacuzino-Pascanu House, 8 V. Alecsandri St., is an 18th-century building currently housing the Press House.

Costache Ghica House, 16 Universității St., built in 1760, was an exquisite residence between 1795 and 1806 and the headquarters of the first Romanian university in 1860.

Mavrocordat House, 10 N. Bălcescu St., a former residence between 1785–95, housed the United Institutes School whose teaching staff included the great Romanian poet Mihail Eminescu (1850–89).

Alecu Balş House, 29 Cuza Vodă St., built in 1815, houses the Moldova Philharmonic Orchestra.

National Theatre, 18—9 Mai St., is an imposing neo-Baroque edifice built between 1894 and 1896. It has one of Romania's most beautiful performance halls.

Statues

Stephen The Great, prince of Moldavia (1457–1504). His sculpture is by Emmanuel Fremiet (1883); Piaţa Palatului Culturli.

Miron Costin, a chancellor of Moldavia, writer, and chronicler (1633–91). His sculpture is by Wladislaw Hegel (1888), and the remains of the chronicler are buried under the socle of the statue; Cuza Vodă St.

Gheorghe Asachi, a man of learning, who helped establish the basis of the Romanian education and the press and theater in Moldavia (1788–1869). His sculpture is by Jean Georgescu (1890), and his remains lie under the socle of the statue; 64 Ştefan cel Mare St.

Vasile Alecsandri, poet, playwright, and statesman of European fame (1821–90). His sculpture is by W. Hegel (1905); Piaţa Teatrului Naţional.

Mihail Kogălniceanu, the statesman who proclaimed Romania's national independence on May 8, 1877. The sculpture was done by Raffaen Romanelli (1911); 11—23 August St.

Alexandru Ioan Cuza, prince of the United Principalities (1859–62) and of the Romanian National State (1862–66). His statue was sculptured by R. Romanelli (1912); Piaţa Unirii.

Mihai Eminescu, regarded as Romania's greatest poet (1859–89). This sculpture is by Schmidt-Faur (1929); Biblioteca Centrală.

Alexandru D. Xenopol, historian, philosopher, university teacher, and academician (1847–1920). His sculpture is by C. Barashi (1934); 11—23 August St.

Group of Princes' Statues, sculptures by Dimitiu-Bîrland, I. Dămăceanu, and E. Bîrleanu; Casa Tineretului (Square of the Youth House).

Alley of Statues of writers, painters, musicians, and other Romanian men of culture; Copou Park.

Lion's Obelisk, erected from a design made by Gheorghe Asachi, under supervision of the architect Singurov (1834); Copu Park.

Independence Statue, by Gabriela Adoc (1979); Independence Square.

Parks

Botanical Gardens, 7–9 Dumbrava Roşie St.

Copou Gardens (here is found Eminescu's famed linden tree), 23 August St.

Gr. Cobălcescu Natural Reservation, on Repedea Hill.

Useful Addresses

Nicolina is a well-known spa famous for its sulfurous chlorosodium iodate and bromate water springs; 2 Hatman Şendrea St.

Iaşi County Tourist Office, Piaţa Unirii, block 12; phone: 981-43037 or 14364.

Romanian Automobile Club, L 13-15, 30 Decembrie St.; phone: 981-53245.

CFR (Railways Travel) Agency, Piaţa Unirii; phone: 981-13673.

Tarom (Romanian Airlines) Agency, 3 Arcu St.; phone: 981-15239.

Post Office, 3 Cuza Vodă St.

Telephone, 21 Al. Lăpusneanu St.

Peco (Filling Stations), Şoseasua Păcurari, phone: 981-17142 (open 24 hrs.); Şoseaua Bucium, phone: 981-32891 (open 24 hrs.).

Auto Service Stations, Piaţa Unirii, phone: 981-13001; Şoseaua Păcurari 98, phone: 981-43137.

Hotels

Unirea (restaurant, brasserie, bar, confectioner's), Piaţa Unirii; phone: 981-42110.

Traian (restaurant, brasserie, bar), phone: 981-14320.

Moldova (restaurant, brasserie, bar, confectioner's), Anastasie Panu St.; phone: 981-42225.

Continental (bar, tea shop), phone: 981-14320.

Restaurants (Romanian Cuisine)

Bolta Rece, 10 Rece St.; phone: 981-13167.

Trei Sarmale, Şoseaua Bucium; phone: 981-32832.

Ciric (forest, lakes, camping); phone: 981-79520.

Motels, Camping

Ciric (camping), phone 981-79920.

Bucium (inn, camping).

GALAŢI

The city of Galaţi is a major river port on the left bank of the Danube River not far from the Soviet border. Located in the eastern part of Romania, the city is situated where the Danube, after flowing north, bends to the east for its final run to the Black Sea. Galaţi is the county seat of Galaţi County and has a population of about 300,000 people, ranking it as the seventh largest city in size in the country. The city lies 152 miles northeast of Bucharest by highway. The site of the city is just north of a point where the Siret River joins the Danube after flowing in a southerly course from Romania's northern boundary with the Soviet Union. Several rail lines run into Galați, with one of these running eastward into Soviet territory. Galați lies on a plateau between the Siret and Prut rivers.

Galați is a major shipbuilding center for Romania and has the country's largest shipyards. Oil tankers, freighters, and other ships are launched there. An iron and steel plant built in the mid-1960s with support from the West makes steel plates for the shipyards. Using imported iron ore, the plant has become the main focus of the country's iron and steel industry, replacing Transylvania in importance in this industry. The Danube River is a major highway for moving coal and iron ore. Galați is a major port for the shipping of grain, petroleum products, and lumber. Other industries in Galați include textiles, chemicals, food processing, building materials, and machine building. The city is also an important center for fishing activity and the canning of fish. Apiculture is widely practiced around Galați. One can see the beehives along roads, especially near fields planted in sunflowers. From Galați to the Sulina mouth of the Danube, the distance is about 90 miles.

The city was founded in the 3rd century B.C. with some historians giving credit to a leader of the Gauls named Brennus for laying its foundations. Its site was occupied by the Romans, who developed it into an important port and center of trade. These functions were still important to the town during the Middle Ages. The Turks occupied the town during the 16th century and directed most of its trade and exports toward the Bosporus and Constantinople. During the 17th century its trade centered largely on cattle and grain. Turkish forces remained in Galați until 1829, and following their departure the port began to rejuvinate with new trade and industries. After 1837 it was declared a free port, and in 1856 the city became the headquarters of the European Danube Commission, regulating usage of the Danube River. In 1887 docks were built along its waterfront to accommodate shipping. Galați also serves as a naval base. The American Red Cross was very active in Galați in 1919, where it had two cantines that fed over 1,500 people daily.

Over the centuries the city experienced wars, several major fires, and disease epidemics. The Germans destroyed much of its port and parts of the city while retreating before the Russian army during World War II. Due to all the damage it sustained from its many disasters and its subsequent rebuilding, the city presently has a modern 20th-century look to most of it.

Galaţi's main cultural features and points of interest include several historic churches, the **Precista Church** (fifteenth century; restored in the 17th century); the **Mavromol Church** (17th century); and **Vovidenia Church** (18th century). There is also a natural history museum and several other museums containing art treasures and objects of historical interest; the state theater; and a technical college. Lake Brateş, a large fresh-water lake, is popular for its swimming, fishing, recreational activities, and lovely gardens. Excursions can be made from Galaţi into the Danube delta. There is hydrofoil service between Galaţi and Tulcea.

Useful Addresses

Tourist Office, 6 Republicii St.
Galaţi Hotel (first class), 1 Republicii St.

BACĂU

Bacău is located in northeast Romania in the historic province of Moldavia and is the county seat of Bacău County. The city lies on the Bistriţa River about six miles north of the point where it flows into the Siret. By highway, Bacău is 179 miles north-northeast from Bucharest. It also lies on a major rail line which runs north, crossing into the Soviet Union. Nearby cities are Piatra-Neamţ (38 miles northwest) and Gheorghe Gheorghiu-Dej (33 miles southwest). The foothills of the Subcarpathians lie near the city. Bacău has a population of 181,000 people.

The city is an important industrial and commercial center. Among its plants are those for sawing timber and wood processing, pulp and paper manufacture, leather working, shoes and boots, equipment for mining and the oil industry, textiles, clothing, building materials, and engineering works. Important petroleum deposits are located west of the city. The area around Bacău raises livestock and grows cereals. Food processing is important in the city.

Bacău was first mentioned in documents dated in 1408, which note its function as a customs post. In the late 1400s the town served as the court and residence of the prince of Moldavia. The town has a few tourist attractions, including its **Historical Museum, Art Museum,** and **Museum of Natural Science.** Its old **Precista Church** dates from the 15th century. Bacău also has a state theater, several lovely parks, and a symphony orchestra.

Useful Addresses

Tourist Office, 10 Calea Mărăsesti.

Hotels
Bistrița (first class), 3 Calea Mărăseti.
Decebal (first class), 6—6 Martie St.

BOTOŞANI

Located in northeast Romania on the Moldavian Plain, Botoşani is enveloped by rich agricultural lands. The city lies 277 miles by highway from Bucharest. It has a population of 110,000 people and is the county seat of Botoşani County. Several highways pass through the city and radiate out from it. It has connections by both highway and a branch rail line with the Soviet Union, whose border is along the Prut River to the east and north of the city.

The name Botoşani is derived from that of Batu Khan, a grandson of Genghis Khan. The Mongols invaded the area in the 13th century, and the town was founded a century later. Since World War II, industries have helped to spur its growth. Its main enterprises include textiles, flour milling, clothing, food processing, and the production of vegetable oils. Livestock raising is important around the city.

The city's main tourist features include a number of old churches: the **Church of St. George** and the **Uspenia Church** founded by the wife of Petru Rares in the 16th century; and the **Popauti Church** built at the close of the 15th century by Stephen the Great. All three churches underwent restoration in the 18th century. The **Monastery of Stephen the Great** (late 15th century) contains some beautiful frescoes, and **Cosula Monastery** (16th century) is another exquisite structure.

Useful Addresses

Tourist Office, 1 Piaţa 1907.

SUCEAVA

Located in a picturesque hilly area (1,082–1,263 feet in elevation) on the banks of the Suceava, 268 miles by road north from Bucharest, the Suceava Municipality is the turn-table of tourism in the north of Moldavia and one of the most attractive towns in the country. One should make a stop in this old residence of the Moldavian princes (14th-16th centuries) where you will find: a modern town; hundred-year-old monuments set amidst the panorama of new constructions; pleasant sites for walks and relaxation; nice hotels providing excellent accommodations; restaurants with special dishes of the Moldavian cuisine; and the traditional hospitableness of the inhabitants of this ancient Romanian city.

The beginnings of its settlement are lost in the dim past. Archeological excavations at Scheia, in the western part of the city, reveal traces of inhabitation of the Dacians in the 2nd-3rd centuries A.D. Diggings in other parts of the town have produced evidence of continuous settlement here.

As the old capital of Moldavia, Suceava is mentioned in documents of the 14th century (Prince Petru Muşat I. erected the Princely Citadel here after 1388, still intact to date). Suceava was a famous commercial center and customs site in the 15th and 16th centuries. The city experienced expansion during the reign of Stephen the Great (1457–1504), who paid it special attention, reinforcing the Princely Citadel and restoring the Princely Court and building numerous edifices. Suceava was ravaged occasionally by the attacks of foreign troops or by devastating fires. Yet, on May 21, 1600, when the armies of Michael the Brave entered the Princely Citadel without a struggle, the town experienced great relief and exhilaration. His victorious march enabled the prince to achieve the first union of Wallachia, Transylvania, and Moldavia. For 143 years, between 1775—when the north of Moldavia came under Hapsburg rule—and November 6, 1918, the town was under foreign occupation. In the period between the two world wars, its main importance was that of a commercial center

Moldavia

for the exchange of goods between the mountains and the lowland areas.

Suceava has recorded, especially in the last two decades, a rapid pace of economic and town-planning development, evidenced by new buildings and dwellings, and industrial enterprises (among these the Aggregate Works of Wood Processing, the Aggregate for Cellulose and Paper, the Zimbrul Knitwear Factory, and the Stradunina Leather and Footwear Factory).

The municipality, now the capital of Suceava County, has a population of about 80,000 inhabitants and is visited by numerous tourists all year round.

The province of Bukovina, in which Suceava is located, was awarded in 1975 the international prize "Pomme d'Or" by the International Federation of Tourist Journalists and Writers for its carefully preserved monuments, for the originality of its folk art and folklore, and for its picturesque landscape.

Bukovina has genuine masterpieces of universal architecture and art (Voronet, 1488–1547, described in UNESCO's *Great World's Monuments* catalog; Arbore, 1503–41; Humor, 1530–35; Moldovița, 1532–37; and Sucevița, 1581–1601) with exterior frescoes of exquisite coloring. The bright colors of the frescoes, preserved throughout centuries with their specific predominant hue, such as the blue of Voroneț or the green of Sucevița, lend a distinct personality to each building or dwelling.

You may also visit the Putna Monastery and Museum (1466–1662); the wonderful Dragomirna Monastery (1609); and the monasteries in Rișca (1542), Slatina (1561), and Solca (1620). Local centers of folk art with various and original items and themes showcase folk songs and dances, folk dresses, household implements, ancient customs, and traditions. These are genuine tourist spots. Lovers of folk art may admire the peasant architecture of the houses of Ciocănești, the wonderful textiles and costumes of Arbore, the furred vests of Gura Humorului, the famous black pottery of Marginea, or colored pottery of Rădăuți, as well as the marvelous wood carvings of the area. The museums in Suceava—Rădăuți, Gura Humorului, and Fălticeni—exhibit many old household utensils. There is also a unique museum in Cimpulung Moldovenesc, The Museum of Wood Art, with its Ioan Tugui ethnographic collection of 4,500 spoons made of wood.

Tourist programs include rides on *hutsul* horses (Rădăuți studs), which are located in Bukovina and have a long tradition in the breeding of horses. Museums devoted to the composer Ciprian Porumbescu in the Ciprian Porumbescu village, to the sculptor Ion Irimescu in the town of Fălticeni, and to the poet Nicolae Labiş in the Mălini village are also visited by many tourists.

The main year-round health resort and spa in Bukovina is Vatra Dornei. For further information on this spa see the chapter on health resorts and spas, or contact the Suceava County Tourist Office, 2 N. Bălcescu St.

During your stay in Suceava, do not miss the majestic view of the town from the heights of the Princely Citadel. It will help you to understand better the following lines by the writer Geo Bogza about the place: "Ever since the Romanians asserted their existence in the light of history, making a country and erecting towns which they gave names to, not many were those which had such an echo throughout ages . . . as Suceava."

What to See

Museums

County Museum, 33 Ştefan cel Mare St.; open from 10 A.M. to 6 P.M. The History Museum sheltered in this building displays records of the past events and deeds of the people who inhabited this area from the earliest times to the present. In this museum are medieval armor, documents from the reigns of princes, coins, tools, and some 350,000 objects and documents related to modern and contemporary history. Of particular interest is the Hall of the Throne, which recreates the setting and atmosphere of Stephen the Great's court, including furniture, weapons, and various and richly ornate costumes.

Folk Art Museum (Princely Inn), 5 Ciprian Porumbescu St.; open from 10 A.M. to 7 P.M. It is housed in an old building dating from the end of the 16th century which is the oldest civil building in Suceava County. Initially it was probably used as an inn. The museum displays a collection of pottery from the famous centers of the county (Marginea and Rădăuţi), folk dresses, towels, rugs, and various wooden objects. A room is devoted to the customs and traditions in the area.

Natural Science Dept., 23 Ştefan cel Mare St.; open from 10

A.M. to 6 P.M. Interesting collections of paleontology, flora and fauna of the area are on display.

Fine Arts Dept., 23 Ştefan cel Mare St., open from 10 A.M. to 6 P.M. It is housed in the same building as the Natural Science Dept. On show are works of art and sculpture and graphics by well-known classical Romanian and foreign artists.

Documentary Memorial Funds "Simeon Florea Marian," 4 Aleea Simeon Florea Marian; open from 8 A.M. to 3:30 P.M. The setting of the life and work of the folklorist and ethnographer S. F. Marian (1847–1907) is commemorated by means of his personal belongings, publications, and manuscripts. He was the author of such well-known works as *Romanian Folk Ornithology, Holidays with the Romanians,* and *Wedding Rituals with the Romanians.*

Astronomical Observatory, 3 E. Bodnăras; open from 8 A.M. to 8 P.M.

History and Art Monuments

The Princely Citadel, Cetăţii Park. It stands on a high hill on the east side of the town. The Princely Citadel was originally erected to serve as a fortified castle for Prince Petru Muşat I, who moved Moldavia's capital from Siret to Suceava. Around 1400, Alexander the Kind changed it into a citadel with a strong military presence. Thick walls of 9.8–13 feet, supported by bulky bastions and towers, were also erected by Stephan the Great. Throughout its history, up to 1675 when it was demolished, the Suceava Citadel was impregnable. Its gates halted even Constantinople's conqueror, Mohammed II, in 1476.

Scheia Citadel, in the northwest area of the town. The citadel was erected in the 14th century out of stone and mortar on a hill at 1,260 feet altitude. Only vestiges of it are left now. It was meant to strengthen the defense of the capital and of the independence of the Moldavian state. It has the shape of a rhombus, with walls 9.8 feet thick.

Zamca Medieval Group, Zamca St. It was erected in 1606 on a plateau on the west side of the city. The composition of its architecture blends elements of Gothic and classic tradition with motifs of oriental influence. The surrounding wall forms a trapezoid with two parallel sides, one of which is 193.6 feet long and the other 216.5 feet in length. The other two sides are 229.6 and 242.7 feet long.

Monument of Medieval Architecture Mirăuți, 17 Mirăuților St., was founded by Petru Mușat I (14th century), restored by Stephen the Great, and then restored again in the 17th century. It acquired its present form in the past century. The building was the site of the coronation of the first princes of Moldavia.

Princely Court, Ana Ipătescu Blvd. It was first built of stone by Stephan the Great on the ruins of a wooden palace dating from the reign of Petru Mușat I. Prince Petru Rareș reconstructed it from brick. Recent archeological investigations brought to light two rooms more than 62 feet long as well as cellars made of two naves separated by pillars standing 9.8 feet from one another.

Monumental Complex of Ioan Vodă Viteazul, No. 2 St. It is an impressive building with a Gothic cupola erected between 1514 and 1522 by Prince Bogdan III and his follower, Prince Stefanita. Its masterful artwork is the painting preserved on a great surface in the interior and the remarkable vestiges on the exterior.

Monument of Medieval Architecture, Karl Marx St. It was founded by Prince Petru Rareș in 1534–35. The votive painting in the interior represents the portraits of Petru Rareș, Princess Elena, and two of their sons. In the yard stands a 98-foot-high tower built in 1562 by Prince Alexandru Lăpușneanu.

Equestrian Statue of Prince Stephen the Great, Cetății Park. Standing on the hill in the vicinity of the citadel, it is one of the most impressive equestrian statues of the prince in the country. This bronze work of sculptor Eftimie Bîrleanu, unveiled in 1977, is 72 feet high. The bas-reliefs on the pedestal show scenes of the great battle of Vaslui (1475) against the Ottoman armies.

Statue of Petru Mușat I, Ștefan cel Mare St. Located in front of the House of Culture, the statue is 11 feet high and is the work of architect Paul Vasilescu.

Useful Addresses

County Municipal Council, 36 Ștefan cel Mare St.; phone: 987-22548.

Municipal People's Council, 58 Ștefan cel Mare St.; phone: 987-12696.

Militia of the Municpality, 19—1 Mai Blvd.; phone 987-10498.

Suceava County Tourist Office, 2 N. Bălcescu St.; phone: 987-21297 or 10944.

Moldavia

Branch of the Romanian Automobile Club, 8, N. Bălcescu St.; phone: 987-10997 or 12345.
Tourism Office for Youth, 1 Meșteșugarilor St.; phone: 987-15235.
Tarom Agency, 2 N. Bălcescu St.; phone: 987-14686.
CFR Travel Agency, 8 N. Bălcescu St., phone: 987-14335.
Adas (State Insurances), 35 Ștefan cel Mare St.; phone: 987-13676.

Hotels-Camping
Arcașul (first class), 4–6 Mihai Viteazul St., phone: 987-10944.
Balada (first class), 3 V.I. Lenin St., phone: 23198.
Bucovina (first class), 5 Ana Ipătescu Blvd., phone: 17048.
Suceava (first class), 4 N. Bălcescu St., phone: 22497.
Casa Tinererului (second class), 5 V. I. Lenin St., phone: 987-13192.
Suceava Camping (second class), Ilie Pintilie St.; phone: 987-17048.

Restaurants
Arcașul, 4–6 Mihai Viteazul St.; phone: 987-10944.
Bucovina, 5 Ana Ipătescu Blvd.; phone 987-17048.
Suceava, 12 Ștefan cel Mare St.; phone: 987-22838.
Crama, 2 N. Bălcescu St.
Bachus Wine Cellar, 2 Ana Ipătescu Blvd.; phone: 987-10177.
București, 2 N. Bălcescu St.; phone: 987-17441.
National, 3 N. Bălcescu St.; phone: 987-15380.
Brădet, Cetății Park; phone: 987-10533.
Select, Karl Marx St.; phone: 987-26697.
Dorna, G. Enescu St.; phone: 987-26829.

Shops
Bucovina (general stores), Ștefan cel Mare St.; phone: 987-16785.
Tourist (gifts, handicrafts), 22 Ștefan cel Mare St., N. Bălcescu St.
Galeriile Fondului Plastic (Plastic Arts' Galleries), 26 Ștefan cel Mare St.; phone: 987-16288.
Casa Cărții (House of the Book).
Adam, Eva (department stores), phone: 987-25637.
Auto-Moto-Velo (spare parts), Calea Obcinelor, Block T 64; phone: 987-23875.

Comturist (shops with sale of goods on free convertible currency), at Arcașul, Bucovina, and Suceava hotels.

Higher Education Institutions
Pedagogical Institute, 1 Emil Bodnăraș St.; phone: 987-16147.

Theaters, Cinemas
House of Culture, 20 A. Ștefan cel Mare St.; phone: 987-20699.
Modern Cinema, 1 Dragoș Vodă St.; phone: 987-10075.

Parks
Central Park (you can see the busts of Prince Petru Rareș and composer Ciprian Porumbescu), Ștefan cel Mare St.
Cetății Park, Parcului St.
Arenia Stadium, 7—1 Mai Blvd.; phone: 987-16145.
Artificial Skating Rink, E. Bodnăraș St.; phone: 987-27703.

Medical, Health Facilities
County Hospital, 21—1 Mai Blvd; phone: 987-14897.
Pharmacy No. 1 (24 hrs.), 2 N. Bălcescu St.; phone: 987-17285.
Pharmacies, 1 Mai Blvd.
Telephone, 10 N. Bălcescu St.; phone: 987-16660.
Post Office, I. C. Frimu St.

Transportation Facilities
Suceava Nord Station (Ițcani District), 4 Gării St.; phone: 987-10037.
Suceava Station (Burdujeni District), 7 N. Lorga St.; phone: 987-13897.
Suceava Airport (Salcesa commune), phone: 987-14885.
Bus Station, 2 V. Alecsandri St.; phone: 987-16239.
Peco Station, 25—1 Mai Blvd., phone: 987-10123; Ilie Pintilie St., phone: 987-15645.
Service Station, Fălticeni Highway, phone: 987-13684; Ilie Pintilie St., phone: 987-13510.

GHEORGHE GHEORGHIU-DEJ

This town is named after a former secretary of the Romanian Communist Party. Under the concept of centralized state planning, the government established a petrochemical complex here between

1953–55, and the settlement soon grew into a city. Today, the city numbers over 50,000 persons living around oil refining and chemical plants. The complex produces plastics, synthetic rubber, chlorine, and other related products. Both oil and salt deposits are located nearby. The city lies at the juncture of the Trotus and Tazlau rivers in Bacău County. It is 33 miles by road to Bacău.

Useful Addresses

Tourist Office, Piaţa Magistralei.

CHAPTER 6

Monasteries of Bukovina

Situated in the north of Moldavia, Bukovina is a region blessed with a luxurious nature wrapped in a diffused light which tones down colors and blends them with the blue of the sky. Bukovina presents itself to the tourist like an art album with the names Voroneț, Humor, Sucevița, Arbore, Moldovita, and Putna written on it. Here history lies asleep in monasteries and citadels, in churches containing treasures of old Romanian civilization, and in traditions and beliefs sprung from the rich Romanian folklore.

The monasteries lie in the general vicinity of the city of Suceava in the northern part of the country (see map of Romania). Voroneț Monastery lies a short distance from Gura Humorului, which is located on Highway 17 about 22 miles southwest of Suceava. Humor Monastery lies due west of Suceava in the village of Humor, which is about 4 miles north of Gura Humorului on Highway 17. Arbore Monastery is located about 29 miles northwest of Suceava via Highway 2. About 36 miles northwest of Suceava is Sucevița Monastery, surrounded by the green hills of the Carpathians. To reach Sucevița from Suceava, take Highway 2 north to Radauti, then Highway 17A west. Northwest from Sucevița is Putna Monastery, which lies 19 miles northwest from Radanti.

The monasteries of Bukovina were built during the 15th-16th centuries and bear the stamp of the personality of Prince Stephen the Great, an illustrious army commander and Moldavia's spiritual leader. During his reign, which lasted almost half a century (1457–1504), he was able to keep the country in the rhythm of medieval times. In spite of the frequent wars, culture blossomed, and the ruling prince had numerous monasteries, churches, and citadels built. It was during the reign of Stephen the Great that the Moldavian style of art came into being; later that term was to enter world art history to define a harmonious blend of folk artistic traditions with certain Byzantine and Gothic influences which had reached Moldavia through Serbia, Russia, and Poland. The Moldavian style brought numerous constructive and ornamental innovations into the heritage of Romanian art.

The exterior frescoes of local churches represent one of the most astonishing treasures of Moldavian art. They represent a genuine illustrated Bible, unique of kind and in artistic value. The idea of painting a Bible on churches in images that could be understood by the masses was in fact a real educational achievement of the Middle Ages. The range of images develops like a color film including tales and legends, customs, and great historical events (the fall of Constantinople, for example). Wall painting is an influence from the Western world, as it was used for the adorning of churches and public edifices in Italy, Switzerland, and Slovakia. However, in Bukovina it makes up a coherent iconographic display that covers the whole surface of the facades, which is unusual.

In Bukovina, the fresco, "the most difficult and most daring way of painting," as Michaelangelo described it, has been preserved for almost five centuries.

The Romanian state takes special care of these art monuments that have become an asset, preserving them for future generations. As a token of the appreciation of the unmatched value of these art treasures—masterpieces of both painting and architecture—in this part of the country and of the way they were preserved and cared for, Bukovina was awarded the prestigious "Pomme d'Or" prize by the International Federation of Writers and Journalists on Tourism in 1975.

VORONEȚ—THE SISTINE CHAPEL OF THE EAST

Voroneț is a fairyland world painted on a patch of sky. In the middle of a village lying at the foot of the mountains, amid fir trees and oak trees and little houses with whitewashed walls and florid verandas, a little church has been standing for about five hundred years. This princely shrine is wrapped from top to bottom in the gorgeous attire of frescoes.

Voroneț was built in three months and three weeks in 1488 by Stephen the Great and enlarged and painted on the outside in the time of ruling Prince Petru Rareș (1527–38 and 1541–46). Hundreds of paintings, ranging from the frail child (the symbol of the soul in the scene of the "Last Judgment") to the immense composition of "Jesse's Tree," were developed amid an explosion of blue.

The inner wall painting comprises such scenes as "The Holy Supper." In the nave is the commemorative picture of Stephen the Great, Mistress Maria Voichita, and Bogdan, their son. The folk influences and certain elements of the local life can be seen in the painting of the naves. The wall paintings in the nave and on the altar were made in 1547. The artistic magnificence and fame of Voroneț are greatly indebted to the outer frescoes dominated by the specific blue color (the Voroneț blue). The complete painting of the exterior—explained not only as an intention to seed the fear of sin and to perpetuate obedience to the great landowners but also as a stimulus of the people to fight against the Ottoman yoke—is clear in themes such as "The Siege of Constantinople" and the "Last Judgment," the most valuable composition of the ensemble.

Voroneț represented a new facet of Byzantine art. The church has a trefoil form representative of the Moldavian architectural style of its time, an original synthesis of Byzantine and Gothic elements. While advancing north, Byzantine art halted here in the shade of the Carpathians to receive the baptism of folk lyricism. The Romanians lent it softness and warmth, replacing its sternness with warm humanism, the grace and humor peculiar to its surroundings. The colors were borrowed from nature, with the sky, the flowers, and the forests serving as guides of the Moldavian painters. That is why the angels have the sweet faces of Moldavian women, the archangels blow the *bucium*—a Romanian shepherd's musical instrument similar to an alpenhorn—at the Last Judgment, and the souls carried to heaven are wrapped in Moldavian towels, while the souls doomed to the fire of hell wear the turbans of the Turks (Moldavia's enemy at the time).

The simplest and most dramatic composition is the "Last Judgment," which decorates the whole western facade. The compositions representing the "Last Judgment" on the Voroneţ chapel are a real monumental work achieved with superb artistic craftsmanship. The composition could easily compare with the mosaics in the Kahrie Mosque in Istanbul, the images in San Marco, Venice, Sienna, Assisi, and Orvieto, and the frescoes of Cimabue and Giotto.

In the fire of hell (a grand funnel of live coals opening at the feet of Jesus), the sinners are struggling—illustrious personages, kings, popes. Near the seat of judgment, Adam and Eve are represented, along with bands of prophets, hierarchs, martyrs, and Moses. In another illustration, a hand is holding the scales of justice where the sins of mankind in judgment are being weighed. To the right and to the left, the devils are quarreling for possession of the accused. Among the sinners, there are bands of Turks and Tatars, with harsh faces and fierce looks. The "Resurrection of the Dead," a very dramatic scene, is performed to the sound of the *bucium,* an autochthonous folk element. The animals, too, take part in the judgment, handing back fragments of human torsos to complete the bodies that were torn to pieces by wild beasts. The deer alone has nothing to hand back, for in Romanian folklore it stands for innocence. At the Gate of Heaven there is a great crush, the painter wishing to express humorously how the people hurried to rush into the long-expected Garden of Eden.

The southern wall displays "Jesse's Tree," the fabulous genealogy of Jesus. A fresco including eight panels and almost one hundred personages develops in luxurious interweaving of vine branches and tendrils. Also on the southern side are painted the portraits of Grigore Ros and Daniil Sihastrul (the Hermit). The furniture in the church—the chair and the pews—were made at the time of Petru Rareş; the chair of the ruler is a masterpiece of wood carving.

On the northern wall, more exposed to the elements of the weather, there are still a few scenes representing the Creation of the World and a popular legend, "Adam's Deed" (a compact between Adam and the Devil), a legend also painted on Sucevita and Moldovita monasteries.

This panorama unfolds against a dominant blue background. It is the Voroneţ blue, an artistic definition included today in the publications of international art next to Veronese green and Titan red. Around the church, a wall was built to protect and better preserve this monument.

HUMOR—MINIATURES ON A LAWN

This church is painted on the outside from the eaves down to the foundations. Humor Monastery (3.7 miles from Gura Humorului) looks like a page of a manuscript covered with miniatures, left lying on a lawn.

Founded by Voivode Petru Rareş and the boyar Theodor Bubuiog in 1530, the church is small, with a wide open porch, arched on three sides. Its vault, or treasury, is similar to the one at Moldovita, except that the one at Humor seems to be floating, which makes it greatly admired by art specialists. The well-known art historian Paul Henry stated in this respect: ". . .Italian art has nothing more beautiful and the artist seems to have rediscovered the great Byzantine tradition in the profound sense of the architectural composition that characterizes the baptistry at Ravenna."

The exterior painting is impressive for its compositions and portraits. The southern wall displays the composition known as "Hymn to the Glory of the Virgin," painted after the poem written by Patriarch Serghei of Constantinople and dedicated to the Virgin Mary, who is reputed to have saved the city during the attack of the Persians in 626. At Humor, this poem, represented in embroideries, miniatures, and medieval frescoes, consists of twenty-four scenes.

Under the images of the poem, a historical scene during the siege of Constantinople was designed to evoke the medieval belief in miracle-working icons, and the people's wish to defeat the Turks. Hatred for the enemy was so fierce that the hope in a miracle made the painters of Humor and Moldovita paint a defeat of the Turks instead of an actual historical event. On the south wall is the fresco known as the "Last Judgment." "The Tree of Jesse" on the north wall has greatly deteriorated with time and weathering.

At Humor the hues are brilliant, genuine, and borrowed from nature. Nothing is *rechereche;* everything springs from the soul. The painting has even humor. In one of the scenes the devil is represented as a cunning, jocular, greedy woman, an image that makes the onlooker laugh. On the walls of Humor there are legends, too (the Return of the Prodigal Son, with the scene of the feast and merry-making, and a hora danced by five dancers who ask the guests to come and join in the dance).

Humor Monastery played an important part in the history of the Romanian culture. As early as the 15th century at Humor there was a workshop where painters of miniatures and calligraphers worked; a famous miniature representing Stephen the Great has been preserved here.

ARBORE—A STRANGE VISION

Smaller than the other churches, Arbore has a dimly lit *pronaos*, a nave with large windows, and no cupola because it was not built by a prince, but by a boyar instead. Arbore has preserved eternal frescoes of unprecedented artistic beauty.

Unlike Voroneţ where blue predominates, at Arbore it is green which is uppermost. The green is in five shades, combined with red, blue, and yellow. Every shade is lit up differently, the far darker tonalities expressing a world of mysterious shadows and lights.

The most valuable painting is that on the western wall and on the buttresses. It consists of a succession of small scenes, like miniatures, unfolding on eight panels. The scenes are from Genesis and the lives of the saints. The drawing is delicate and lively, the personages are in motion, and the citadels and buildings are seen in perspective. The personages are lively and graceful, their faces glowing with delicate pink; their clothes are distinctly elegant. The female saints move with soft elastic steps like ballet dancers.

It is noteworthy that in the courtyard of Arbore church two heavy slabs of stone have been preserved since the period when the church was painted. In these, fifteen small holes were cut to serve as containers for the mixing of colors, thus providing the great number of shades used by Moldavian painters.

SUCEVIŢA—A POEM IN GREEN AND LIGHT

Surrounded by gentle mountain scenery, Suceviţa appears like a strong stone citadel, with massive towers, buttresses, and watch roads. The walls of Suceviţa date from the 16th century and enclose within them many legends and tales such as the one of the woman who for thirty years carried in her ox wagon the stone out of which the monastery was built. In memory of the woman who toiled for three decades, the head of a female is carved in black stone, half-concealed under the arch of a buttress. Here, too, another legend is connected with human sacrifice: the artisan who was painting it fell off the scaffolding while he was working on the western wall and died. The wall was left without any beautiful frescoes.

Suceviţa is a monument with a great number of images. It is depicted inside and outside with thousands of portraits and images. From top to bottom, the walls seem to be painted with drops of sky, sunshine, dew, and violet dusk with mother of pearl radiance, all against a green as intense as the bed of a sea or as green as a lawn after the rain.

The northern wall displays a monumental composition, "The Scale of Virtues," wonderfully well preserved, with scenes symbolizing the people's belief in the first judgment of souls after death.

On the southern wall there is again "Jesse's Tree"—the symbol of the continuity between the Old and the New Testament. It is painted against a dark blue background in an interweaving of medallions and delicate winding stones which grow from the body of Jesse, who is seen lying asleep, one hand under his head. Next, there is the frieze of scholars and philosophers of antiquity (Pythagoras, Sophocles, Plato, Aristotle, and Solon) gorgeously clad in Byzantine cloaks—Plato is carrying a small coffin with bones on his head, the symbol of meditation on man's life and death. And again there is the poem of Patriarch Serghei. The "Prayer to the Virgin" is depicted with numerous scenes and personages wearing oriental dress, horses in motion, and citadels and buildings in Italian style. The "Pocrov" (the veil) is another brilliant image representing the Virgin Mary as a Byzantine empress under a large red veil held by angels. Around the apse is the composition "Cinul" (Rank), a suite of all the heavenly and worldly hierarchies (seraphs, angels, prophets, apostles, bishops, and martyrs), all painted in sober colors in which the saturated green background is emphasized by the red of the clothes, the ochre of the faces, and the gold of the halos.

The paintings in Sucevița are of great religious importance and in keeping with the architecture of the church. The painted stories and the background in which they develop present a rare chromatic harmony of oriental brilliance, as in images from the *Arabian Nights*.

MOLDOVITA—A PARCHMENT IN BLUE

Moldovita could be an image in a travel guide marked with three stars, a picture in an art album, or a scene in a color film having won five Oscars. It is in fact a monastery nestling in the shade of the Rarau Massif, among fir forests and flowering clearings where springs well up from the earth.

The church of Moldovita Monastery is larger than the Voroneț or Humor monasteries; it was built in 1532 and painted in 1537. The outside walls are clad in frescoes.

From the eaves down to the base are hundreds of scenes and personages in panels. In the open porch there is the "Last Judgment," a scene less dramatic than the one at Voroneț, and on the southern facade are the "Prayer to the Virgin" and "Jesse's Tree," painted against a dark blue background.

One of the most valuable scenes at Moldovita (on the south wall) is the "Siege of Constantinople," a monumental composition. It seems the "Siege of Constantinople" has been painted only in Moldavia. This historical event was so deeply stamped on the memory of the people that even after one hundred years it was still alive in the people's minds. The Moldavian artist rendered a panoramic view of Constantinople as a citadel with numerous towers and with all the activity existing during such a siege. In the monastery there is still 16th-century furniture engraved and colored with folk art motifs, used in peasant notchings. The princely chair of Petru Rareș with a back six-and-one-half feet high is a syntheseis of Moldavia's 16th-century ornamental art.

There can also be seen the "Pomme d'Or" prize awarded to Bukovina.

PUTNA MONASTERY—THE GREAT CHURCH

This monastery is located in the town of Putna in the Suceava River valley. A rail line connects Putna with Radanti. Putna is but a short distance from the border with the Soviet Union and lies on the eastern slopes of the Carpathians.

The monastery was built by Stephen the Great during 1466–81. A fire destroyed it in 1484, but it was rebuilt only to suffer destruction in warfare during the 17th century. In the 1730's, an earthquake badly damaged it; however, it was restored by the architect Romstorfer in 1902.

Inside the monastery is the tomb of its founder, Stephen the Great, and his decendants dating to the time of Petru Rareş. The monastery was built with high walls for protection, on top of which are battlements. Several towers added to the defense of its walls. During the 19th century a number of buildings were constructed in the courtyard of the monastery. Visitors can see an excellent collection of old Romanian embroidery in the museum of the monastery.

CHAPTER 7

Danube River and Delta

Nearly 1,800 miles long, the Danube drains a basin covering 500,000 square miles, collecting the water of 120 tributaries along its course. Over 80,000,000 inhabitants live in its drainage basin in eight European countries. The Danube runs through Romanian territory for 666 miles, i.e., more than one-third of its total course. It is the second largest river in Europe (only the Volga in European Russia is longer). The Danube springs from the Black Forest in West Germany and flows into the Black Sea. An advantageous means of transport, the Danube has since earliest times been one of the most traveled waterways of the continent. The Danube has been called by many names: "Istros" in Egyptian legends and in the language of the Argonauts; "Phisos" by the Phoenicans; "Danare" by the Romans; "Danubius" in the language of the Scythians; "Rio-Divino" at the court of Charles V; and "Le Rio des Fleuves de l'Europe," according to Napoleon Bonaparte. The river has been sailed by Phoenician ships, Hellenic triremes, Roman galleys, Byzantine ships, Genoese caravels, Venetian galleons, Turkish boats (caiques), Cossack sheiks, tugboats and barges, and motor ships in recent times.

At the end of its journey is the Danube delta, a patch of land and waters eternally struggling against time. Information ages old describes the delta with much inconsistency. Herodotus of Halicarnassus ("the Father of History"), when referring to Darius's campaign against the Scythians in 514 B.C., stated that at its mouths the Danube separated into five arms. Eratosthenes, an astronomer, geographer, and philosopher of Alexandria, the Greek historian Polybius (275–125 B.C.), and other ancient authors described the features of the Danube delta somewhat similarly. Strabon of Pontus, a geographer and historian who lived at the beginning of the 1st century A.D., stated that the Istru had seven mouths, the largest being "the holy mouth" and that in front of these there is an island named Peuce. About the same time, Pliny the Elder, a Roman historian philologist, and man of letters, speaks of six arms of the delta, the island of Peuce, and several lakes, one of which, named Halmyris, was very large (probably Lake Razim). Finally, Claudius Ptolemaeus of Alexandria, an astronomer, mathematician, and geographer and a contemporary of the Dacian King Decebalus, spoke again of seven mouths of the river, including "the holy mouth." In the year 950 a document mentions "Selina," probably Sulina; in 1308 an anonymous chronicler speaks again of seven arms of the river; and in 1318, Pietro Visconte, probably a member of the family of the dukes of Milan, traveled in the delta and proclaimed that Sulina and Sfîntu Gheorghe were suitable places for mooring ships. The maps of the Middle Ages furnished only scant information, and some erroneously show the Danube flowing into the Marmara Sea. Others have it flowing into the Dardanelles or have it pouring its waters into the Black Sea. These same maps give it either one or two arms, or five or six, one of which wanders as far as Constanța. Finally in 1856, the English sea captain Spratt drew a map more to reality. Thus, we do not know how the Danube looked 2,500 years ago.

Every year it becomes about 131 feet longer. This figure might be smaller or larger depending on the year; but it represents the essence of this miraculous waterway and land in a permanent metamorphosis, perpetually changing its shape and dimensions, its aspect and contents. At the point of the "Delta," i.e., the

Danube River and Delta

letter of the Greek alphabet that gave it its name, the first separation of its arms takes place. The average discharge of the Danube is 4,820 cubic yards per second, which means that in two minutes there flows a quantity of water which could serve the needs for a whole day for the population of a city with 1.5 million inhabitants. Similarly, this mass of water carries, on the average, two tons of alluvial sediment per second, the raw material for the foundation of new land born from the water, which is among the youngest land of the European continent. About 502 square miles of the delta are inside Soviet territory.

TULCEA

The main gate to this unique land is the city of Tulcea (51,000 people), the chief town of the county by the same name. This town, built on seven hills, the same as Rome, is of almost the same age as that venerable city. Today, this former dusty oriental-like market town is continually developing as a sea and river port and as the center of the Romanian ocean fish industry. Tulcea is also an aluminum mining center, a builder of ships, and a tourist "gateway." Thousands of Romanian and foreign tourists pass this way, using all sorts of water transport means to reach other parts of the Danube delta.

Ovid, the Roman poet, banished to the remote town of Tomis (Constanța), wrote in the early years of the first century A.D.: "That old city is on the Danube or the Istru (it has strong walls and it is not easy to break into it). Aegyssus built it and it's also called Aegyssus. . . ." Of the old bulwark, little has remained. But the "bulwark" of the delta has been preserved intact.

Useful Addresses

Tulcea County Tourist Office, 2 Gării-Faleză St., phone: 915-14720; telex: 522200.

Tourism Agency, 2 Gării-Faleză St.; phone: 915-11607.

Danube Delta Musuem, 32 Progresului St. (exhibits concerning the past history of Dobrudja and the delta; tools used in fishing, navigation, and the reaping of reed; a diorama; and aquarium).

Independence Monument and Archeological Park with vestiges of the ancient Aegyssus (6th–7th centuries B.C.), Colnicul Horei (The "Hora" Hillock).

Railway Station, on the Promenade.

River Landing Stage (Navrom), on the Promenade.
Tarom, Gării St., block of flats (ground floor); phone: 915-11227.
Peco Filling Station, Şoseaua Babadagului.
Car Service, Şoseaua Babadagului, Bariera Mahmudiei.

Climate

In the delta the climate is continental, favorably influenced by the proximity of the sea and the abundance of inland waters. The annual average temperature is 52° F. The average temperature (at 1 P.M.) in July is 75° F; in September, 70° F. The delta has scant rainfall (the annual average—13.8 inches—is normal to the area). The humidity of the air in summer (at 2 P.M.) is 60 percent inland and 70 percent in the littoral area. In summer a gentle wind blows across the delta.

Hydrographic Network

The Danube delta lies at 45° N. latitude and 29° E. longitude. Its surface consists of 2,178 square miles, 1,729 square miles of which are Romanian territory. It is a comparatively flat area of which 80 to 90 percent is covered by water permanently or temporarily. Its shape looks like a triangle with both base and height apprpoximately 49.6 miles long. The Danube carries annually on an average 50 million tons of alluvial deposits, eight times more than the Tiber and twenty times more than the Rhine. Its annual discharge is 3,825–6,885 cubic yards per second. The temperature of the water (at 1 P.M.) in June was 68° F; in July and August, 71.6° F; in September, 64.4° F. The main water courses in the delta are four arms, three of which flow into the sea.

Chilia, the northern arm and the most active one, has a microdelta of its own (there exist about 40 mouths in the vicinity of the sea). Its length measures 65 miles to Periprava (compared to 1830 this delta has grown by 3.7 miles); its widest breadth is 3,281 feet; its greatest depth is 118 feet. It carries more than 62 percent of the total of all the waters of the Danube. Navigation is mainly of local interest.

Tulcea, an arm between Chilia and Sfîntu Gheorghe, has on its right bank the town of Tulcea, capital of Tulcea county. Its length is 11.8 miles; its maximum width is 984 feet; and its maximum depth is 112 feet. The Tulcea carries about 38 percent of the waters of the Danube and is the main waterway of that river.

Sulina, the shortest, straightest, and the best navigational arm through which the Danube flows into the sea is 44 miles in length and has a maximum breadth of 820 feet. Used as a maritime traffic canal, it is maintained at a depth of 24 feet. Ships of 7,000 tons can sail through it.

Sfîntu Gheorghe is the oldest arm through which the Danube flows into the sea. Its length is 70 miles (compared to 1857 it has grown by 1.34 miles); its maximum width is 1,804 feet, and its maximum depth is 85 feet. It carries 20 percent of the waters of the river, and navigation on it is mainly of local interest.

Secondary Hydrographic Network of the Danube delta broadly consists of four components: *sahale* (former arms of the Danube now clogging up); brooks (very small *sahale*); channels (straightened and dredged *sahale*); and *peribonias* (splits in the littoral mouths through which exchanges of water are effected).

To these are added formations of simple depressions and of lacustrian nature: lakes (which never dry up; their depth varies between 1.6–9.8 feet); estuaries (at the mouths of small rivers); lagoons (former maritime gulfs); marshes (waters of small depth, which can dry up); *japse* (small depressions which fill with water only when there are high floods); and lakes in depressions, such as Pardina, Sontea, Fortuna, Dranov, Matiţa, and Obretin.

The delta hydrographic network also includes the offshore bar, a marine area situated along the shore, 6.2–9.3 miles wide, with a depth less than 82 feet. It is influenced by the waters flowing into the sea, sometimes as far as 18.6 miles offshore.

The Fauna

The fauna of the delta are a vast mosaic of species, unparalleled on the European continent and consist of specimens unique in the world. This is due to the very nature of this extraordinary laboratory, which offers ideal conditions for the life and procreation of its species.

Birds

The ornithofauna of the Danube delta include some of the most unique in the world, numbering more than 250 species, 70 of which are extra-European. In the perimeter of the delta you can see birds from the north of Europe and Asia, from the southern areas of the globe, Africa, Iran, and India. It is not surprising if we remember that the Danube delta is situated at parallel 45° N. latitude, which is half the distance between the Equator and the North Pole, thus representing a natural halting place for migratory birds. Five great air migratory routes concentrate on the Danube delta and separate afterwards: the Pontic (from the plains north of the Black Sea), the Sarmatian (from the north of Europe); the littoral (from the area of Caucasus); the east Elbic (from the area of central Europe); and the Carpathian (from the north of Europe, across the Carpathian Mountains).

A general survey of the ornithological fauna of the delta led to the establishment of five main types: Mediterranean (herons, eastern flossy ibis, small cormorants, golden eagles, black-winged eagles, "Ciocintorses"—avocets, shelldrakes, pelicans); European (songsters—reed nightingales, buntings, "Boicusi," sea swallows, seagulls, fishing eagles, and sea eagles); Siberian (singing swans, plovers, polar grebes, half snipes, and cranes); Mongolian (golden eagles and saker falcons); and Chinese (egrets, mute swans, large cormorants, and Mandarin ducks).

Among the enormous number of birds, there are some species which have been the object of special attention because of the scarcity of the specimens or for the special way in which they behave or for their beauty. About 2,000 pairs of white pelicans find refuge in the protection of the delta reserves.

The birds of the delta may be divided into two groups: "white monuments"—those having shining white feathers (the roseate pelican, the Dalmatian pelican, the spoonbill, the great white egret, the small egret, the mute swan, and the singing swan); and the "polychrome monuments"—showing feathering which combines white and black with green, yellow, rust, brown, and blue (the black-winged marshbird [similar to a stork] the avocet, the shelldrake, ruby shelldrake, and the sea eagle).

Fish

The Danube delta is also important for the amount and quality of its fish: 110 species are known, 36 of which belong to the delta proper. The delta accounts for 50 percent of the fresh-water fish production of Romania.

In the arms through which the Danube flows into the sea, where the course is more rapid, there are usually sterlets, large beaks, great sturgeon, common sturgeon, sevruga, mackerel, carp, sheat Fish, perch, pike, barble, rapacious carp, and asprus. In the calmer waters of the multitude of lakes between the arms of the river are found crucian, perch, bream, pike, and carp while the saltwater-fish milieu of the Razim–Sinoe lagoonlike system consists of fish ranging from perch and pike to grey mullet and flounder depending on the salinity of the water. The marine area in front of the delta shelters mostly sturgeon and common sturgeon and Danube mackerel.

Some of these species of fish are found in other waters in Romania but specific to the delta are the valuable sturgeon (the great sturgeon, the common sturgeon, the sevruga, and red sterlet) which are full of the famous black roe (caviar); the great mullet, of which there exist four species of the Mugil type; and the Danube mackerel.

In the Danube delta fishing is done all the year round except for a period of sixty days when the fish deposit the roe. Annually, specialists have fixed the date of the respective period as from April 1. In an effort to protect the faunistic species, hunting is forbidden in the Danube delta. Information on the laws and the best fishing areas can be obtained at the County Association of Amateur Fishermen and Hunters, Tulcea, O. 10 Isaccea St.; phone: 915-11404. Fishing in the region of fish farms is forbidden.

Mammals

A large variety of mammals live in all the higher areas not reached by the waters. Some of them are otter, mink, muskrat, hare, wild boar, fox, wolf, polecat, and wild cat. Also found are tortoises, the adders, and the colonies of snakes on the islands of Lake Razim.

The Flora

The vegetation of the delta is extremely varied and consequently difficult to describe. Briefly it can be divided into floating plants (their roots in water and their leaves above the surface); submerged plants (wholly under water); emergent (with roots in mud and leaves above the surface); riparian (growing on the banks of the water); and the vegetation of the sand banks and that of the salt marshes.

A few examples of the types of vegetation are:

Plants with floating leaves: white water lilly, yellow water lily, frog bit, marsh thistle, epi d'eau.

Riverine and floating reed islets: about 80 percent of local reed is Phragmites genus and 20 percent is mace reed, water fern, sorrel, forget-me-nots, brook mint, and water hemlock. Reeds cover over half of the delta area.

Plants growing on land: white willows, poplars, alder, and ash, representing the forests on the Letea and Caraorman sandbanks.

Forests

The whole surface of the land of the delta is rich in vegetation, especially willows. Recently, poplars have become present everywhere. Of special interest are, however, the forests of the Danube delta.

Letea forest (1,750 acres) is situated 4.4 miles south of the locality of Periprava (on Chilia Arm) and stretching along Letea sandbank as far as the village by the same name. It is characterized by a development in stripes (called *hasmacuri*) and by an abundance of creeping plants, some of which are Mediterranean in origin and form massive garlands, and lianas between the trees of the forest—grey oak trees (some more than 150 years old and more than 82 feet high), "Giinita," elms, alder, white and black poplars, willows, and fluffy ash (a botanical rarity). In general, no area appears as an equatorial forest. White-tailed eagles watch from the tops of trees while snakes and adders can be seen hiding among the leaves covering the ground.

Caraorman forest (1,000 acres) is situated west of the sandbank by the same name between the Sfîntu Gheorghe and Sulina arms. Unlike Letea, the trees here develop in clusters. It has almost the same flora and fauna as Letea forest.

Sandbanks

Sandbanks form one of the main characteristics of the configuration of the delta. They are constituted of alluviums deposited in the course of time either by the water of the river (river sandbanks) or by the water of the sea (maritime sandbanks), or they represent fragments of plain left between the waters; they all lend a special character to the landscape and facilitate the growth of specific vegetation.

Letea is the largest maritime sandbank in the delta (12 miles long, 9.3 miles in width) and comprises 42,500 acres. Its highest elevation is about 43 feet. The area is shaped like an isosceles triangle, with its point at Periprava and its base in the proximity of Sulina Arm. The soil consists of sand gathered in dunes which sometimes are more than 10 feet high. More than 1,800 species of insects are found there, among which is one species of night butterfly which has disappeared from the rest of Europe.

CARAORMAN is a maritime sandbank situated south of the Sulina Arm. It is also shaped like an isosceles triangle with its point at Crisan and its base near Sfîntu Gheorghe Arm (11 miles long, 5 miles in width, totaling 17,500 acres). The highest elevation here is 264 feet. The sandy soil is undulated in endless sanddunes which can attain a height of 23 feet, creating the image of a real desert. In the western part of the sandbank grows the Caraorman forest.

Sărăturile (salt sandbank) is a maritime sandbank situated north of the village of Sfîntu Gheorghe (5.6 miles in length, 6.2 miles in width, covering 18,500 acres). Its highest elevation is 13 feet. According to some authors, it's the former Peuce Island mentioned by the ancient geographer Strabon. The soil is sandy, with dunes over 6 feet high and a poor vegetation consisting of halophyte plants (adapted to salt marshes) and xerophites (adapted to drought). When the sand is burning hot it can cause the phenomenon known as a mirage.

Chilia is a sandbank situated north of the locality by the same name (9.3 miles long, 3.1 miles broad, and totals 13,950 acres).

Ştipoc is a remnant of predeltaic land formed of river alluviums and is an extensive sandbank located between pardina (Chilia Arm) and the south of the Chilia sandbank. It is 18.6 miles long, about 1.5 miles in width, and consists of 8,750 acres. The highest elevation here is about 10 feet.

Crasnicol is a maritime sandbank situated south of the locality of Sfîntu Gheorghe. It is 11 miles long, set amidst numerous larger sandbanks, and covers approximately 8,750 acres. In this marshy area the land can appear or disappear overnight. It is inhabited by migratory birds, or birds of passage.

Natural Reserves

The limits of natural reserves were determined some twenty years ago, and the main reserves and the secondary ones in the Danube delta were set aside to preserve the natural evolution process, i.e., the protection of the specific fauna and the flora. In this way scientific research is ensured the detailed observation of the existing species and subspecies and the often puzzling manifestations of certain specimens of the fauna and flora. The total surface of the reserves amounts to about 100,000 acres, divided into three large permanent units and a few temporary small ones.

Roşca-Buhaiova-Merhei-Hrecişca-Letea are the landmarks of the perimeter of the 38,500 acres of this reserve. It is located in the Matita depression between the Letea and Chilia sandbanks, north of the large "M" on the Sulina Arm. The nucleus of the reserve consists of Lakes Roşca, Argintiu, and Buhaiova; a combination of lakes, marshes with reed, and floating reed plots shelters large colonies of pelicans, egrets, yellow herons, flossy ibises, and spoon bills.

Sfîntu Gheorghe-Perişor-Zătoane is a reserve extending south of the locality of Sfîntu Gheorghe on 36,500 acres that has as its eastern limit the sea littoral. It is a succession of sandbanks with isolated lakes, marshy areas, river waters and sheets of saltish water, sandy ponds, and reeds, all crossed by parallel sanddunes. The nucleus of the reserve consists of Lakes Zătonul Mare and Zătonul Mic, which are halting and hatching places for the silent swans, white, red, and yellow herons, and cormorants and generally mixed colonies in which pelicans are present.

Periteaşca-Leahova-Gura Portiţei reserve continues toward the south of the above-mentioned protected area and amounts to almost 9,750 acres. The reserve is conspicuous for its sandbanks, some dry and others bathed by the water of the sea or of Lake Razim, offering favorable conditions for shore birds used to salt water and birds of passage.

Its tourist character is "par excellence," but it is also of scientific interest too. The Danube delta has become an object of observation by numerous specialists at home and abroad. In each of the three areas mentioned, a reduced protection surface is reserved to specialists where fishing and other activities are highly regulated.

Entrance to the scientific reserves in the Danube delta is allowed only with a pass issued by the Academy of the Socialist Republic of Romania—the Commission for the Protection of the Monuments of Nature—and only after the date of June 15.

Hunting, the collecting of biological material, breaking the quietness of the fauna, the throwing about of scraps of paper and other wrappings, the use of portable radio sets, camping, and the lighting of fires are forbidden in the reserves. Entrance is allowed only to those reserves lying along the channels and canals which are specially authorized for admission.

Special measures have been taken for the protection of the

ornithofauna to ensure the nestling and to protect the migration routes and the nestling and migration areas which have been established. Certain favorite traditional points of the migration areas have been established: Gorgova, Iigani, Crişan (on Sulina Arm), Independenţa, Uzlina, Plopul (on Sfîntu Gheorghe Arm), the Sacalin Island lakes, Dranov, Goloviţa, the islands of Popina and Lupilor, and Gura Portiţei—all south of the locality of Sfîntu Gheorghe. Considered temporary reserves, they occupy approximately 20,000 acres.

Law No. 9.1973 regarding the protection of the environment states that terrestrial and aquatic fauna constitute one of the country's riches due to the part they play in maintaining the ecological equilibrium and in meeting the necessities of the nation's economy. For the purpose of protecting the fauna, it is forbidden to:

(a) naturalize or take captive the wild fauna without an authorization issued by the state;
(b) to commercialize the wild fauna;
(c) to introduce any foreign species of fauna into the wild nature of the country without the advice of the state.

Within the reserves, it is forbidden to carry on any activity which might lead to the degradation or modification of the scenery, of the structure of the fauna and flora, or of the ecological equilibrium, except in cases when the law should authorize this kind of activity. Furthermore, the Academy of the Socialist Republic of Romania establishes specific rules regarding the preservation, upkeep, and scientific exploring and entering reserves.

The infringement of the provisions of the law regarding the protection of the environment entails disciplinary, material, civil, or penal responsibility and might be considered an offense.

Navigation in the Danube delta with private motorboats is forbidden by law. Use of such craft is allowed only on the Danube.

What to See

Aghghiol is a village 11 miles southeast of Tulcea, a health and climatic resort of local interest (saltwater and mud in a neighboring lake); a paleontological reserve (fossils and ammonites, fauna of the Triassic Age); and the place where a princely tomb of the 4th century B.C. was discovered with its particularly rich inventory.

BABADAG is a town situated 23 miles south of Tulcea, on the shore of a lake, at the foot of forests by the same name. Its oriental origin can be translated as "the Father of the Mountain." The locality possesses the elements of a climatic resort and is considered "Dobrudja's Sinaia." It has an art musuem, a museum house of oriental character, a mosque (16th-17th century), and the Kalaigi drinking fountain (19th century). On the shore of the lake are the vestiges of a settlement dating from the Iron Age over which traces of life in La Tène (4th century B.C.) were superimposed over those of the Roman-Byzantine epoch (6th century A.D.). Around June 15 there is a great picnic in the lime tree forest in the proximity. The town has a camping ground—Doi Iepuraşi—a Peco filling station, and auto service.

Beştepe is a village situated 12 miles southeast of Tulcea on the road to Independenta at the foot of five hillocks—which explains its name of oriental resonance. Roman vestiges and the remains of an earthen walled city can be seen.

Bisericuţa, an island on Lake Razim, is located approximately 6.5 miles east of Unirea. Remains of settlements dating from the Bronze Age and Byzantine times can be seen.

Caraorman is a village situated on the sandbank of the same name—"the black forest" south of the locality of Crişan (Sulina Arm). Around it are sanddunes nearly four feet high and an oak tree forest.

Chilia Veche is a village situated 50 miles northeast of Tulcea on Chilia Arm. It was one of the earliest deltaic human settlements and probably the Achillea of Greek antiquity, the Licostomo (two wolf's mouth) as known by the Genoese, and Eskil-Kalé during the Turkish domination. In the 15th century it was one of the main Moldavian towns. In 1479 Prince Stephen the Great rebuilt the walled city at Chiliá (today in the Soviet Union) utilizing 800 bricklayers and 17,000 workers. It is the most striking example of the degree of development of the technique of construction reached in Moldavia during the reign of the great prince. At that time, Chilia Veche was situated about 3 miles from the seashore; at present, it is situated 25 miles from the sea. Its monumental church, with steeples more than 90 feet high, is visible from some distance. There is also a fisheries station. The locality, presently undergoing development, is becoming one of the main industrial-agrarian localities of the Danube delta.

CRIŞAN, a village situated on the banks of Sulina Canal, is the main starting point for a trip both toward the north (Matiţa, Letea) and toward the south (Caraorman, Litcov, Roşu-Roşulet). A monument here commemorates inauguration of the Sulina Canal (1859). It has a fisheries station, hotel, and camping.

DENISTEPE (Dealul Mare) lies north of the town of Babadag (876 feet in elevation), which has a name of oriental influence—"the hillock of the seas"—in translation. A legend has it that the Argonauts who had set out in search of the Golden Fleece from Colchis moored their ship here by tying it to the iron ring fixed at the top of nearby rocks. Scientists from Grusia (USSR) investigated the tale of the Golden Fleece and discovered a method utilized in antiquity by the inhabitants of Colchis in order to obtain gold from the rivers of the Caucasus with the aid of a ram's hide tanned in a special manner.

Dranov is a lake and an important canal connecting the Sfîntu Gheorghe Arm and the Razim lagoon complex. Its fisheries station and a chalet are at the southern mouth of the canal.

Dunavaţu (de Jos and de Sus) (Lower and Higher) is situated 4.5 miles to the southeast of the village of Independenţa. Its orgin dates from an ancient settlement probably named Ad Stoma or Halmyris, the name of Lake Razim in antiquity. It is on an important connecting canal with the southern lagoon system, at the confluence of which there is a fisheries station and a chalet.

Enisala is a village situated 5 miles east of Babadag. In ancient times it was a walled city by the same name, later a Roman military camp, then a Genoese and Turkish fortification, ruled over a time (14th century) by Mircea cel Bătin (Mircea the Old), ruling Prince of Wallachia. It is an important station for the artifical breeding of fish.

Gura Portiţei connects the waters of the Razim-Goloviţa complex with the sea about 7 miles from Unirea. It has been marked on European maps since 1710. There is a fisheries station and a tourist center. Over a mile to the south is a chalet on the Grindul Lupilor (the Wolves Sandbank).

Independenţa (former Murighiol), a village situated 25 miles southeast of Tulcea, sits in the great bend made by Sfîntu Gheorghe Arm. A health resort of local interest, it is also named Morughiol, i.e., "the violet lake," because of the color of the lake, which has therapeutic properties. Nearby salt marshes, a natural reserve, are the favorite nesting place of the "wader." One can reach Sfîntu Gheorghe Arm by boat. In the vicinity are the remains of a Genoese fortification. A camping ground is available.

Letea is a village on the sandbank by the same name, south of the village of Periprava (Chilia Arm). In the proximity is the Letea forest.

Mahmudia, a village situated 22 miles east of Tulcea on the road to Independenţa, is a river port. Vestiges of a Roman-Byzantine fortress named Salsovia are seen. The village is now the chief town of a bishopric. It is claimed that this is the place where Licinnius was killed by order of Constantine the Great, with whom he shared the throne of Byzantium in A.D. 325. There is a hotel in the village.

Malicu is a village on the Sulina Arm of the Danube. It has a museum and a hotel. Maliuc is an important starting point for trips to Lakes Fortuna and Păpădia, and Şontea Brook. It has a campground.

Mile 23 is a typical fishing settlement located in the first loop of the "Great M" (on the Old Danube). It has a fisheries station and is a locality of tourist interest for trips to Lakes Leghianca, Matiţa, and Roşca, and to the sandbanks of Stipoc and Chilia, which are about 7.5 miles from the village of Crişan.

Nufăru, a village 6 miles southeast of Tulcea, is situated on the right bank of the Sfîntu Gheorghe Arm. It was mentioned in the 10th century under the name of Prislava. The remains of some old fortifications are visible, and in the past there was likely a bridge here over the Sfîntu Gheorghe Arm.

Periprava is a village situated 65 miles northeast of Tulcea, in the proximity of the third and last inland delta of Chilia Arm. A typical fishing settlement of tourist interest, it is a starting point for trips towards the Letea sandbank and forest, Lakes Merhei and Matiţa, the Lopatna Canal, as well as Mile 23 village.

Popina is an island in the northern part of Lake Razim which was also known as Pochina on 19th-century maps. Its surface covers 225 acres; and its height, a record for the whole Danube delta, is 154 feet in elevation. It is a natural microreserve—a place where red winter ducks and shore swallows like to nestle.

Sfîntu Gheorghe, a village situated at the spot where the arm of the Danube by the same name flows into the sea, lies 70 miles southeast of Tulcea. Mentioned in records as early as 1318, the

Danube River and Delta

settlement was later utilized as a base by the Ottoman fleet. It is an important locality of tourist interest, with its a typical deltaic architecture. It possesses a fisheries station for the processing of black caviar, a new lighthouse (187 feet high), and an old lighthouse (1856). It has the most extensive sea beach on the littoral. In its proximity is the Sărăturile sandbank and Sacalin Island (formed in 1897), which is a microdelta of Sfîntu Gheorghe Arm.

Sulina, the second town of the delta, is an important river and sea port situated at the spot where the river arm by the same name flows into the sea. The town has a shipyard, light manufacturing, and a food industry. Around 950 it was a Byzantine port, then a Genoese port in 1318, and later a naval base for the Ottomans. Early in the 20th century it became a free port, the Porto Franco described at length in the novel *Europolis* by the Romanian writer Jean Bart (Eugeniu Botez). An old lighthouse of typical deltaic architecture (dating from the 19th century) stands in the middle of the town. The town has a hotel and an extensive maritime beach.

Unirea (former Jurilovca), a village on the shore of Lake Golovița, is a typical fishing village founded in the 18th century. Its architecture, costumes, and customs are of Lipovan tradition. A museum and a hotel cater to tourists. From the port of the fisheries station, motorboats start at regular hours for the tourist center of Portița. At Dolojman Cape are the remains of a Greek town, probably Argamum (Orgame), the earliest ancient settlement on the territory of Romania mentioned in the literature of the time of Hecateus of Milletus (5th-6th century B.C.).

Uzlina, a village 40 miles southeast of Tulcea, is one of the few fishing settlements on the left bank of Sfîntu Gheorghe Arm. A nature reserve, it is home to numerous birds that come to build their nests here.

Useful Information

Ways of Access

DFR (Romanian Railways): fast and slow trains, Bucharest-Medgidia-Tulcea (5–8 hour journey); slow trains, Constanța-Tulcea (4 hours).

ITA (Motor Transport Company): regular buses, Constanța-Tulcea, Galați-Tulcea (Danube crossing by ferryboat), Brăila-Tulcea (Danube crossing by ferryboat).

Tarom (Romanian Air Transport): regular flights, Bucharest-Tulcea (45 minutes).

Navrom (Romanian Water Transport): Brăila-Galaţi-Tulcea-Sulina (8 hours); Tulcea-Sulina (3 hours); Tulcea-Chilia Veche-Periprava (5 hours); Tulcea-Sfîntu Gheorghe (6 hours); Crişan-Mile 23 (1 hour). Special Rapid Craft: Brăila-Galaţi-Tulcea-Sulina (4 hours); Tulcea-Sulina (1½ hours); Tulcea-Sfîntu Gheorghe (2 hours).

Accidental delays, modifications of the timetable, or canceling of certain trips do not entitle travelers to refunds.

Excerpt from the Tariff for Travelers' Transport (NAVROM)

The transport of travelers is effected in two classes, at the traveler's choice and within the limits of available seats. Craft with a single class of travelers is the fastest, and only first class tickets are valid plus extra payment for speed and a reserved seat. All classes of tickets entitle the traveler to carry with him on board the craft 30 kg. of personal luggage.

Insuring Travelers

The tariffs for travelers' transport include legal insurance for the value of the ticket, while the State Insurance Administration (ADAS) insures travelers against the risks of the journey.

Hotels

Tulcea: *Delta* (first class), 2 Garii-Faleza St., phone 915-14728, can accommodate 234 persons in double rooms. It has a restaurant, brasserie, and snack bar. *Egreta* (first class), 1 Pacii St., phone 915-17109-4-5, single and double rooms. It can accommodate 218 and has a restaurant; it also has a self-service unit.

Malicu: *Salcia* (second class) can accommodate 52 in double rooms; restaurant.

Crişan: *Lebăda* (first class) can accommodate 148 in double rooms; restaurant.

Sulina: *Sulina* (first class) can accommodate 150 in single and double rooms; restaurant and bar. *Farul* (third class) can accommodate 40 in two or three bedded rooms; restaurant.

Unirea: *Albatros* (second class) can accommodate 12 in double rooms; restaurant.

Danube River and Delta

Mahmudia: *Plaur* (first class) can accommodate 34 in double rooms; restaurant.

Baia: A hotel (second class) can accommodate 18 in two or three bedded rooms; a restaurant.

Camping Grounds

Independenţa, 230 places; restaurant.
Gura Portiţei, 175 places; restaurant; transport by motorboat from Unirea.
Doi Iepuraşi, 28 places; restaurant.
Pescarul-Crişan, 200 places; restaurant.

Organized Excursions

The geography of the deltaic area—its network of water with frequent modifications of direction and depth, the generally long distances to cover between the various sightseeing spots, the protection of the enclosures declared to be natural reserves—has led to the organizing of a number of types of excursions able to offer visitors genuine images of the Danube delta. This is a sparsely populated area offering limited tourist facilities.

Itineraries

Taking into account the duration of the excursions and the conditions of some of the channels and canals, the itineraries generally follow a few of the most interesting waterways:

Tulcea—Sfîntu Gheorghe Arm—-Canal Ivancea—-Lakes Roşu-Roşulet—Sulina—Crişan—Lake Matita—Lopatna Canal—Mile 23—Şontea Canal—Lake Fortuna—Maliuc—Tulcea.

Tulcea—Litcov Channel (one of the longest in the delta)—Lakes Roşu—Roşulet—Sulina—Tulcea.

Tulcea—Sfîntu Gheorghe Arm (as far as 33.5 miles)—Dunavat Channel—Lake Razim—Tulcea.

Tulcea—Sfîntu Gheorghe Arm (as far as 28 miles)—Dranov Channel—Lake Razim—Tulcea.

Excursions Organized by:

Carpati-Bucureşti National Tourist Office, 7 Magheru Blvd.; phone: 90-145160; telex: 112700 Carpat R.

Tourism Central Office ONT Litoral; Tourist Services Agency-

București Hotel in Mamaia; phone: 918-31152; telex: 14266 Romlitoral

Oficiul Județean de Turism—Tulcea, Gării-Faleză St.; phone: 915-11607; telex: 52220.

The excursions in the delta take one or more days. They offer attractive tourist and special programs which include stopovers for taking pictures and filming the flora and fauna of the delta, campfires with specially baked carp, tasting of various wines, rowing boats, amateur fishing. Excursions are made by fast motorboats, slower motorboats, hydrofoils, and river ferryboats.

Depending on the water level, the agency organizing the excursions may partially modify the itinerary and in special cases cancel an excursion.

Practical Advice

Do not forget to pack: rubber-top boots, a waterproof hat and coat; warm clothes and blanket (in autumn); some cloth and gauze for canopy; torch; binoculars; penknife; small medical pouch; light fork, knife, and spoon; and food such as garlic, pepper, vinegar, sugar, biscuits, tea, jam, mineral water.

Do not try to spend the night in the open, particularly in the months of May, June, and July when the mosquitoes are in full activity; if you haven't a tent, use a canopy.

Never drink Danube water, except in an extreme case, after having decanted and boiled it.

Do not go sailing on brooks and channels without someone who knows these places well (a guide).

CHAPTER 8

Health Resorts, Spas, Treatments

Romanian spas and health resorts, mineral springs, and mud baths are widely renowned for their therapeutic effects on a wide variety of ailments. The Romans knew and used some of these during their occupation of the country. In modern times the country's richness in mineral springs, therapeutical muds, *mofettes* (natural emanations of carbon dioxide), and a number of drugs and treatments developed there have attracted many foreigners in the hope of alleviating or curing their aches and pains, diseases, allergies, skin infections, and other disorders. Many geriatric and other patients prize the treatments they have received in Romania's spas, resorts, and clinics. Some of the drugs and treatments do not have the stamp of approval of U.S. health authorities; nevertheless, Romania continues to attract many foreign patients, especially the elderly. More will be said of some of the controversial drugs and medications available in Romania later in this chapter.

Romania has more than 160 spas and health resorts spread throughout the country in geographical areas with varied climates and altitudes. In a few geographical areas there are many mineral springs with varied degrees of chemical composition which make possible the simultaneous treatment of diseases and secondary ailments. Many of the spas and resorts are noted for their beautiful natural surroundings, comfortable accommodations, entertainment facilities, and high standard of medical services. Some of the more popular resorts and spas are:

BĂILE FELIX

This spa is located in northwest Romania in Bihor County at the foot of the Craiu Hills. It lies five miles southeast of the city of Oradea in the Simleu valley near Băile 1 Mai at an altitude of 459 feet. Surrounding the spa is a forested hilly area. By auto it is approximately 370 miles from Bucharest. From Oradea airport take trams No. 4 and 5, plus bus. It can also be reached by train from Oradea.

The Felix spa thermal waters were discovered 1,000 years ago, but the resort was not developed until 1885. Most of its developments and improvements have been made since World War II. Its location accounts for its microclimate which is mild with small temperature variations. The climate is conducive to year-round treatment. The annual average temperature is 50° F (January and August means are 34° F and 68° F, respectively). Precipitation is light in the area, and winds are low in speed. The resort is modern looking and contains both outdoor and indoor pools.

Cure indications for the resort include those for: inflammatory rheumatic diseases; degenerative rheumatic diseases; abarticular rheumatic diseases, posttraumatic affections; affections of the central and peripheral nervous system; and metabolic, nutritional, endocrine, and gynecological diseases.

The natural cure factors of the resort include thermal-mineral waters that are bicarbonated, rich in sodium, sulphate, calcium, silicum, and slightly radioactive. The temperature of the waters

Health Resorts, Spas, Treatments

ranges between 68° and 118° F. The thermal waters have a very rich flow (30,000 m^3/daily). Muds mixed with peat are heated with thermal water and applied in the form of hot wrappings. The stable, mild climate favors rehabilitation treatments.

Cure facilities and treatment include: hot mineral water baths in tubs and pools, hot mud wrappings, kinetotherapy in pools with mineral-thermal water, vertebral traction, electro- and hydrotherapy, paraffin wrappings, gynecological therapy, rehabilitation and medical gymnastics, indoor and outdoor pools with thermal-mineral water, laboratories for clinical explorations and check-ups of patients, a radiology section, and consulting rooms.

Hotels

Belvedere (deluxe B), 500 beds in double rooms; swimming pool, dollar shop, currency exchange. Phone: 992-61445 or 61051.

Poienita (first-class A), 304 beds in double rooms; swimming pool, dollar shop, day bar. Phone: 992-61551.

Somes (first-class A), 344 beds in double rooms; bar, dollar shop, confectioner's, bowling, billiards. Phone: 992-61248.

Felix (first-class A), 291 beds in double rooms; day bar, dollar shop. Phone: 992-61545.

Unirea (first-class A), 304 beds in single and double rooms; bar, restaurant-terrace, dollar shop. Phone: 992-61124 or 61125.

Termal (first-class A), 300 beds in double rooms; day bar, dollar shop, indoor pool. Phone: 992-61214 or 61222.

Lotus (first-class A), 400 beds in double rooms; day bar, disco room, cinema hall, dollar shop. Phone: 992-61361.

Nufărul (first-class C), 150 beds in double rooms; dollar shop, TV. Phone: 922-61142.

Tourist Agency Scheduled Trips (phone: 992-61475)

Tour of Oradea—historical and architectural monuments, museums.

Evening in Oradea—Romanian dishes, wine tasting, folk program, gifts.

Beiuş town—old cultural center of Transylvania, Rieni (wooden church).

Bears' cave at Chiscau—rich in stalactites and stalagmites.

Stina de Vale (health resort)—departure point for hiking in the Apuseni Mountains, winter sports.

Maramureş—one of Romania's major ethnographic and folkloric centers—famous for the wood-carving craft and old Romanian traditions.

Gepiş—in the woods, trout-fishing.

BĂILE HERCULANE

This spa is located in the Southern Carpathians in the southwest part of Romania on the Cerna River. It lies in Caraş-Severin County about 13 miles north of the Danube River. Herculane spa stretches down to the foot of the Domogled Massif (3,609 feet in elevation), a nature reserve well known for the beauty and rarity of its floristic species. The spa itself lies at 524 feet in elevation and enjoys a mild climate. It has an annual average temperature of 49° F, with an average of 16° F in January and of 73° F in July. The thick forest skirting the spa keeps strong winds out. Winters are mild with little snow; summers are cool; spring is short and arrives early; autumn is long lasting. There is frequent sunshine from March through late October. Extreme air pressure readings are registered in October-November and July-August. The spa is about 242 miles by road from Bucharest.

The spa is one of the best-known resorts in Romania and flourished at the time of Roman occupation. The Romans built public baths, temples, and statues in the area. The most famous statue is one dedicated to Hercules, hence the origin of the name of the resort.

Cure indications for the resort include those for: diseases of the locomotor apparatus (chronic degenerative and inflammatory rheumatism); the peripheral nervous system; posttraumatic locomotor sequelae; myosities; and tendonities. Other cure indications include those for: chronic gynecological problems, chronic infections of the upper respiratory tract, digestive disorders, chemical poisoning, diabetes mellitus, obesity, and eye diseases. The spa is highly recommended for treating rheumatic afflictions.

The thermal-mineral waters of the spa range from 105° F to 140° F. The waters spring from deep in the ground; due to their great heat and rich mineral content, they stimulate physiological activity and are very effective therapeutically. The waters are rich in sulphate, calcium, and magnesium and have a positive effect on the metabolism.

Cure facilities and treatment include: electrotherapy—infrared

Health Resorts, Spas, Treatments

rays, ultraviolet rays, ultra-sounds; hydrotherapy—air-bubble baths, Turkish baths, galvanofaradic baths, and several types of douche-massages; kinetotherapy—medical gymnastics, electrokinetotherapy, therapeutic thermal pools, outdoor thermal water swimming, mineral waters, saunas.

Băile Herculane has facilities for radiology, stomatology, and a laboratory for clinical tests. Acupuncture is also applied at the spa, and there is a section of medical rehabilitation. A branch of the Bucharest-based National Institute of Gerontology and Geriatrics offers year-round treatments with Romanian products: Gerovital and Aslavital. There is original Romanian drug therapy with Boicil Forte and Pell-Amar. Medicinal herbs are also used in treatments.

Hotels
Roman (first-class B), 301 beds in single and double rooms and suites; inside pool, sauna, bowling, billiards, library, music hall. Phone: 965-60390.

Hercules (first-class B), 500 beds in single and double rooms and suites; day bar, solarium, dollar shop, dance band. Phone: 965-60030.

Minerva (first-class B), 400 beds in single and double rooms and suites; day bar, disco, indoor pool, sauna, dollar shop. Phone: 965-60767-8-9.

Diana (first-class B), 400 beds in single and double rooms and suites; day bar, disco, indoor pool, dollar shop. Phone: 965-60130.

Afrodita (first-class B), 400 beds in double rooms and suites; day bar, indoor pool, solarium, beauty parlor, hairdresser, sauna. Phone: 965-60730-34.

Cerna (first-class B), 128 beds in two- and three-bedded rooms; day bar, nearby pool, terrace. Phone: 965-60440.

Tourist Agency Scheduled Trips (phone: 965-60454).

Iron Gates area (hydro-power and navigation complex). Orşova (new town on the Danube), Drobeta-Turnu Severin (Danube port, commercial and tourist center).

Sailing from Orşova toward the Danube gorges.

Tour of Caraş-Severin County.

Tismana—historical and feudal art monument (16th century), Tirgu Jiu, the Brâncuşi sculptural complex.

The Cerna valley.

Kladova in Yugoslavia, Szeged or Budapest in Hungary; Sofia or Vidin in Bulgaria.

Băile Herculane can be reached by plane to Caransebeș Airport, and then by train from there. A local bus runs from the train station to the resort.

SOVATA

Sovata lies in the central Transylvanian plateau at the foot of the Gurghiu Massif in a depression skirted by century-old forests. The spa is located in Harghita County 224 miles by road north from Bucharest. There is an airport at nearby Tîrgu Mureș, which is 38 miles by train or bus from Sovata.

This old spa and health resort has won its reputation due to the exceptional therapeutic properties of the salt water of its heliothermal lakes. Millions of years ago the area was a sea lagoon. A warm climate then accelerated in time the process of water evaporation and what was left became huge deposits of salt, the largest in the country. Dolines (large funnel-shaped sinkholes) started their formation in these salt deposits, and the lake mud and water developed their healing properties under these conditions. Heat from the rays of the sun was absorbed in the salt water and mud, and its energy were stored in these substances.

Situated on the fringe of thick forests at an elevation of 1,740 feet in a hilly area, Sovata enjoys a dry, constant sub-Alpine climate. There are no strong winds in its purified air. Winters are mild, summers cool, and autumns prolonged. Annual average temperature is 47° F, with January and July-August means recording 38° F and 65° F, respectively. The air pressure remains fairly constant in this area, and precipitation is light. The landscape here is very picturesque.

Cure indications for the spa include those for: affections of the locomotor apparatus, such as degenerative rheumatism, inflammatory rhuematism, abarticular rheumatism, posttraumatic disorders, and affections of the peripheral nervous system; gynecological affections including chronic ovary disorders, secondary sterility, postoperative and postinflammatory adhesion syndromes, uterine problems, and secondary hypomenorrhea; secondary disorders including endocrine insufficiencies and disfunctions connected with ovarian, thyroid, and pituitary hypofunction; and cardiovascular disorders.

The natural cure factors for Sovata are related to the sodium chloride water of five lakes; Ursu, Alunis, Negru, Rosu, and Verde with concentrations varying from 77 to 213 grams per liter. Ursu is the largest of the lakes and is 62 feet deep. The temperature of Ursu (Bear's Lake) varies with depth, actually increasing in warmth at depths where salt layers acting like an insulator prevent the loss of accumulated heat. In summer the surface water temperature is 67° F, increasing to over 104° F at about 5 feet in depth, then generally decreasing toward the bottom of the lake. Water salinity rises with increased depth.

Another natural cure factor is related to the mud taken from Negru Lake, which is rich in chlorine, sodium, potassium, and organic substances and is effective in the treatment of various forms of rheumatism and some chronic gynecological ailments. Heliotherapy is also an important cure factor associated with baths in the lake. The stable, dry, and clean air of the area together with its luxuriant vegetation make Sovata an excellent place for rest and physical rehabilitation.

Treatment facilities at Sovata include laboratories, consulting rooms for gynecology, stomatology, radiology, podiatry. Galvanizations, glavanic baths, massages, douches, gymnastics, kinetotherpy, and saunas are associated therapies. Treatments with Romanian-developed drugs are also used. Recreation facilities include bowling, swimming, boating and disco rooms.

Hotels

Sovata (first-class), 324 beds in double rooms and suites; day bar, reading room, confectioner's. Phone: 954-78798 or 78159.

Făget (first-class), 274 beds in double rooms; day bar and restaurant. Phone 954-78297 or 78651-52.

Aluniş (first-class), 274 beds in double rooms; day bar and restaurant. Phone: 954-78601.

Brădet (first-class), 194 beds in double rooms and suites; bar, dollar shop, exchange, and pool. Phone: 954-78311 or 78422.

Tourist Agency Scheduled Trips (phone: 954-78639)

Sovata and Tîrgu Mureş—historical and architectural monuments and museums.

Sighişoara—medieval borough with old historical, artistic, and architectural monuments.

Gurghiu village—annual "Maiden Fair" in the latter half of May, an old folkloric event.

Izvoru Muntelui Lake—the largest intramountain storage lake

in Europe, also the Bicaz gorge and Lacu Rosu, another health resort.

Northern Moldavia—historical and feudal art monuments and churches.

BĂILE TUŞNAD

This resort is located in the valley of the Olt River in a wooded area of the Eastern Subcarpathians. It is situated along the border of Covasna and Harghita counties about 40 miles north of Braşov. Twenty miles to the south lies Sfîntu Gheorghe. Băile Tuşnad can be reached by Highway 12 and by rail from Sfîntu Gheorghe. It is both a resort and a spa. Bucharest is 146 miles to the south by road.

Located at 213 feet in altitude, the spa has a sub-Alpine climate that is both fortifying and stimulating. Its average summer temperature is 59° F. The area has low cloudiness and is surrounded by wooded slopes. The spa has had good results in treating a number of ailments. Its mineral springs have been used for this purpose for nearly four centuries. The waters have a content rich in carbon, bicarbonates, sodium, calcium, magnesium, chlorine, and iron. They are hypotonic and slightly radioactive; some of them are mesothermal. The springs are used both for external and internal cure. *Mofettes* here are also used in treatments.

The spa has a open-air pool with mesothermal carbogaseous water. The treatment center has a gymnastics center and a clinical laboratory for functional and blood tests and performs surgeries of different types. There are also consulting rooms for psychiatrists, general practioners and dentists. The medical staff speaks various foreign languages.

Ailments treated in the spa include: disorders of the central nervous system (asthenic neurosis with anxiety and depression, secondary asthenia, physical and intellectual fatigue); cardiovascular ailments (valvular and mycardium problems—without cardiac insufficiency, postmyocardic infarct states, peripheral arteriopathies, high blood pressure, postphlebitis states, and varices); chronic diseases of the digestive tract and of annex glands (stomach and intestine troubles, liver and biliary complaints); and endocrine problems (light hyperthyroiditis, parathyroid insufficiency, and suprarenal insufficiency).

Associated diseases treated include: nutritional complaints (diabetes, gout, obesity); troubles of the urinary tract; blood disorders and complaints of the hematopoietic organs. It is recommended that, as far as possible, patients should bring their physicians' recommendations and recent lab tests.

The spa has a modern treatment center linked with the Tusnad Hotel, which is provided with the following equipment and facilities: carbogaseous baths, galvanic baths, paraffin packs, hydro therapy, vertebrotherapy, baths, massage, and aerosols. Electrotherapy is also utilized.

Băile Tuşnad offers a variety of recreation and entertainment. Water sports can be enjoyed on the lake at the spa. Walks and hikes are common in the surrounding fir and oak forests (Stînca Şoimilor, Poianna Indrăgostiţilor, Piscul Cetăţil). Mountain climbing is available, and hikers can enjoy the beautiful landscape. Trips can be arranged to: Sfînta Ana Lake (3,740 feet in altitude—2½ hours' hike), a lake of volcanic origin located in an extinct crater in the Ciucul Mountains; nearby Lacu Sfînta Ana chalet (4,134 feet in altitude) and Mohoa peat bog (natural reserve); to Brăşov, an important economic, cultural, and tourist attraction, or to Poiana Braşov, an internationally known tourist resort. Trips can also be arranged to other localities. In winter one can practice skiing, sledding, and skating in the resort (national skating competitions are held in Tuşnad). A club, library, disco, and restaurants with dance bands and dance floors will add to your entertainment.

Hotels

Tusnad (first class), 220 beds in double rooms; restaurant, snack bar, currency shop; linked directly to the treatment center and the laboratories.

Olt (first class), 260 beds in double rooms; indoor pool, currency shop, snack bar.

Ciucas (first-class), 160 beds in single and double rooms and suites; snack bar, currency shop, restaurant.

Villas

Nearby villas offer various categories of comfort. Their single and double rooms provide a cosy atmosphere. The villas are situated either close to the Olt River or at the foot of the mountains.

BUZIAS

In the southwest of Romania lies the region of Banat (along the boundary of Yugoslavia) crossed by the lazy waters of the

Timiş River. There, guarded by the vine-covered slopes of Silagiu Hill stands one of the best-known Romanian health resorts, Buzias. The resort is located in Timiş County, about 22 miles east of the city of Timişoara. It can be reached by highway or by train, which stops at a nearby local station.

The therapeutical effects of its mineral waters gained their fame during Roman times. Buzias was turned into a resort in 1819. More recently, it has become a balneologic development, with new accommodation and treatment capacities being built and older ones being modernized.

The climate of Buzias is a mild continental type with no great seasonal variations in temperature. Its mean annual temperature is 52° F. Spring comes early, autumn sets in late, and winters are short and mild (above 32° F). Precipitation is moderate with the highest rainfall recorded at the beginning of summer. Buzias lies at 420 feet in elevation.

The natural cure factors of the spa include: mineral, carbogaseous waters rich in bicarbonate chloride, sodium, calcium, and magnesium; *mofettes;* and its favorable climate. The mineral water of Buzias has a pleasant taste and is bottled and used as table water.

The therapeutical indications of the spa include those for the cardiovascular and nervous systems. The resort is particularly recommended for treating cardiovascular disorders. Other diseases given treatment include those of the digestive tract, hepatobiliary ducts, metabolic and nutritional disorders, and asthenic neurosis. Cure facilities and procedures at Buzias include warm tub baths with carbogaseous mineral water, herb baths, *mofettes,* gymnastics, electrotherapy, hydrotherapy, massages, pools with mineral water, lab tests, X-rays, acupuncture, and treatment with Romanian medications.

Local entertainment includes tennis courts, volleyball, badminton, swimming, theater, library, a club, and band concerts. Romanian and international dishes are served at the spa.

The local tourists agency is located at 1 Florilor Street, phone: 963-31060. It can arrange for local and distant tours.

Hotels

Timiş (first class), 288 beds in double rooms; bar, restaurant, treatment facilities. Phone: 963-32360.

Parc (first class), 288 beds in double rooms; bar, dollar shop, exchange, hairdresser. Phone: 963-31920.

Busias (first class), 98 beds in double rooms and suites. Phone: 963-31060.

VATRA DORNEI

In the heart of the Northern Carpathians in the depression of the Dornas River valley (or Dorna Land) is one of the best-known health and balneary cure resorts in Romania—Vatra Dornei. Situated at an altitude of 2,625 feet on the right bank of the Dorna, it is surrounded by mountains (Giumaldau, Rarau, Bistrița, Calimani, Bîrgău, and Rodna) covered with rich forests of birch, beech, and coniferous trees which protect the spa from strong winds. The spa lies 98 miles northwest of Piatra–Neamț and 68 miles southwest of Suceava in Suceava County. The town of Vatra Dornei sits at the junction of the Dorna with the majestic Bistrița River. It is a lumbering and cheese-making center. The Dorna valley has cool but sunny summers. The average annual temperature is 41° F, with a mean of the monthly highs of 59.5° F in July and of the monthly lows of 21.2° F in January.

The natural cure factors associated with Vatra Dornei include mineral waters rich in carbogases, iron, bicarbonates, sodium, calcium and magnesium. The spa has four major mineral springs. The mineral waters are used in both external and internal cures. Local peat mud, rich in organic substances, is also used in treatments. The sub-Alpine climate of the resort is also considered to have its beneficial therapeutic effects.

The natural cure factors have therapeutic indications that are recommended for: affections of the cardiovascular system (arterial hypertension, valvopathy, ischemic cardiopathy); disorders of the locomotor apparatus (degenerative rheumatic disorders, abarticular rheumatic conditions, posttraumatic affections; neurologic affections; and associated diseases—endrocrine, digestive, urinary, gynecological, and dysmetabolic (obesity, diabetes, atherosclerosis).

Vatra Dornei has two treatment centers—Calimani and Dorna—with medical equipment. Therapeutic procedures and equipment include warm baths in mineral water, warm mud wrappings, artificial *mofettes,* electrotherapy, hydrotherapy, gyms, mechanotherapy, massages, paraffin wrappings, saunas, and pools for kinetotherapy.

Of local interset is the Cynegetic and Natural Sciences Museum in which are exhibits of the rich fauna and flora of the area.

Another interesting museum is the Bukovinean Ethnography Museum, displaying local folk art. In the vicinity of Vatra Dornei there is a cable car running to Dealul Negru peak (4,268 feet high). In the winter the area becomes a favorite of skiers. Snow lasts four to five months a year, and there is a ski lift for the slopes.

Hotels

Calimani (first class), 304 beds in double rooms and suites; dollar shop, tourist agency, therapeutic treatments. Phone: 988-73921.

Bradul (first class), 300 beds in suites and double rooms; dollar shop, exchange, snack bar, therapeutic treatments. Phone: 988-73922.

Dorna (first class), 300 beds in suites and single and double rooms; dollar shop, snack bar, private treatments. Phone: 988-71021-22.

SLĂNIC-MOLDOVA

This health resort is located in the valley of the Slănic River about 11 miles from the town of Tîrgu Ocna in Bacău County on the slopes of the Subcarpathians. The resort can be reached by train from Bucharest to Tirgu Ocna (184 miles) and then by bus or auto (11 miles) for the last distance. One can also take Tarom Airlines to Bacău (a 45-minute trip), which is near the resort, and then take a bus or car from there to the spa (about 53.5 miles). The nearest major town to the resort is Gheorghe Gheorghiu-Dej, about 20 miles distant.

The spa is situated at an altitude of 1,739 feet in a depression in the mountains. In July its average temperature is 64° F, while in May it averages 25° F. There are 20 sources of mineral water in the area. The waters are rich in sodium, chlorine, bicarbonates, and carbogases. The moderate climate and local *mofettes* are other natural cure factors associated with the resort.

Therapeutic indications for Slanic-Moldova include those for: the digestive tube and its annex glands; inflammations of the intestines; nutritional maladies; infections of the respiratory system (chronic bronchitis and bronchial asthma); and cardiocavular disorders. Medical cure procedures at the spa include those of bathing in mineral waters, the use of aerosols and inhalations, medical gymnastics, saunas, massages, physiotherapy (electro-, thermo-, and hydrotherapy), and a sanatorium for bronchopulmonary infections.

Recreational facilities at the resort include bowling, volleyball, tennis, a theater, library, and hiking. Local tours can be arranged into the mountains and to the Slănic waterfall.

Hotels

Perla (First-class), 93 rooms, bar, exchange, shop, snack bar.

A new hotel built in Tîrgu Ocna will likely be open by the time this book is published. It will contain 200 rooms, shop, bar, and exchange.

CĂLIMĂNEŞTI-CĂCIULATA

Located about one mile apart, the two health resorts of Călimăneşti-Căciulata lie in the valley of the Olt River in the Subcarpathians in Vilcea County. Both resorts are noted for their mineral springs which are recommended for the treatment of a variety of diseases. Located among densely forested hills of the spectacular Olt Pass, the spas' waters have become widely renowned. Napoleon III of France, who was afflicted with kidney stones, ordered water from the springs of these resorts to treat his condition. The mineral waters of the spas have been recognized for their value in treating digestive tract problems, kidney and urinary complaints, and locomotor deficiencies. The local waters have been attributed to having positive effects on the peripheral nervous system, metabolic and nutritional diseases, and allergic diseases. The waters contain sodium chloride, sulfur, bromide, and iodine. The spas lie about 118 miles northwest of Bucharest. The largest city nearby is Piteşti, about 48 miles to the southeast. Several old monasteries lie in the vicinity of the spas, which have an altitude of about 920 feet. Călimăneşti has an all-season hotel, the *Vilcea*.

LACU ROŞU (Red Lake)

This health resort and winter sports center is located about 37 miles southwest of the city of Piatra-Neamţ in the Eastern Carpathians. From Lacu Roşu the road winds 16 miles southwest to the town of Gheorgheni. Lacu Roşu lies in Harghita County at an elevation of 3,200 feet. The resort lies around a storage lake (Lacu Roşu) formed naturally in 1837 when a side of Mount Ghilcos fell in. The trunks of sunken trees can still be seen in the water. The surrounding forests, mountains, and the lake offer spectacular scenery. The resort is visited by many individuals suffering from conditions of stress and asthenia, i.e., lacking in strength. Asthenia is a debilitating disorder orginating in muscular or cerebellar disease. Villas can be rented in the area, and there is a second-class hotel, the *Ceahlău*, in nearby Bicaz.

COVASNA

Located in the northwest area of the Vrancea Mountains in the Eastern Carpathians, this health resort and spa has mineral springs and associated thermal facilities. Its post-volcanic phenomena include *mofettes*, carbogaseous water, and mineral mud. The therapeutic properties attributed to this resort include their value in treating respiratory ailments, cardiovascular disorders, digestive afflictions, urinary disorders, metabolic and nutritional diseases, and neurosis. Covasna lies about 19 miles east of Sfîntu Gheorghe in Covasna County. The resort is due north of Bucharest, about 145 miles by road. Its hotel is the first-class *Cerbul*.

BĂILE OLĂNEŞTI

This small health resort is located 12 miles northwest of the city of Rîmnicu Vîlcea in the Subcarpathians at an altitude of 1,478 feet. By road the spa lies 121 miles northwest of Bucharest. Băile Olăneşti does not have the reputation of some of Romania's other health resorts. The spa lies in a narrow valley with heavily forested slopes overlooking it. It is noted for its mineral waters which flow from some 30 springs in the vicinity. The therapeutic properties of the waters are reported to have positive effects in the treatment of respiratory ailments, digestive disorders, urinary infections, metabolic and nutritional diseases, and allergic reactions. The spa is open in all seasons.

BĂILE GOVORA

This is another small health resort located in the same general area as Băile Olăneşti. It lies in a forested hill area about 13 miles southwest of Rîmnicu Vîlcea at an altitude of 1,360 feet. Noted for its mineral waters which are pumped from more than 1,000 feet beneath the surface, the spa is an all-season resort. The mineral waters are often mixed with muds high in mineral content for therapeutic purposes. The mineral waters, which may be taken internally, contain sulfur, salts, and iodine. The waters are used in the treatment of locomotor disorders, peripheral nervous dysfunctions, gynecological diseases, and respiratory ailments.

SINGEORZ-BĂI

Also one of the small, lesser-known resorts of Romania, this spa is located in Bistriţa-Năsăud County in northern Transylvania. It lies in the valley of the Someşu Mare River where it flows off the slopes of the Eastern Carpathians. A highway runs through the spa, with a rail line skirting it on either side. By highway, Singeorz-Băi is 48 miles northeast of the city of Dej. The spa is a thermal resort whose therapeutic properties are claimed to have beneficial effects on digestive disorders, metabolic and nutritional diseases, and neurosis.

BLACK SEA COAST

The Romanian Black Sea coast is looked upon as a major resort area and source of health treatment by a growing number of tourists and patients going there looking for remedies to ailments. The seacoast stretches for 152 miles of sandy shoreline. The resorts lie largely from Mangalia on the south to Navodari on the north. In between these is Constanţa, the major political, economic, and administrative center of the region.

People speaking about the "miracle" of the Romanian sea coast are referring to its therapeutical benefits. Many patients, some considered irrecoverable, suffering from chronic rheumatism, infections of the upper respiratory tract, circulatory conditions, or arthritis pains have been helped or restored to some measure of health at the resort-spas of this area. Actually, there is a complex of natural cure factors, modern equipment, as well as human care, that comprises the curative capacity of the Romanian sea coast. The well-known resorts of Eforie Nord, Eforie Sud, Neptune, and Mangalia stand out as important treatment centers and have acquired a good reputation in this regard. One should also mention the small Techirghiol resort, named after the neighboring lake, another health center noted for the exceptional qualities of its mud and water. Environment and natural cure factors of the region include:

The Climate. The Black Sea coast has a steppe climate, moderately endowed with marine elements, including chlorine, magnesium, iodine, and bromine. The high intensity of solar radiation on the coast is also said to have stimulating effects. In summer, a very warm season at the seaside, temperatures range on an average between 72° F at Eforie and 71.5° F at Mangalia. The summer months have an average of 25 sunny days each. In mid-June, the sun shines for about 9½ hours daily, in July for 11 hours daily, and in August for some 10 hours daily, amounting to 2,300–2,500 hours annually. The location of the seacoast results in a high amount of solar radiation in the morning. The air pressure in summer ranges between 758 and 766.6 mm of mercury; in the winter it is higher. The relative humidity ranges between 70 and 82 percent and is lower at noon in the summer.

The Sea. The breeze from the Black Sea helps to ensure thermal stability, uniform rainfall, and a permanent refreshing of the air (factors which help to make the area well known for its therapeutic effects). By storing the sun's radiation, particularly in the summer, the Black Sea becomes a repository of natural heat which influences the thermal aspect of local seasons along the seacoast, resulting in much longer summers and mild autumns. The sea water ranges between 75° F and 82° F in summer, which reportedly helps blood and lymph circulation and the general metabolism of bathers and swimmers.

The Salt Water of Techirghiol Lake. Rich in sodium, magnesium, potassium sulfates, and bromides, the water of the lake is reported to play an important role in intensifying the activity of the circulatory system, having positive effects in the treatment of neuromuscular and various types of rheumatismal disorders. Techirghiol water is used in treatments on the sandy beaches of the lake, as well as for curative purposes in indoor swimming pools or in tubs with warm mineral water.

The Sapropelic Mud of Techirghiol Lake. The mud is oily and finely granulated and is the outcome of the anaerobic decomposition and fermentation of the lake fauna. It is rich in mineral and organic substances, estrogenic substances, and enzymes which activate and regenerate tissues. The mud also contains vitamins C, E, B_2, and B_{12}, which are bistimulating substances. Its antiinflammatory bacteriostatic properties are very beneficial. Thermic and chemical action in the mud activate the circulatory system and provide ionic equilibrium. The mud is smeared on the body and heliotherapy is applied, followed by baths in the sea or lake and swimming. The mud may also be applied in warm wrappings (mud baths, vaginal pads, massages).

Therapeutic indications for the natural cure factors of the Romanian seaside resorts include: disorders of the locomotor systems inflammatory chronic rheumatism, degenerative rheumatism barticular rheumatism, orthopedic afflictions, disorders of the peripheral nervous system, skin diseases, chronic gynecological complaints, metabolic disorders, rickets, poliomyelitis, lymphatic problems, and metabolic disturbances. The inhalations and aerosols of the seaside are reported to have positive effects on asthma-like bronchitis, rhinitis, and sinusitis. The natural cure factors of the seaside are also claimed to have counterindications for arterial hypertension, cardiovascular diseases, cancer, pulmonary tuberculosis, psychoses, epilepsy, hyperthyroidism, and other afflictions.

EFFIE NORD

This quiet, old spa of varied architecture stretches between the Black Sea and Techirghiol Lake. Its setting is favored by charming natural surroundings—high cliffs, a well-kept beach, lush vegetation, a recreation lake, and sports grounds. It is an all-season resort.

The Effie Nord Treatment Center is connected by warmed corridors to the hotels Delfinul, Meduza, and Steaua de Mare. The indoor pool has heated sea water used for kinetotherapy and recreation. Other pools contain water from Techirghiol Lake; there are mud wrappings, mud baths, and baths in tubs with salt water from the lake. Therapeutic provisions at Effie Nord include those for hydrotherapy, electrotherapy, aerosols, vertebral elongations, medical and recuperative gymnastics, massages, saunas, and herb baths. There are consulting rooms for balneology, gynecology, radiology, internal diseases, and dermatology. There is also a clinical laboratory and acupuncture rooms.

Hotels

Europa (deluxe), 242 single and double rooms and suites; day bar, dollar shop, exchange, pool, hairdresser. Phone: 917-42590 or 42685.

Delfinul (first- class A), 462 beds in 218 double rooms and two-bedded suites; pool, day bars, restaurant. Phone: 917-42630 or 42632.

Steaua de Mare (first-class A), 462 beds in 218 double rooms and two-bedded suites; pool, day bars, restaurant. Phone: 917-42480 or 42482.

Meduza (first-class A), 462 beds in 218 double rooms and suites; pool, suites have TV and refrigerator. Phone: 917-42770 or 42772.

Bega (first-class A), 246 beds in 218 double rooms and suites; snack bar, pool. Phone: 917-41468.

Bran (first-class A), 246 beds in 123 double rooms; pool and snack bar. Phone: 917-41421.

Brad (first-class B), 246 beds in 123 double rooms; snack bar, pool. Phone: 917-41418.

Astoria (first-class A), 53 beds in double rooms; bar, dollar shop, exchange. Phone: 917-47475.

EFORIE SUD

This resort lies immediately south of Eforie Nord. Eforie Sud lies on a strip of narrow land between the Black Sea and Lake Techirghiol. The resort is about 12 miles south of Constanța on a cliffed coastline that gives it a beautiful view of the sea. It is the oldest resort on the Romanian seacoast. Villas and holiday houses stand side by side with elegant hotels. This is a summer resort, which looks like a large park because of all the flowers, trees, and gardens surrounding its facilities. The mud and water from Lake Techirghiol are used in treatment facilities, baths, and sanatoria in the area. Eforie Sud has several theaters, an archeological museum, minigolf links, tennis courts, swimming pools, folklore programs, and folk music. A number of the hotels have restaurants with orchestras, and a few hotels have discos and juke boxes.

Hotels

Flamingo (deluxe), tourist information desk. Phone: 917-42530. First-class hotels include the *Parc, Gloria, Riveria, Cosmos,* and *Excelsior.* Second-class hotels include the *Turist, Suceava.*

NEPTUNE

Neptune is one of the more recently built resorts strung along the southern part of the Black Sea coast. Neptune is located about 22 miles south of Constanţa along the coastal highway. It lies along a sandy strip of beach with a small lake, Tatlageac, located on its west side. Neptune lies between Costineşti on the north and Jupiter on the south. Opened in 1960, the resort has grown steadily since then. Its recreation lakes and an old oak forest make up a beautiful landscape, rounded out by the outlines of modern hotels. Neptune is an all-season resort.

Natural treatment factors at Neptune include hypothermal, sulfur, and mineral water; sea water; the curative mud from Lake Techirghiol; and the sea bioclimate high in aerosols and solar radiation. Therapeutic indications for Neptune include those for degenerative rheumatic disorders; inflammatory rheumatic conditions; peripheral neurologic disorders; gynecological problems; endocrine, metabolic, and nutritional diseases; respiratory ailments; and dermatological diseases. Neptune has out-patient treatment with mud and heated sea water or therapy at the Doina Hotel, which has sea water tub baths, hot mud wrappings, massages, douch massages, electro- and hydrotherapy, and geriatric sections for treatment by the well-known Romanian therapeutical products. Other attractions of the resort include swimming pools (several of them covered), water sports, theaters, disco, bowling, tennis, minigolf, and a park for children. Neptune has more than three dozen modern hotels.

Hotels

Neptune (deluxe), 126 rooms: sauna, snack bar, pool, disco, dollar shop, exchange. Phone: 917-31020.

Doina (deluxe), 330 double rooms; pool, day bar, dollar shop, exchange, treatment services. Phone: 917-31818.

Bilea (first class), 300 double rooms; currency exchange, day bar, tourist bureau. Phone: 917-31617.

Amfiteatru is also considered deluxe.

First-class hotels include the *Delta, Sulina, Arad, Panoramic,* and *Belvedere.*

In addition, there is the *Sat de Vacantă* (the Holiday Village) with bungalows and small houses, several campgrounds, over 30 restaurants, day bars, confectionary and pastry shops, and food stores.

MANGALIA

The southernmost resort on the seacoast, Mangalia, is a town of noted tourist and archeological interest (with the preserved remains of Callatis Citadel). The resort harmoniously blends traditional architecture with new, modern, and comfortable buildings. Mangalia is an all-season resort. It lies about 28 miles south of Constanţa, near the border with Bulgaria. Greek and Roman remains abound in the vicinity. Mangalia sits where the Dobrudja plateau slopes off to the sea, and in its vicinity are the Vomorova Forest and Lake Mangalia.

Mangalia is old, having been founded in the 6th century B.C. by the Greeks. Both the Greeks and Romans knew the city by the name of Callatis. Between the 13th and 16th centuries it was called Pangalia, and it took its present name at the end of the 16th century. Of interest in the city is the Archeological Museum, which contains a collection of ancient statutes, coins, urns, and other Greco-Roman antiquities from ancient Callatis. It is open between 10 A.M. and 5 P.M. and located on Izorului Street. Also of interest are the 15-century Esmahan Sultan Mosque and ancient tombs.

Mangalia is most noted as a resort and for its therapeutic indications, particularly those related to infections of the digestive tract, the kidneys, and liver. The spa has balneary treatments in the winter. Mangalia has amusement parks, water sports, horseback riding, and horse-driven carriages, many nice restaurants, and sports grounds.

Hotels

Mangalia (first class), 293 rooms; pool, hairdresser, sauna, disco, shop, exchange, information bureau, and in-house treatment facilities. Phone: 917-51968.

Scala (first class), 144 rooms; snack bar, shop, exchange. Phone: 917-51287.

Other first-class hotels are the *Zefir* and *Scala*. Second-class hotels include the *Orion, Zenit* and *Astra*.

MAMAIA

This major resort on the Black Sea is located about 4 miles north of Constanţa on a narrow neck of land with the sea on the east and Lake Siutghiol on the west. Mamaia is more important as a resort than a spa, but it has the climatological aspects of the other Black Sea spas and is also a balneological center. The well-known Roman poet Ovid is said to have spent some time here, and there is small island in a nearby lake named in honor of him. Mamaia is the largest and most important of the seaside resorts.

Hotels
International (deluxe).

First-class hotels include the *Alcor, Vega, Amiral, Condor, Dorna, Parc, Doina, Tomis, Ovidiu,* and *Histria*. The *Peria Hotel* has a tourist agency (phone: 31334 or 31316), as does the *Bucureşti B Hotel* (phone: 31152).

OTHER RESORTS

The resorts listed above are largely known for their health and therapeutic efforts, but many visitors travel to them for their recreational and sports facilities. A number of other Romanian resorts may be more appropriately categorized as the recreational type, although some of these are recommended for their health treatment value as well. Resorts that fall more in the recreational and entertainment category follow.

SINAIA

This resort town is located in the valley of the Prahova River in the Subcarpathians about 79 miles north of Bucharest. Set in the Bucegi Mountains with forested slopes overlooking it, Sinaia has a picture-postcard look to it. The town and resort not only is well known in Romania but has an international reputation as well. It was the first modern settlement of the area (17th century), built on a culture hearth of the Bronze Age. The name

Sinaia was given to the spot by Mihail Cantacuzino, a nobleman in the 1600s, after he had made a journey to biblical Mount Sinai. He founded Sinaia Monastery on the site in 1695, which is one of the interesting places to visit in the area. A railway was built to the town in 1878 to connect it with Bucharest. A highway had been built through it previously in 1846. Already by 1871 it had become a place for holidays and mountaineering. In that year the journals of the time wrote that the Sinaia hotel was full of guests. The sub-Alpine climate, with cool days in summer and temperate ones in winter, together with the charming town located between the forest-covered slopes of the Furnica (6,900 feet in elevation) and Batu Mare (6,217 feet) soon made Sinaia into a health resort called the "gem of the Bucegi." Villas, hotels, and casinos were built as "pleasure seekers" from Bucharest sought its charms.

In 1875 the Romanian royal family began the construction of Peles Castle at Sinaia and continued to modify it until 1896. The castle became the summer residence of the monarchy, and Romanian society followed the royal family to Sinaia each summer, where politics and match-making took their course. In the royal castle, King Ferdinand, Queen Marie, and Princess Ileana lived amidst a wooded park covering hundreds of acres. A twisting roadway led to the palace located on the side of a mountain. Queen Marie had blonde hair and blue eyes and was one of Europe's most beautiful and elegant ladies. Her jewels were famous and worth a fortune. Her great-grandfather was the Russian Tsar Alexander I, and her grandmother was Queen Victoria of England. Two of her children married into the Greek royal family, and one became the wife of King Alexander of Yugoslavia. Marie was a woman of great intellect and worked hard for her country. She published many children's stories and several books.

In the days of the monarchy, Sinaia's fine hotels and casinos made it Romania's playground of the rich. Young and old flocked to it, while social life centered around the royal palace. The Sinaia of the pre-World War II era was well known for its outdoor restaurants, where many of the upper classes gathered. The wealthy men and women spent lavishly and wore the latest fashions from Paris and Rome.

In the last twenty years or so, the town has continued to develop. Industries have been built, including those of food processing, metallurgy, and building materials. New hotels, motels, and camping sites have been added; and the balneary treatment centers have been equipped with modern technology. The local springs are rich in a variety of minerals, and their waters are used in bathing and the treatment of a variety of diseases. Annually, over 200,000 visitors arrive in Sinaia.

Sinaia's climatic conditions and mountainous slopes account for it being one of the major resorts for winter sports in the country. The great variety of slopes and its bobsled track permit Sinaia to host national and international ski, sled, and bobsled competitions. Cable cars run from Sinaia to the upper slopes of the nearby mountains. A number of ski lodges and hotels are located on the mountainous slopes. The ski slopes have different degrees of difficulty and length. Snow persists in the area from December through April. The average January temperature for Sinaia is 25° F, while in summer the average temperature is 59° F.

Entertainment at Sinaia is varied: tennis courts, volleyball, basketball, skiing, indoor swimming, archery, mechanical games, theatrical and cinema shows, "Romanian evenings" with folklore shows, discoes and bars. Excursions can be made to Sinaia Monastery (now a museum), the Bucegi nature reserve, and nearby towns and cities. Hiking trips into the mountains can be arranged. The resort hotels have money exchanges and rent-a-car services. For beginners in the art of winter sports and for children, there are ski schools where lessons are taught individually or in groups by skilled coaches. Sports items and outfits can be rented at the Montana, Sinaia, Alpin, and International hotels.

Hotels

Sinaia (first class), 480 rooms in suites and single and double rooms; indoor pool, sports equipment for hire, sauna, shop, exchange, snack bar. Located at 30 Carpati Blvd. Phone: 973-11551-55.

Montana (first class), 353 beds in suites and double and single rooms; indoor pool, sauna, wine cellar, mechanical games, sports equipment rental, shop, exchange. Located at 24 Carpati Blvd. Phone: 973-12750-55.

International (first class), 392 beds in suites and single and double rooms with balconies; shop, bar, hairdresser, sports equipment rental, exchange, snack bar. Located at 1 Avram Iancu St. Phone: 973-13851.

Palas (first class), 275 beds in suites and single and double rooms;

snack bar, disco, shop, exchange, conference rooms. Located at 1—30 Decembrie St. Phone: 973-12051.

Caraiman (first class), 142 beds in suites and double rooms; snack bar, exchange, confectioner's, reception halls. Located at 4 Carpati Blvd. Phone 973-13551.

Paltinis (first class), 220 beds in single and double rooms; snack bar, exchange, disco. Located at 67 Carpati Blvd. Phone: 973-13555.

Alpin (first class), 161 beds in suites and double rooms; bar, disco, exchange, medical room, sports equipment rental. Located at Cota 14000. Phone: 973-12351.

Cerbului (first class), 128 beds plus 80 beds in bungalows; restaurant. Located on highway DN 1. Phone: 973-14751.

Izvorul Rece (second class), 79 beds plus 160 beds in bungalows; restaurant. Located on highway DN 1. Phone: 973-14751.

POIANA BRĂŞOV

Poiana Brăşov is a modern health resort and winter sports center located at the foot of Mount Postavaru in the southeastern Carpathians, 7 miles from Braşov, at an altitude of 3,379 feet. The nickname of the resort is "clearing of sunshine." Its mountain climate is refreshing, and the resort has an average yearly temperature of approximatly 41° F (July 58° F; January, 23° F). This resort lies about 171 miles north of Bucharest.

Its bioclimate has clean air devoid of dust and allergic factors and has an atmosphere rich in ultraviolet rays. Treatments exist for asthenic neurosis, physical and intellectual overexertion, benign hyperthyroidism, rachitic and child growth problems, and secondary anemia. The area is well known for winter sports. The snow layer has an average thickness of 19.5 feet and persists from December through April. There are 12 ski slopes with different degrees of difficulty, some of them lighted. Ski lifts are available as well as coasting paths equipped with mechanical lifts for cable transport. There is a ski school with teachers certified by the Romanian Ski Federation; sports equipment is available for.

The resort has a covered swimming pool, an open-air swimming pool of Olympic size, sauna, sports facilities (tennis, minigolf, handball, basketball), a gymnastic hall, and a skating rink. Buses with regular timetables connect the resort to Braşov.

Restaurants

Sura Dacilor. It is built and decorated in an architectural style reminding one of the homes of the Dacians (the ancestors of the Romanian people). Traditional Romanian meals and drinks are prepared from special recipes. The Romanian folk music band is popular.

Coliba Haiducilor. It has a rustic charm and appearance and offers fine Romanian dishes, wines, and a folk music band.

Miorita. Old traditions of Romanian folk art blend with its modern architectural features. One must see its hand-woven carpets, pottery, fine raw-silk towels, and brightly colored table cloths. Its homemade dishes and fine Romanian wines draw many visitors to the shore of Poiana Lake, where the restaurant is located. Entertainment is a Romanian folk music band.

Vinatorul. This restaurant is decorated like a hunting lodge and serves excellent venison and good wines.

Ruia. Decorated in the style of traditional Romanian folk houses, it serves Romanian and international food. It has a good wine cellar.

Poiana Ursului. A traditional peasant-style decoration, Romanian cooking, and a folk music band are its attractions.

Capra Neagra Its cosy atmosphere, dim lights, good food, and shows are popular with people of all ages.

Favorit. In this amphitheater-shaped restaurant, guests can watch films produced in Romania or abroad (between 12:30 A.M. 3:30 P.M.) and variety shows (from 6:30 P.M.).

Recreation Activities

Invitation to a Sheepfold. This event occurs in a genuine sheepfold, where visitors can witness ewes' milking. Shepherd-made milk products and Romanian dishes are prepared by the shepherds' fire, and Romanian wines add to the festivities.

Horseback Riding. The local riding center has ponies for children and thoroughbred horses for others year-round. Rides on horseback, in sleighs, carts, and horse-driven wagons are organized along special routes. Riding equipment is available for hire.

Lawn Tennis. Played in the vicinity of the hotels Poiana and Piatra Mare, the courts and equipment can be rented.

Table Tennis. Tables are available in the hotels Sport, Piatra Mare, Ciucas, Brandul, and at the Favorit Multifunctional Complex.

Other Activities. These include minigolf, roller skating, archery, swimming, bowling, billiards, bicycling, fishing, and boating.

Favorit Multifunctional Complex. This is an entertainment complex for all ages. It contains a conference hall, exhibition center, library, mechanical games room, bowling alley, reading room, and other recreational pursuits.

Mountaineering. The Poiana Braşov area is popular with those who like mountain climbing and hiking the slopes and forest trails or like to go for short or long walks. The marked paths with different degrees of difficulty are:

ROUTE 1: Poiana Braşov—Ripa Dracului—Cheisoara—Cheia Chalet. Duration 3 hours, easy route.

ROUTE 2: Poiana Braşov—Junilor Chalet—Poiana Neagului—Risnov. Duration 3 hours, easy route.

ROUTE 3: Poiana Braşov—Junilor Chalet—Cristian Village. Duration 3 hours, easy route.

ROUTE 4: Poiana Braşov—Racadau Valley—Braşov. Duration 4 hours, easy route.

ROUTE 5: Poiana Braşov—Poiana Ruia—Cristianu Mare Peak—Poiana Ruia—Timpa. Duration 4-5 hours, easy route.

ROUTE 6:—Poiana Braşov—Poiana Ruia—Cristianu Mare Peak—Poiana Ruia—De Lapte Cave. Duration 3-4 hours, easy route.

ROUTE 7: Poiana Braşov—Poiana Ruia—Postavarul Chalet—Poiana Trei Fetite—Spinarea Calului—Mount Carbunarul—Poiana Secuilor Chalet—Trei Braxi Chalet—Predeal. Duration 5-6 hours, difficult route, recommended only to experienced hikers.

ROUTE 8: Poiana Braşov—Cristianu Mare Chalet—Cristianu Mare Peak—Timisu de Jos. Duration 4-5 hours, long and difficult route, recommended only to experienced hikers.

ROUTE 9: Poiana Braşov—Cheisoara—Cheia Chalet—Glajeria Valley—Malaiesti Chalet—Omu Peak and Chalet. Duration 12 hours, long and difficult route, recommended only to experienced hikers.

First-Class Hotels

Alpin, 280 beds in suites, one-room flats, double rooms with phone and TV; central heating, lifts, restaurant, bar, indoor swimming pool, sauna, car park. (Phone 92-262111 or 262262.

Ciucas, 509 beds in one-room flats and in double or three-bedded rooms with phone and TV; sauna, central heating, lifts, restaurant, bar, car park. Phone 92-262111 or 262262.

Health Resorts, Spas, Treatments

Caraiman, 132 beds in one-room flats, double rooms with phone and TV; central heating, lift, restaurant, bar, cafe, car park. (Phone 92-212226 or 262377.

Soimul, 314 beds in double rooms; central heating, lift, phone and TV, restaurant, bar, cafe, sauna, car park. Phone 92-262111 or 262262.

Piatra Mare, 348 beds in one-room flats and double rooms with phone and TV; central heating, lift, restaurant, bar, cafe, hairdresser, disco, car park. Phone 92-262226 or 262377.

Teleferic, 298 beds in one-room flats, double rooms and suites with phone and TV; central heating, restaurant, bar, cafe, sauna, hairdresser, outdoor swimming pool, car park. Phone 92-262277 or 262277.

Bradul, 120 beds in three-bedded rooms; central heating, bar, car park. Phone 92-262255 or 262313.

Sport, 243 beds in single, double, three-bedded rooms and in suites with phone and TV; restaurant, cafe, disco, hairdresser, tourist information desk, car park. Phone 92-262255 or 262313.

Poiana, 119 beds in single, double, and three-bedded rooms with phone and TV; bar, acupressure room, car park. Phone 92-262255 or 262313.

Intim, 64 beds in double rooms; central heating, phone and TV, restaurant, car park. Phone 92-262123.

First- and Second-Class Villas
These have private kitchens and dining rooms, 10 to 30 beds, and central heating.

BUSTENI

Busteni is a small town and resort located in the Prahova valley 5 miles north of Sinaia at the foot of Caraiman Massif—7,822 feet in elevation. The resort itself lies at 2,887 feet in altitude and is on highway DN 1. It is an important center for mountaineering activities. With the towering high peaks of the mountains around the resort, the scenery is spectacular. On the south side of the town is the Hotel Silva from which a cable car extends up the mountainous slopes to the Babele Chalet located at 7,238 feet in altitude. In winter the area is covered with a blanket of snow, and skiers throng to Busteni. The mountains have marked paths through them for climbers. Founded in the early 1800s,

Busteni has several small industrial enterprises. Its hotels are the 7-storied *Silva* and the *Caraiman*.

PREDEAL

This town lies 8 miles north of Busteni, with the town of Azuga in between them. Predeal lies in the Prahova valley along highway DN 1. Beyond Predeal is the Timiş valley and Braşov. Predeal is the highest town in Romania, lying at 3,412 feet in elevation. It is a winter sports resort with marked paths, ski slopes, chair lift, ski lift, and chalets. Many residents of Bucharest visit Predeal, especially on weekends during the winter. Predeal, Azuga, Busteni, and Sinaia all lie on the rail line connecting Bucharest with Braşov. The resort industry of the Prahova valley only began to grow in the 1830s, but the area is fast-developing and is one of Romania's major centers of this activity.

The ski slopes around Predeal offer varying degrees of difficulty and length. Several ski lifts and cable cars run up and down the slopes on the east side of the town. There are classes and skilled instructors for teaching skiing. Centers for renting sports materials and outfits are located at the hotels Orizont, Cioplea, and Clabucet-Sosire.

Hotels

Orizont (first class), 316 beds, bar, disco, indoor pool, gymnastics, massages, sauna. 6 Trei Brazi St. Phone: 922-55150.

Cioplea (first and second class), 292 beds, bar, disco, sauna, gymnastics. 102 R.S.R. Blvd. Phone: 922-56870.

Bulevard (first class), 84 beds; bar, restaurant. 129 Gh. Gheorghiu-Dej Blvd. Phone: 922-56022.

Cirus (first class), 72 beds. 2 Avram Lancu St. Phone: 922-56035.

Carmen (first class), 60 beds; bar, restaurant, sports grounds. Gh. Gheorghiu-Dej Blvd. Phone: 922-56517.

Clabucet-Plecare (first class), 93 beds; restaurant, bar. Phone: 922-56312.

Clabucet-Sosire (second class), 60 beds; restaurant, bar. Phone: 922-56449.

Trei Brazi (first class), 83 beds, restaurant. 4.3 miles from Predeal. Phone: 922-56264.

PIATRA-NEAMŢ

This resort town located in northeastern Romania is the capital city of Neamţ County. The town lies 217 miles north of Bucharest on the east bank of the Bistriţa River. It is situated at the foot of the Subcarpathians where the Bistriţa leaves behind the surrounding peaks of Cozia, Pietricica, and Cernegua. Among these peaks is one of the largest deposits of fossil sea fauna in Romania. In the same area stand the Giants' Cauldrons, huge hollows carved out by the wind in the gritstone.

Piatra-Neamţ has a population of more than 110,000 inhabitants and is the site of ancient settlements. Artifacts unearthed here predate the Bronze Age. Excavations around the city resulted in the discovery of Petrodava, an ancient Dacian city which Ptolemy spoke about in the 2nd century B.C. During the Middle Ages, Piatra-Neamţ was a trading and market center and hosted medieval fairs. Its old church of St. Ion Domnescu (St. John) was constructed by Stephen the Great in 1497. He also had built the St. Ion Tower, often identified as Stephen's Tower, which houses an old clock in its belfry. The city's Archeological Museum contains fine specimens of pottery from the Neolithic Age. About 3 miles from Piatra-Neamţ is the Bistriţa Monastery built in 1402 and reconstructed in 1554. It is the burial place of Alexander the Good, its founder. Stephen the Great added a tower to it in 1498.

Piatra-Neamţ is also a diversified industrial center. It contains textile and food-processing plants, saws timber into lumber, manufactures paper, refines oil, and produces metallurgical and chemical products. The city also promotes itself as a climatic resort and a picturesque area with forested mountains. The area's rich folk culture and architecture attracts many tourists who come to hear local folk musicians play and view the art, architecture, traditional clothing, and handicrafts of the people. The *Central* is regarded as the city's main first-class hotel (132 rooms), but the *Ceahlaŭ* (146 rooms) is also an excellent first-class hotel.

OCNA SIBIULUI

This small health resort complex is located 8 miles northwest of Sibiu at an altitude of 1,338 feet. The resort lies around mineral springs and salt lakes whose waters and muds are used in the treatment of a variety of ailments. It is a bathing resort with both hot and cold baths. The resort is open year-round.

VENUS, SATURN, JUPITER

These three resorts lie on the southeastern coast of the country along the Black Sea. They are part of the chain of resorts (some discussed previously) stretching from north of Constanţa to Mangalia on the south. Jupiter, Venus, and Saturn (accordingly from north to south) are all within a short distance from one another. These resorts are relatively new but have grown fast since their establishment. They are among the finest resorts in Romania. Their hotels are modern; and they offer the tourist a variety of activities to choose from, including swimming, sunbathing, nice restaurants, bowling, minigolf, tennis, water sports, theaters, and a sports complex.

Hotels

Jupiter: *Capitol, Cometa, Meteor, Scoica, Dunarea, Tismana,* and *Cozla.*

Venus-Aurora: *Onix, Corina, Anca, Florica, Silvia, Raluca, Vulturul, Lidia,* and *Veronica.*

Saturn: *Balada, Horia, Saturn, Diana, Alfa, Siret, Cleopatra, Cerna, Prahova,* and *Gama.*

ROMANIAN DRUGS AND TREATMENTS

Romanian doctors and researchers have developed a number of drugs and treatments which have for decades lured many foreigners to the country looking for cures for their particular diseases, aches and pains, and disorders. These drugs and treatments receive mixed blessings by doctors and health authorities outside Romania. Yet patients by the thousands visit Romania each year, particularly the elderly. The Romanian drugs and treatments are controversial at least, and most have not been rigorously tested by American standards.

One of these drugs is Gerovital H_3, a drug licensed by Dr. Ana Aslan in 1957 after experimental work on it from 1946-56. This drug is widely used in many countries. Its basic ingredient became known in Switzerland and Germany in 1956. Known originally as novocaine, its pharmacologic term became procaine in the 1950s. The first clinical results of Gerovital H_3 were reported in 1951. In Gerovital H_3, the H_3 stands for a symbol of its vitamin-type action, with para-aminobenzoic acid as vitamin H. According to literature by Dr. Aslan and the Romanian Ministry of Health, Gerovital H_3 is indicated in physical and intellectual asthenia; prevention and management of aging of the skin, hair, and nails; articulation diseases of rheumatic origin; the treatment of atherosclerosis; arterial hypertension; angina pectoris; infarction; sequelae; Parkinson's disease; neuritis; neuralgia; arthrosis; spondylitis; osteoporosis; psoriasis; bronchial asthma; gastroduodenal ulcer; some hormonal disturbances. Gerovital H_3 is available in the form of injections, infiltrations, tablets, hair lotion, and face cream.

Another medicine developed by Dr. Aslan is Aslavital, which is aimed at fighting old age. In addition to procaine, it contains an activating factor and an antiarteriosclerosis one, which is said to be useful not only in the prophylaxis and treatment of aging but also in diseases of the central nervous system and of the cardiovascular system. Aslavital is also indicated as effective in generalized or predominantly cerebral, coronary, or peripheral atherosclerosis and the prevention or control of thromboembolic accidents and postneurologic sequelae. The drug is also said to be effective in the phychical and physical underdevelopment syndrome in children and in cases of encephalomyelitis sequelae. Some of the reported special efforts of a Gerovital H_3 and Aslavital cure are memory improvement, increased physical and intellectual capacity, elimination of nervous breakdown, improvement of sleep, better adaptation to the stress of hurried life, better brain and heart blood circulation, and revitalization of internal organ and skin tissues.

Pell-Amar drugs, another Romanian product, were developed by Dr. Ionescu-Călineşti from mud extracts. As early as the 19th century some Romanian resorts—Amara, Techirghiol, and others—became well known for the purported healing properties of their lakes. Due to specific climatic conditions and to mineral composition, some Romanian lakes contain important bottom deposits of sapropelic muds and mineral organic compounds. Research carried out by the Romanian medical school for spa treatment revealed the therapeutic properties of muds, each with its own chemical characteristics. The action of the chemical substance in muds on the ailing body led researchers to isolate active substances found in the black mud mass. The result was a sapropelic mud extract called Pell-Amar. The drug is made by extracting the mineral and organic components of the mud. Pell-Amar drugs are used in cases when mud baths are contraindicated because of temperature or hydrostatic pressure. The drugs are rich in chlorine, sodium, sulphate and magnesium, enzymes, amino acids, and organic phosphorus. The drugs are recommended for a wide range of disorders: rheumatism, diseases of the peripheral nervous system, gynecological, and some skin diseases. The product is applied in the form of foam baths, local and general gel applications, injections, oral administration, or ointments.

Boicil Forte is a relatively new Romanian drug devised by Dr. Vasile Boici. It is recommended in the treament of rheumatic diseases, where it is reported to eliminate pains, muscular contractions, deficient vascular circulation, migraines, arterial peripheral disturbances. The drug is administered by a micro-infiltration technique. Reports say that within minutes pain disappears or is much reduced and the ankylosed patient is able to move and walk around. In many cases, Boicil Forte arrests the evolution of the diseases it is used in treating.

Ulcosilvanil, a drug developed by Dr. Ioan Puşcas, is reported to be very effective in the treatment of ulcerous diseases. Different treatment plans are recommended, some for 10-24 days and others for as little as 2-5 days. A 98 to 99 percent healing rate is reported. Ulcosilvanil treatments are available in Felix spa. The other drugs and treatments described above are available at most of the spas and health resorts previously described.

CHAPTER 9

Practical Information

Visa Regulations

Tourist or transit visas in Romania are granted upon request at border crossings without prior formalities or applications. Should one wish to obtain the visa beforehand, the Romanian Diplomatic Missions or Consular offices abroad will grant it upon request (the Romanian Consular Office, 1607 23rd St. NW Washington DC 20008; for Canadian citizens the Romanian Consular Office is at 655 Rideau St., Ottawa, Ontario.

Tourists traveling on the basis of re-entry permits must obtain their entry visas in advance from the Romanian Consular offices mentioned above. A tourist visa will be granted to any foreign citizen wishing to visit Romania who possesses a valid passport recognized or accepted by the Romanian State, against a tax in dollars or in any other freely convertible currency.

Customs Formalities

No duty is collected and no special permit is required from tourists for bringing into Romania items of personal use.

Gifts brought into the country should not exceed the value of 2,000 lei; tourists may take out of the country goods purchased with lei exchanged by authorized banks or currency offices, as well as presents carried in their luggage up to a total value of 1,000 lei. Works of art and books of documentary, scientific, or artistic value can be taken out of the country on the basis of the "permitted for export" certificate issued by the shop which sold them.

The following products may not be taken out of Romania: meat, edible oil, flour, maize, sugar, rice, coffee, cocoa, honey, olives, distilled alcohol, vegetables, fruit, pepper, and imported spices.

Currency Regulations

Tourists entering Romania individually or in groups with prepaid arrangements for the duration of their stay and submitting confirmations issued by travel agencies are exempted from mandatory currency exchange.

A minimum exchange of U.S. $10 per person per day of stay is required from travelers without prepaid arrangements (not applicable to children under 14 years of age). This minimum currency exchange must be made at points of entry for an amount defined by the number of days for which the visa is issued. Subsequent visa extensions require currency exchange in the same ratio.

Tourists of Romanian origin who are foreign citizens or without citizenship and tourists who are Romanian citizens residing abroad and have valid Romanian passports, as well as parents, wife/husband and children of tourists mentioned above are exempted from the mandatory currency exchange provided their entrance visitor visas are obtained from the embassies of the Socialist Republic of Romania abroad. Import or export of Romanian currency is forbidden. Upon leaving the country, unused amounts of Romanian currency obtained from exchange at the National Tourist Office desks or banks can be reconverted to the initial currency at any exchange desk (minimum daily exchange amounts are not included in this provision).

Tourist Seasons in Romania

Romania attracts tourists all year around. Museums, historical sites, concerts, theaters, folklore performances and exhibits, and sports events are always accessible, though each season offers special attractions: the Black Sea resort season is between May 15 and September 15; winter sports resorts operate from December through March.

Food and Drink

Romanian cuisine is varied and has achieved considerable prestige throughout Europe. Breakfast is normally served between 7 and 10 A.M., and lunch between 12:30 and 3 P.M., which is the principal meal. Dinner is served between 7 and 10 P.M. In general, Romanian menus consist of three main courses. Dessert is varied, including many cakes and pastries. The basic course consists of garnished grilled beef, pork, or chicken. The highly seasoned grilled meatballs, *mititei*, are famous at home and abroad. Romanian cuisine also includes cold or hot dietary menus, served in special restaurants or lunch counters.

Show Times

Concerts, plays, and operas generally start between 6-7 P.M. There are no performances on Mondays. Make reservations for performances in advance. Ticket prices: opera—18-50. lei; concert—18-35lei; theater—15-30 lei.

Credit Cards and Travelers Checks

Diners Club, American Express, Master Card, Access Card, Carte Blanche, Eurocard, and Visa are accepted. Travelers checks and Eurocheques are also accepted at all entry points and tourist offices.

Electricity

Power supply in Romania is mostly 220 volts. Always check whether your razor or other electrical appliances are compatible.

Use plug adaptor, European standard. The official time is two hours ahead of Greenwich Mean Time and seven hours ahead of Eastern Standard Time.

Photography

You can photograph or film any tourist sight in Romania (public structures and monuments, natural sights, town views, and historic buildings).

Admission Fees

Museums and exhibitions generally charge a fee of about 5-10 lei. Museums are closed on Mondays.

Barber Shops

Prices are fixed according to category and are always displayed. Generally, a shave costs 10-25 lei; a haircut, 15-25 lei.

Beauty Parlors, Hairdressing Salons

At your hotel or in town, these establishments provide the usual services at very reasonable prices: wash and set, 25-50 lei; cut, 15-48 lei; manicure, 15-20 lei; facial, 90-120 lei; and pedicure, 28 lei.

Business Hours:

Shops are open from 9 A.M. to 1 P.M. and 4 P.M. to 8 P.M. (closed on Sundays); department stores, from 9 A.M. to 6 P.M.; food markets, from 7 A.M. to 6 P.M.; exchange counters in banks, from 8 A.M. to 12 noon. (exchange desks at hotels and tourist offices from 8 A.M. to 8 P.M.). Official institutions, ministries, municipal offices, and commercial and industrial enterprises are open from 8 A.M. to 4 P.M.

Movie Theaters

Performances, which are non-continuous, start (in some cinemas) in the morning and finish at midnight. Films are subtitled in Romanian only and dubbing is rare. Prices of tickets vary from 5 lei to 14 lei.

Nightclubs and Entertainment

Nightclubs with or without entertainment are found in various cities throughout the country but especially on the Black Sea coast. Admission fee varies with the club's category and program.

Dining and dancing are popular in Romania, and most restaurants and hotels have a band and often a vocalist.

Independent Travel to Romania

Romania can be easily reached from all parts of Europe and by all means of transportation. A number of international highways provide access to Romania from Yugoslavia, Hungary, Bulgaria, and the USSR. At all border crossing points, customs and Romanian tourist offices are open twenty-four hours.

Highways and Entry Points

From Hungary: International highway E 68 via Artand-Bors (frontier point); Oradea—highway Amko-Nagylak-Nadiac (frontier point)—Arad (by national highway).

Bekescsabo-Gyulo-Varsand (frontier point)—Chisineu Cris (DN 79A northward to Oradea and southward to Arad); or via Petea Satu Mare (frontier point).

From Yugoslavia: International highway via Vatin—Moravita E 70 (frontier point)—Timişoara; highway Sprska Crnja-Jimbolia (frontier point)—Timişoara; highway Iron Gates E 752 (frontier point)—Drobeta-Turnu Severin.

From Bulgaria: International highway E 70 and E 85 via Russe-Giurgiu (frontier point)—Bucharest; international highway E 87—via Varna; Vama Veche (frontier point)—Magalia—Constanţa; highway Varna-Egru Voda (frontier point)—Constanţa via national highway DN 38; Vidin Calafat (frontier point)—Craiova via national highway DN 56. The crossing of the Danube between Vidin and Calafat is via ferry.

From the Soviet Union: International highway E 85 viaPorubnoie—Siret (frontier point)—Suceava; highway Leuseni—Albita (frontier point)—Husi (via national highway 24B).

By Ship: Entry via the Black Sea (landing at the port of Constanța) or on Danube (landing at Giurgiu for Bucharest and at Cernavoda for the Black Sea coast).

Cruises on board the Romanian M/S *Oltenita, Carpati,* and *Steaua Dunaril* start in Vienna and end in Bucharest or at the Black Sea resorts.

By Rail: Direct international trains, such as Wiener Walzer, North Orient Express, Balt Orient Express, Danubius Express, Transdanubium, Carpati Express, and București Express, connect all European countries with Romania throughout the year. Romania is affiliated to the International Rail Tariff systems RIT and Inter-Rail.

By Air: Romanian Airlines (Tarom) provides direct connections between many world capitals and Romania as well as between main Romanian cities.

In addition to Tarom the following airlines operate scheduled flights to Romania: Aeroflot, Air Algerie, Air France, ALIA, Alitalia, Agency for Civil Aviation (China), Aua, Balkan, CSA, El AL, Interflug, Iraq Airways, Lot, Lufthansa, Lybian Arab Airlines, MALEV, Syrian Arab Airlines, and Swissair. Tarom and Pan Am operate direct flights between New York and Bucharest.

Motoring

Romania provides first-class conditions for sightseeing by car; a network of well-kept, uncrowded roads, service and filling stations, and accommodations and restaurants in towns and along the highways. Drivers must possess a national or international driver's license issued by competent authorities. Driving in Romania is free on any road, in all areas, without road or bridge taxes (except crossing the Danube for the Black Sea coast). All roads are accessible to trailers throughout the year.

Rent-a-Car (general renting conditions)

1. Rent-a-car without driver. A car without driver may be rented to any person who owns free convertible currency and a national or international driving license (at least one year old. Renting is possible for at least three hours or for one day.

2. Tariffs include: technical checkup and maintenance of the car; oil changing and replenishing; transport of the car from the garage to the renting institution; replacing the faulty car.

3. Tariffs do not include: petrol, garage fee, fee for transfers during renting period, and damages not covered by the insurance. Insurance covers loses due to damage, theft, or deterioration of the items from the car inventory (with the exception of losses due to carelessness or deliberately caused). Renting is recorded in a written agreement signed by both parties. The reception and handing over of the car may be performed at the following places: in Bucharest: Agency of International Tourist Services, 7 Magheru Blvd., phone 167791; Otopeni Airport, ONT desk, phone 337501; National Tourist Office desks in the hotels București, Athenée Palace, Inter-Continental, Dorobanti, Flora, Nord, Modern, Capitol, Majestic, Union, Gara de Nord (north railway station); and in the country at tourist offices.

Gasoline and Lubricants

There are many filling stations in Romania situated in towns or at intervals of about 30 miles on all main roads. Fuel can be obtained against coupons purchased at National Tourist Office agencies, at border crossing points, and at major hotels across the country. Gasoline, 88-90 octane, is U.S. $.80 per liter; gasoline, 96-98 octane; is U.S. $.85 per liter; diesel oil is U.S. $.70 per liter.

Speed Limits

On highways: for cars over 1,800 cubic centimeters, 90 km/h; for cars between 1,100-1,800 cubic centimeters, 80 km/h; for cars up to 1,100 cubic centimeters, 70 km/h. In cities, towns, or other localities, speed limits are 60 km/h. The Carpati-București National Tourist Office through its branches in main cities offers the following services: Free road service within a 30-minute drive on highways serviced by the A.C.R.; free towing service (maximum distance is 30 km); repair, legal, and medical service against letters of credit; broadcasting of emergency messages to motorists on the road. Gasoline coupons are available at border points or at National Tourist Office desks, which are to be found throughout the country. Coupons must be paid for in any freely convertible currency. Accommodations are booked when available. Information on weather and road conditions can be obtained as well as general tourist information and assistance.

Addresses of Romania's Tourist Information Offices Abroad

Austria—Rumanisches Touristenamt, 6-8 Wahringerstr. 1090 Vienna, Austria; telex: 111072 Carpro A: phone 343157.

Belgium—Office National du Turisem Roumain, 26 Lace de Brouckere, Brussels 1, Belgium; telex: 23447 Mintur B; phone: 2180079; 2186382.

Czechoslovakia—Romanian National Tourist Office, 11000 Parizka ul.e 20, Socialist Republic of Czechoslovakia; telex: 122147 Rotu C; phone: 2317578.

Denmark—Romanian National Tourist Office, 55 A Vesterbrogade, Copenhagen, Denmark; telex: 19419 Romont DK.; phone: (01) 246219.

Federal Republic of Germany—Rumanisches Touristenamt, 1 Neue Manizerstrasse 6, Frankfurt/Main, Federal Republic of Germany; telex: 414089 Totur D; phone: (0690) 236941-42-43. Rumanisches Touristenamt, 16 Corneliusstrasse, 4 Dusseldorf, Federal Republic of Germany, telex: 8587410 ONT D; phone: (0211) 37104748.

France—Office National du Turisme Roumain, 38 Avenue de l'Opera, Paris 75002, France; telex: 220109 Otrp-F; phone: 7422714; 7422542.

German Democratic Republic—Rumanisches Touristenamt, Frankfurter Tor 5, 1034-Berlin, German Democratic Republic; telex: 113186 Bera DD; phone: 5891726.

Great Britain—Romanian National Tourist Office, 29 Thurloe Place, London SW7 2HP; telex: 262107 Carpat g; phone: (01) 584-8090.

Holland—Roemeens National Bureau Voor Toerisme, Weteringschans, 165 Amsterdam C-1017 X.D; telex: 13624 Caron NL; phone: 020-239044.

Israel—Romanian National Tourist Office, 1 Ben Yehuda, Tel Aviv, Israel; telex: 341454 Roto 11; phone: 663536.

Italy—Ente Naxionale per il Turismo Della Romania, 100 Via Torino, Rome, Italy; telex: 611158 Romtur 1; phone: 4742983 or 460267.

Spain—c/o Embassy of the Socialist Republic of Romania, 157 Avenida Alfonso XIII, Madrid 16, Spain; telex: 22433 E-Rocom; phone: 4587895.

Switzerland—Rumanisches Informations Bureau for Touristik, 10 Schweizergasse, 8001 Zurich, Switzerland; telex: 813730 Inru Ch; phone: 2111730-31.

Sweden—Romanian National Tourist Office, 33 Vasahuset Gamia Brogatan, 11120 Stockholm, Sweden; telex: 10421 Carpat-S; phone: 08-210253-63.

U.S.A.—Romanian National Tourist Office, 573 Third Ave., New York, NY 10016, U.S.A.; telex: 422990 RNTONYC; phone: (212) 697-6971.

Other Useful Addresses

Embassy of the Socialist Republic of Romania, 1697 Twenty-third St. NW, Washington, DC 20008. Phone: (202) 232-4747; (202) 232-4748 for the Consular office.

Tarom—Romanian Airlines, 200 E. 38th St., New York, NY 10016. Phone: (212) 687-6013.

Romanian Commercial Office, 575-577 Third Ave., New York, NY 10016. Phone: (212) 682-9120.

Romanian Library, 200 E. 38th St., New York, NY 10016. Phone: (212) 687-0180.

U.S.A. Embassy in Romania, 7-9 Tudor Arghezi St., Bucharest. Phone: 124040

American Library in Romania, 5-7 Alexandru Sahia St., Bucharest.

Romanian Ministry of Tourism, 7 Magheru Blvd., Bucharest. Phone: 145160.

Embassy of the Socialist Republic of Romania and Consular Office in Canada, 655 Rideau St., KIN 6 A 3, Ottawa, Ontario. Phone: (613) 232-5345.

Embassy of Canada in Romania, 36 N. Iorga St., Bucharest. Phone: 505956.

Otopeni International Airport (Information Bureau), Bucharest. Phone: 333137.

Inter-Continental Hotel (Information Bureau), 4 N. Balcescu Blvd., Bucharest. Phone: 137040 or 140400.

National Tourist Office (Carpati), 22—7 Noiembrie St., Braşov. Phone: 921-12840.

Useful Words and Vocabulary

English	Romanian	Pronunciation
Hello	buna ziua	[booneh szeuah]
My name is	ma numesc . . .	[mah noomaesc]
What is your name?	cum te cheama?	[chum ta kheama]
Where is the telephone?	unde este un telefon?	[oondae aestae co telefonn]
Where are the restrooms?	unde este toaleta?	[oondae aestae toalatah]
Hotel	hotel	
Taxi	taxi	
Restaurant	restaurant	
Money	bani	[bahnii]
Food	mincare	[mahnkharae]
Something to drink	ceva de baut	[tchevah dae baut]
How much does it cost?	cit costa?	[khit costa]
(Can you) help me?	ajuta-ma	[ajutamah]
Policeman	militian	[myllytzyan]
How can I find . . (place)	unde este . . . ?	[oondae aestae]
How far is that from here?	cit de departe este?	[kit dae daepartae aestae]
Airport	aeroport	[aaerport]
Bus station	statia de autobuz	[statzia dae autobu]
Train station	gara	[gharah]
Car	masina	[mashina]
What time is it?	cit e ceasul?	[kit ae tcheassul]
Do you speak English?		

—just ask, and they'll say yes or no.

I am American	eu sint american	[aeu suhnt america]
Who speaks English (around here)?	cine vorbeste engleza aici?	[tchinae vorbaesch- tae aenlaezza aytch]
Can you turn on the heat?	poti sa dai drumul la caldura?	[potsi sah dhay droomool lah khaldoorah]

It's cold here	e frig	[yeh fryg]
Clothes	haine	[hhaynnae]
Suitcase	valiza	[vahliszah]
Purse	geanta	[dgeantah]
Wallet	portofel	[portophell]
When	cind	[kuhnd]
Why	de ce	[dae tchae]
How	cum	[khum]
Yes	da	[dah]
No	nu	[noo]
Please	poftiti	[poftits]
Thank you	multumesc	[mooltsomesk]
How much	cit	[kat]
Good morning	buna dimineata	[buna dimineatsa]
Good afternoon	buna ziua	[buna zi'ua]
Good evening	buna seara	[buna sea'ra]
Goodbye	la revedere	[la reve-de're]
Town	oras	[orahsh]
Theater	teatru	[tea'troo]
Cinema	cinema	[cinemah]
Opera	opera	[o'pera]
Shop	magazin	[mahgahzin]

DISTANCES IN MILES BETWEEN EUROPE'S MAIN CITIES AND BUCHAREST

Amsterdam	1518	London	1611
Athens	770	Madrid	2206
Belgrade	450	Moscow	1227
Berlin	1346	Oslo	1763
Berne	1328	Paris	1501
Bonn	1313	Prague	916
Brussels	1496	Rome	1343
Budapest	558	Sofia	255
Copenhagen	1617	Stockholm	1938
Helsinki	1813	Tirana	733
Istanbul	440	Vienna	688
Lisbon	2575	Warsaw	1123

TRAINS FROM BUCHAREST TO BRAŞOV
FROM GARA DE NORD
North Railway Station

6:35 A.M.	9:50 A.M.
6:43 A.M.	1:05 A.M.
9:30 A.M.	

TRAINS FROM BRAŞOV TO BUCHAREST

12:59 P.M.	5:26 P.M.
2:26 P.M.	7:05 P.M.
4:06 P.M.	8:26 P.M.
4:18 P.M.	

AVERAGE TEMPERATURE (F°)
Bucharest Sea Coast Mountains

Month	Day Night	Day Night	Day Night
Jan.	33—20	37—25	33—18
Feb.	38—24	41—30	34—20
March	51—33	46—35	42—26
April	63—41	55—42	51—33
May	74—51	66—52	61—42
June	81—58	75—60	67—48
July	86—61	82—63	70—51
Aug.	86—60	82—63	70—49
Sept.	76—53	72—57	64—53
Oct.	65—44	62—49	55—36
Nov.	49—35	51—38	45—29
Dec.	37—26	43—32	36—24

ROMANIAN MENU TERMS

The following offers a sample of the wide range of Romanian cuisine. Many of these dishes are eaten throughout the country, but ingredients vary among the regions and provinces and there are many local specialties. In the countryside the people usually keep a pig for meat. *Slanina*, or bacon, is traditionally smoked with garlic and paprika added to it. Then it is stored for months before being cut into thick slices. Sausages (*cirnati*) are prepared in natural casings, customarily with salt, pepper and garlic mixed in.

Potatoes, beans, tomatoes and cucumbers are basic foods in Romania. Onions are used in many recipes. Salads are commonly eaten, with a dressing of vinegar and oil. Eggs are used in many salads and other dishes. *Mamaliga* is a widely eaten dish that is satisfying and filling. It consists of a thick mush of corn meal, a type of polenta, which is stirred often as it is cooked. An all-purpose food, is served hot or cold and in a variety of ways with other dishes.

Two very popular Romanian dishes are *parjole* and *sarmale*. Parjole are highly seasoned, flat meatballs. *Sarmale* consists of cabbage leaves stuffed with meat. The recipe for each of these dishes is given below.

Parjole

   meat (either pork, lamb or beef)
   1 slice of bread
   1 medium onion
   3 or 4 cloves of garlic
   1 egg
   salt, pepper, parsley or dill

The meat is ground and mixed with bread, egg, salt, pepper, parsley, and an onion sauteed in 3 tablespoons of cooking oil. Take a generous spoonful of meat, roll it in flour on a sheet of aluminum foil, pat it flat, and deep fry.

Sarmale

   1 lb. of ground pork
   1/2 lb. of smoked bacon
   1 medium onion
   2 tablespoons of rice
   1 lb. of sauerkraut
   1 fresh cabbage

1 bayleaf
1/4 teaspoon of oregano
20 black peppercorns
1 tablespoon of tomato paste

Romanians typically use a pickled cabbage with thin leaves. The meat and other ingredients are rolled in the cabbage leaves, which are then either poached or baked.

Another commonly eaten Romanian food is borshch, a hearty, sour soup similar to that served in Russia. Its major ingredients include potatoes, beans, carrots, onions, peppers, *leavege* (similar to parsley) salt and meat boiled into vinegar and water. It may be served hot or cold.

Mititei is a popular mincemeat made with pork and highly seasoned with pepper, paprika, and salt. It is kneaded in a bowl and then cooked on a grill.

Other well-known Romanian dishes include *tocana*, a highly seasoned stew made with a variety of meats (mutton, beef, or pork) and vegetables; and *patricieni*, a type of frankfurter.

Several delicious desserts include: *cozonoc*, a bread-like cake made with eggs, flour, salt, sugar, oil, cocoa, vanilla extract, yeast, and milk with sugar added after cooking; and pasca, a cheesecake, made of rice eggs, sugar and salt.

Index

Aghyhiol, 153; 4th-century tomb, 153
Alba Iulia, 95–101; Balthyanaeum Documentary Library, 96; history, 95–96; history and art center, 95, 97–98; hotels, 98; sights, 96–98; sights, nearby, 99; Sebes, 100; today, 96; size and location, 95; useful addresses, 98–101
Arad, 82–87; history, 82–83; hotels, 85–86; restaurants, 86; sights, 83; size and location, 82; today, 83; useful addresses, 85–87
Arbore, 138–139; green, use of, 138; location, 133–34; stone slabs, 138–139
archeological sites, 43, 49, 53, 60, 64, 69, 75, 80, 90, 95, 99, 101, 101–102, 105, 110, 111, 124, 145, 154

Babaday, 154; Iron Age settlement, 154
Bacău, 122
Baia Mare, 92–92; St. Stephen's Tower, 93; size and location, 92; WW I and II, 93
Bacăile Felix, 162; cure factors, 162–63; cure indications, 162; scheduled trips, 163; hotels, 163; location, 162
Băile Govora, 174
Băile Herculane, 164–66; cure factors, 164–65; cure indications, 164; hotels, 165; location, 164; scheduled trips, 165–66
Băile Olăneşti, 174
Băile Tuşnad, 168–69; cure factors, 168, 169; cure indications, 168–69; hotels, 169
Batthyanacum Documentary Library, 96
Bega River, 70

Bicaz Gorges, 4
birds, 147–48
Black Church, 67–68
Black Sea Coast, 175–77; attractions, 175; climate, 176; therapeutic indications, 176–77
Brăila, 47–49; churches and museums, 48; sights, 48; size and location, 47–48; today, 147–48
Braşov, 65–69; history, 65, 66–67; sights, 67–68; size and location, 65–66, 67; today, 65, 66; useful addresses, 69
Brukenthal Museum, 88
Bucegi Mountains, 4
Bucharest, 25–39; churches, 33–34; economic importance, 26; history, 27; hotels, 38; museums, 28–33, 35; restaurants, 36; sights, 28–35; theaters, 38; today, 26; university of, 34; useful addresses, 35–39
Bugias, 169–71; cure factors, 170; cure indications, 170; hotels, 170
Bukovina, 133–35; frescoes, 134; history, 134; monasteries 133–41; *see also* listings for individual monasteries.
Busteni, 187–88; mountaineering, 186
Buzău, 58–59; history, 59; size and location, 58; today, 58
Călimăneşti-Călciulata, 173
camping, 58, 73, 87, 99, 120, 129, 154, 159, 183
Caraorman Sandbank, 151
Carol II, 17
Carpathians, 3–7; Eastern, 3–4; Southern, 4–6; Western, 6–7
cave paintings, 11–12
Ceauşescu, 18–19
chamois (mountain goat), 6
Chilia (arm of Danube), 146
Chilia Veche early settlement, 154

churches, wooden, 83
climate, of Romania, 3, 205
Cluj-Napoca, 75–79; history, 75–76; restaurants, 79; sights, 77; size and location, 75; today, 77; useful addresses, 99; WW I, 77
collectivization, 18
Communist Party, 17, 18
Constanta, 41–47; climate, 42; history, 42–43; museums, 44–45; Piata Independentei, 45; sights, 44–47; size and location, 41–42; today, 42, 43–44; theaters, 47; useful addresses, 47
Corvin Castle, 106
Craiova, 52–58; culture, 53; gardens and parks, 56; history, 52; hotels, 56; museums, 53–55; restaurants, 57; sights, 53–56; size and location, 52; theaters, 57; today, 53; useful addresses, 56–58
credit cards, 195
cula (fortified house), 23–24
cultural centers, 25, 53, 62, 92, 95, 102, 113–14, 125
currency, 194; exchange, 194

Dacians, 8, 12–13, 27, 42–43, 52, 60, 82, 95, 99, 101, 109–110, 114–15, 124, 189; sacred sanctuaries, 110; calendar, 110
dances, traditional, 83
Danube delta, 9, 143–160; climate, 146; fauna, 147–149; flora, 149–150; forests, 150; growth, 144–45; history of, 144–45; hydrographic network, 146; sandbanks, 150; Tulcea, gateway to, 145; *see also* Danube Delta Museum and Danube River
Danube Delta Museum, 145
Danube River, 60, 143–160; excursions, 159–160; history, 143–44; hotels, 158–59; Iron Gates Dam, 61; sights, 153–57; size, 143; useful information, 157
Denistepe, 155
Denşus, Monument of, 106

Deva, 101–108; architecture, 101; citadel, 102–103; Corvin Castle, 106; Horea's Oak, 107; Geoagiu-Băi Spa, 104; Monument of Densuş, 106; Retezat Park, 107; sights, 102–103; nearby sights, 104–108; Ulpia Traina Sarmizegetusa, 105; useful addresses, 103–104
Dobruja, 9
Domogled, Mount, 5
Dracula, Count (Vlad Dracula), 19–21; birthplace, 108
driving in Romania, 198–99; gasoline, 199; renting a car, 198–99; speed limits, 199
Drobeta-Turnu Severin, 60–61; history, 61; size and location, 60; today, 60; useful addresses, 61
drugs and treatments, 190–192; Aslavital, 191; Boicil Forte, 192; Gerovital H_3, 190–191; Pell-Amar, 191–192; Ulcosilvanil, 192
duty on imports, 194

Effie Nord, 177–78; hotels, 178
Eforie Sud, 178
Eiffel, Gustave, 70
electricity, 195
embassy addresses, 201
embroidery, museum of, 141

fish, 148–49
flora, 149–50
folklore, 19–24, 63, 115, 125, 189; Arad area, 83; Count Dracula, 19–21; 18th–19th century lives, 90–91; Sheep Feast, 21; pottery, 21–23; *cula*, 23–24; peasant houses, 24
fossils, 153, 189

Galati, 120–122; history, 121; shipbuilding, 121; sights, 122; size and location, 120–121; WW I, 121
gardens, 35, 56, 61, 75, 78, 90, 119, 178
Geoagiu-Băi Spa, 104
geography of Romania, 2–10

Getae, *see* Dacians
Gheorghe Gheorghiu-Dej, 130
Golden Fleece, 155
Greeks, 64, 157
history, 11–19; prehistory, 11–12; Geto-Dacians, 12–13; Romans, 12–13; Christianity, 13; first Romanians, 14; Ottoman Empire, 14; Michael the Brave, 15; independence, 15; Balkan War, 16; WW I, 16
Histria, 64
Horea's Oak, 107
Humor, 137–38; frescoes, 137–38; location, 133; portraits, 137
hutsul horses, 125–26

Iaşi, 113–120; churches and houses of historic interest, 117–18; history, 114–15; museums, 115–16; sights, 115–19; size and location, 113; useful addresses, 120
industry, 26, 48, 50, 53, 59, 60, 63, 66, 70, 75, 77, 82, 88, 91, 94, 101, 122, 123, 125
Iron Gates Dam, 61

Jupiter resort, 190

Lacu Rosu, 173
language, 2; useful words and phrases, 203–204
Liszt, Franz, 77
Lorga, Nicolae, 113

Mamaia, 181
Mangalia, 180–81
Mediaş, 101
Michael the Brave, 15
Micia Ruins, 111
mileage between cities, 205
Moldavia, 8, 113–131
Moldovita, 140; location, 140; 'Siege of Constantinople,' 140; Pomme d Or prize, 140
monasteries, 27, 117, 123; Arbore, 138; Humor, 137; Moldovita, 140, Putna, 141; Sucevita, 139; Voronet, 135; *see also* Bukovina

and Suceava
mountaineering, 186, 187
museums, 25, 28–33, 44, 51, 53–55, 71, 77, 88, 96–97, 100, 109, 115–116, 126; archeology, 44, 110, 111; Brukenthal, 88; embroidery, 141
museums of the Social Republic of Romania, 29–33; Arts Museum, 29–30; History Museum, 30–31; Library of the Academy, 32–33
nature preserves, of the Danube, 151–53; Periteaşca-Leahova-Gura Portitei, 152–53; Retezat, 5, 107
Neptune, 179–80; hotels, 179–80

Ocna Sibiului, 189–90
Oradea, 79–82; history, 80; sights, 81; size and location, 79–80; today, 80; useful addresses, 81–82

Paleolithic, 11–12
Peles Castle, 182
people, 10–11; nationalities, 10; population by county, 206
Peştera Muierlor (Women's Cave), 75
photography, 196
Peatra-Neamt, 189
Pietrosu, 4
Piteşti, 59–60; history, 59; sights, 60; size and location, 59; today, 59
Ploieşti, 49–52; archeology, 50; history, 50–51; sights, 51; size and location, 49; today, 49; useful addresses, 51–52; world wars, 49–50
Podul Uriaşilor (Giants' Bridge), 5
Poiana Brăşov, 184; hotels, 186–87; location, 184; mountaineering, 186; recreational facilities, 185–86; restaurants, 185
Pomme d' Or award, 125, 134–35; on display, 140
pottery, 21–23; traditional methods, 23; museum of pottery and glass, 33

Index

Predeal, 188; hotels, 188
Punta Monastery, 141; location, 141; tomb of Stephan the Great, 141

resorts, 49, 66, 181–90; Busteni, 187–88; Mamaia, 181; Mangulia, 180–81; Neptune, 179–80; Ocan Sibiulu, 189–90; Piatra-Neamt, 189; Poiana Biăsov, 184–48; Predeal 188; Sinaia, 181–84; *see also* spas
Resita, 94–95
Rîmnícu Vîlcea, 63
religion, 11; early Christianity, 13
Retezat Mountains, 5
Retezat National Park, 5, 107

sanitoria, 39
Sarmizegethusa, 109–111; capital of ancient Dacia, 109; Dacian calendar sanctuaries, 110; Roman amphitheater, 110–11
Satu Mare, 93–94
Saturn resort, 190
Scarişoara Glacier, 7
Sebes, 100
Sfîntu Gheorghe, 109, 147
Sheep Feast, 21
Shipbuilding, 60, 121, 145
shipping, 42, 121
Sibiu, 87; Brukenthal Museum, 88; history, 87–88; sights 88–89, nearby, 90–91; size and location, 87; useful addresses, 89–90
Sighişoara, 108; birthplace of Dracula, 108
Sinaia, 181–84; history, 181–83; hotels, 183; location, 181; today, 182–83
Signeorz-Băi, 175
Slănic-Moldova, 172; cure factors, 172; cure indications, 172–173; location, 172
Slatina, 63
Sovata, 166; cure factors, 166; cure indications, 166–67; hotels, 167; location, 166; mud, 167; scheduled trips, 167–68

spas, 71, 161–181; Băile Felix, 162–64; Băile Olăneşti, 174; Băile Govora, 174; Băile Herculane, 164–66; Băile Olăneşti, 174; Baile Tuşnad, 168–69; Buzias, 169–71; Călimăneşti-Căciulata, 173; Covasna, 174; Effie Nord, 177–78; Eforie Sud, 178; Geoagiu-Bai, 104; Lacu Roşu; Mamaia, 181; Mangulia, 180–81; Neptune, 179–80; Slănic-Moldova, 172–73; Singeorz-Băi, 175; Sovata, 166–68; Vata-Bai, 105; Vatra Dornei, 171–172
sports, winter, 107, 173, 183, 184, 187, 188
Stephan the Great, 154, 189; tomb of, 141
Subcarpathian Hills, 8
Suceava, 124; frescoes, 125; history, 124–25; hotels, 129; *hutsul* horses, 125–26; Pomme d' Or, 125; restaurants, 129; sights, 126–28; Suceava Citadel, 127; today, 125; useful addresses, 128–130
Sucevița, 139–140; location, 134
Sulina, 147

temperatures, 205
Timişoara, 69–75; Bega River, 70; Eiffel-designed bridge, 70; history, 69; hotels, 73; restaurants, 73; sights, 71–72; size and location, 69; spa, 71; today, 69; useful addresses, 72–75
Tîrgoviste, 61–63; history, 62; sights, 62–63; size and location, 61; today, 62
Tîrgu Mureş, 91–92; sights, 92; size and location, 91; today, 91
tourist offices, 200–201
train schedules, 202
Transylvania, 7–8; 65–111
travel to Romania, 197; distance to cities in Europe, 205; entry points, 197–98; motoring, 198–99; *see also* Tulcea *tuica* (plum brandy), 63

Tulcea (city), 145–46; gateway to the Danube delta, 144
Tulcea (arm of the Danube), 146
trekking, 4–5

Ulpia Traina Sarmizagetusa, 105
Unirea, 157

Vatra Dornei, 171–72; cure factors, 171; cure indications, 171; hotels, 172; location, 171

visa regulations, 193
Voroneț Monastery, 135–37; frescoes, 135–37; "Last Judgment," 136; location, 133; trefoil from, 135; Voronet blue, 135, 137

Wallachia, 9–10, 41–64
wine, 82, 99, 115
workers' movement, 82–83
WW I, 17, 49, 121
WW II, 18, 49–50, 122

Other Companion Guides from Hippocrene: written by American professors for Americans who wish to enrich the travel experience by understanding the history and culture of their vacation destination.

Companion Guide to the Soviet Union
Lydle Brinkle

Covering all the Soviet cities which can receive visitors from the West, this guide gives a taste of the great diversity of flavors and rhythms of life in a country with over 130 ethnic groups. Newly up-dated, it contains a chapter on the Crimea, parts only recently opened to foreign tourists.

329 pages ISBN 0-87052-635-9 14.95 paper

Companion Guide to Ireland
Henry Weisser

"The warmth, hospitality, humor and friendliness of ordinary Irish people towards Americans are outstanding characteristics," writes the author. In a sympathetic, yet unromantic manner, he explains the troubled background of the Republic, and shows how to make the most of a visit to this magical, emerald isle. Weisser is a professor of history at Colorado State University.
306 pages   ISBN 0-87052-633-2 $14.95 paper

Companion Guide to Portugal
T. Kubiak

Describing the sights, sounds and smells which the visitor will encounter, Kubiak evokes the rich texture of Portugese life, while presenting a comprehensive review of the nation's history and traditions. The author is a professor of geography at Eastern Kentucky University.
260 pages   ISBN 0-87052-554-9 $14.95 paper